The Coding Headquarters

CPC EXAM PREPARATION 2023-2024

Cpc Practice Exams With 400 Q & A And Rationales

Rachel Hardy

RACHEL HARDY

You Are Special

CONTENTS

ABOUT THE AUTHOR

Rachel Hardy is a passionate and accomplished author in the field of medical coding, renowned for her expertise in Certified Professional Coder (CPC) exam preparation. Under the pseudonym Rachel Hardy, she delves into the world of medical coding education, presenting a wealth of knowledge and practice questions to empower aspiring medical coders on their journey to success.

Behind the pen name, lies the brilliant mind of Vini Trivedi, a seasoned healthcare professional with years of experience in medical coding and a profound understanding of the intricacies within the industry.

Rachel's dedication to the medical coding field is evident in her meticulously crafted practice questions book, designed to assist students and professionals alike in honing their coding skills and conquering the CPC exam with confidence. With a blend of real-world scenarios and comprehensive explanations, her book is an indispensable resource for those striving to excel in this demanding domain.

In both her real and pen names, Vini Trivedi, a compassionate mentor, and Rachel Hardy, an inspiring author, converge to enhance the knowledge and expertise of aspiring medical coders, leaving an indelible mark on the world of healthcare education.

ACKNOWLEDGEMENTS

I would like to take this opportunity to express my gratitude to everyone who has supported me throughout the writing of this book on CPC practice exams.

First and foremost, I would like to thank my family for their unwavering support and encouragement. Their belief in me has been a constant source of inspiration and motivation, and I could not have completed this project without them.

I would also like to thank my colleagues in the medical coding field, whose insights and expertise have been invaluable in shaping this book. Their feedback and guidance have been instrumental in helping me to create a comprehensive and informative guide to CPC practice exams.

Finally, I would like to express my appreciation to all those who will read this book. It is my sincere hope that it will be a valuable resource for those seeking to pass the CPC certification exam and advance their careers in medical coding and billing.

Thank you all for your support and encouragement.

PREFACE

The Certified Professional Coder (CPC) exam, conducted by the American Academy of Professional Coders (AAPC), is one of the most challenging and important exams in the medical coding field. Passing this exam requires a thorough understanding of medical terminology, anatomy and physiology, and coding guidelines and regulations.

As an experienced author, I have written this book to provide a comprehensive guide to preparing for the CPC exam. Whether you are a student, a coding professional, or simply someone looking to advance your career in the healthcare industry, this book is designed to help you succeed on the CPC exam.

I would like to thank the American Academy of Professional Coders for their continued dedication to advancing the medical coding field, as well as the students and professionals who have shared their knowledge and experience with me over the years. It is because of your contributions that this book is possible.

With that said, I invite you to dive in and begin your journey to passing the CPC exam. I wish you the best of luck in your studies and your career.

DISCLAIMER

The information contained in this book is intended as a guide to help you prepare for the Certified Professional Coder (CPC) certification exam. While every effort has been made to ensure the accuracy of the information presented here, I cannot be held responsible for any errors or omissions, or for any consequences that may result from the use of this information.

I would also like to note that the opinions expressed in this book are my own, and do not necessarily reflect the views of any particular organization or institution. Additionally, the examples provided throughout the book are intended to illustrate key concepts, and should not be construed as definitive or exhaustive.

Finally, I want to emphasize that the information presented in this book is current as of the publication date, but may become outdated over time as the CPC exam changes and evolves. It is your responsibility to ensure that you are using the most up-to-date information and resources to prepare for the exam.

With that said, I hope that you find this book to be a helpful and informative resource as you prepare for the CPC certification exam. Good luck!

ABOUT CPC EXAM

The Certified Professional Coder (CPC) exam is a certification exam administered by the American Academy of Professional Coders (AAPC) for medical coders. This exam is designed to test a candidate's knowledge of medical coding guidelines and regulations, as well as their ability to apply that knowledge to real-world situations.

Exam format - 100 multiple-choice questions

Online or in-person options

AAPC offers online and in-person proctored exams. Choose to take the exam at home in a quiet, private location or through your local chapter or a licensed instructor. Learn more about the online proctored exam and how to prepare for the current exam.

Time allowed - In-person and online exams are administered in one sitting, with four hours to complete the exam.

Approved code books

AMA's CPT® Professional Edition, as well as your choice of ICD-10-CM and HCPCS Level II code books

Whether you take the exam online or in-person, you must complete the CPC exam within four hours and answer 70% of the questions correctly to pass.

TIPS FOR CPC EXAM

Passing the Certified Professional Coder (CPC) exam can be a challenging task, but with the right preparation and approach, it is achievable. Here are some tips to help you pass the CPC exam:

Study regularly: Set aside time each day or week to study for the exam. Use study materials such as textbooks, online courses, or practice exams to reinforce your knowledge and skills.

Focus on the key areas: Pay particular attention to the key areas tested on the exam, such as medical terminology, anatomy and physiology, and coding guidelines and regulations.

Take practice exams: Take as many practice exams as possible to familiarize yourself with the exam format and types of questions. This will also help you identify areas where you need to improve.

Time management: Manage your time effectively during the exam by pacing yourself and not spending too much time on any one question. Answer the questions you know first and come back to the more challenging ones later.

Use coding manuals: Familiarize yourself with the coding manuals and use them during the exam. Know how to navigate through them quickly and efficiently.

Read the questions carefully: Read each question carefully and make sure you understand what is being asked before selecting an answer.

Eliminate incorrect answers: If you are unsure of the answer to a question, eliminate any obviously incorrect answers to increase your chances of selecting the correct one.

Stay calm: Stay calm and focused during the exam. Take deep breaths and remember that you have prepared for this moment.

By following these tips and putting in the necessary time and effort to prepare for the CPC exam, you can increase your chances of passing and achieving this important certification in the medical coding and billing field.

EXAM A

INTEGUMENTARY SYSTEM

1) Dr. Richard, a plastic surgeon completed a bilateral rhytidectomy of the neck and a suction assisted lipectomy of the right upper arm. What codes should be reported for Dr. Richard's services?
   a) 15828-50, 15879-RT-59
   b) 15826-59, 15879-RT-59
   c) 15828-50, 15878-RT-59
   d) 15826-RT, 15828-50, 15878-RT-59

2) Rachel had a dermal lesion on her left foot. The physician completed a punch biopsy and then removed the lesion by shaving during the same session. The lesion diameter was documented as 3.6 cm. The defect was covered by a

sterile dressing. Rachel was instructed to follow-up in 3 days. What codes should the physician use to report these services?

a) 11308-LT
b) 11308-LT, 11104-59
c) 11303-LT
d) 11424-LT, 11104-59

3)   Dr. Kennedy completed an excision of a malignant lesion from the scalp of a 45-year-old patient. The patient was prepped and draped in the usual sterile fashion and Lidocaine locally injected. Dr. Kennedy documented the size of the lesion as 2.0 cm. The lesion was excised and marked at the 12 o'clock cephalad portion with a silk suture. The total excised diameter of lesion with margins was 4.0 cm. The defect created by the excision was 5.4 cm and closed with layer 3-0 Prolene sutures. How should Dr. Kennedy report her services?

a) 11624, 12032-51, 96372, J2001
b) 11624, 12032-51
c) 11422, 12032-51, 96372, J2001
d) 11626, 12032-51

4)   A 61-year-old patient had a benign 1-cm lesion excised from his right arm, a benign 2.5-cm lesion excised from his trunk, and a benign 2.1-cm lesion excided from his neck. The final excised diameters were documented at 1.9 cm right arm, 3.1 cm trunk, and 2.0 cm neck. All defects were closed by simple suture technique. How should you report these services?

a) 11422, 11404-59, 11402-RT-59
b) 11422, 12004-51, 11404-59, 11402-59
c) 11401, 11403-51, 11423-51
d) 11602-RT, 11604-59, 11622-59

5)   A patient has a pressure ulcer on his left ischial tuberosity. After examination a decision is made to complete debridement. The documented area debrided is 32 sq cm, including muscle and subcutaneous tissue. How should you report this service?
a) 97597-LT, 97598-LT-51
b) 11044-LT, 11047-LT-51
c) 11043-LT, 11046-LT
d) 11043-LT, 11046-LT, 97597-LT-59, 97598-LT-51

6) Amanda, a 45-year-old patient, was scheduled for a biopsy following a diagnostic mammogram that showed a mass in the right breast. Dr. Linda completed a percutaneous automated vacuum assisted biopsy and placement of a percutaneous localized clip in the right breast under ultrasonic guidance. The biopsy revealed a primary neoplasm of the lower-outer quadrant. How should you report Dr. Linda's professional services?
a) 19085, 76942-26
b) 19081
c) 19083-26, 76942-26
d) 19083

MUSCULOSKELETAL SYSTEM

7)   Jack fell from a ladder, six months ago, and broke his left radius. The fracture is not healing as expected and the implant needs to be replaced. Today, Jack underwent a secondary procedure. Dr. Gene completed an open treatment with internal fixation of the radial neck, including replacement of the prosthetic radial head. How should you report Dr. Gene's services?
a) 24666-LT
b) 24366-LT

c) 25607-LT
d) 24587-LT

8) A patient, under general anesthesia, underwent a primary repair to the left ankle for a disrupted ligament. During the same procedure the patient required a percutaneous tenotomy to lengthen the Achilles tendon. How should you report the surgeon's services?
a) 27695-LT, 27606-59-LT
b) 27698-LT, 27685-59-LT, 01472-47
c) 27695-LT, 27685-59-LT, 01472-47
d) 27698-LT, 27605-59-LT

9) Dr. Hewes completed an anterior arthrodesis fusion, with a structural allograft, and minimal discectomy at L1-2, L3-4, and L4-5. Anterior instrumentation was required and inserted for stabilization of the entire lumbar region. How should Dr. Hewes' report this procedure?
a) 22612, 22614 x 2, 20931, 22846
b) 22558, 22585 x 2, 20931, 22846
c) 22558, 22585 x 2, 20931-51, 22846-62
d) 63075, 22558, 22614 x 2, 20931-51, 22846-62

10) A patient is stabbed in the right arm. The stab wound is enlarged, cleaned, and foreign materials removed and inspected, and coagulation of minor blood vessels is completed. What code(s) should you report for this service?
a) 20103, 24200
b) 20103
c) 24200, 24000-59
d) 24000, 20103-59

11) A 62-year-old female patient is referred to Dr. Stegman for increased right groin pain. The patient describes the

pain as worse when sitting and rising from a seated position. The pain is temporarily relieved with intra articular corticosteroid injections. Monday, Dr. Stegman's physical examination documents loss of hip internal rotation, suspected cam lesion, and referral for x-ray with arthrography followed by CT with contrast. Both the x-ray and CT scan verify a cam lesion. Today, one week after the initial consult, Dr. Stegman completed a surgical right hip arthroscopy, including a femoroplasty to repair the cam lesion. How should Dr. Stegman report today's services?
a) 29860-RT, 73525-26, 73701-26
b) 29914-RT, 73525, 73701
c) 29914-RT
d) 27130-RT

12) Which is the correct CPT definition of external fixation?
a)   The usage of skeletal pins plus an attaching mechanism/device used for temporary or definitive treatment of acute or chronic bony deformity.
b)   The usage of skin application for force by an attaching mechanism/device used for permanent or definitive treatment of acute bone deformity.
c)   The usage of skeletal pins plus an attaching mechanism/ device used for permanent or definitive treatment of chronic bony deformity.
d)   The usage of skin and skeletal pins plus an application of mechanism/device used for temporary treatment of acute or chronic bony deformity.

RESPIRATORY AND CARIOVASCULAR SYSTEMS

13) A 20-year-old smoker has a single 8.2-mm lung nodule reported on CT of the chest. The peripheral nodule is not amendable to biopsy by routine bronschoscopy. The

patient agreed to undergo a diagnostic bronchoscopy with computer-assisted navigation under moderate sedation. Dr. Smith completed the procedure and provided moderate sedation with a trained observer. The intra-service time was documented as 45 minutes. How should Dr. Smith report her codes for this procedure?

a) 31622, 31627
b) 31622, 31627-51
c) 31622, 31627-51, 76376, 99152, 99153
d) 31622, 31627, 99152, 99153

14) A patient with a benign neoplasm of the bronchus and lung underwent a bronchoplasty with a cartilage autograft repair. The thoracotomy site was closed with layered closure and a chest tube left in place for drainage. How should you report this procedure and diagnosis?

a) D14.30, 31770
b) C80.1, D14.30, 31775, 20910-51
c) D3A.090, 31825
d) D14.30, D3A.090, 31775, 31825-51

15) A 22-year-old patient who suffers from severe persistent asthma underwent a flexible bronchoscopy with bronchial thermosplasty in the right middle lobes. Dr. Aster's nurse, who is a trained independent observer, monitored the patient during the 45-minute intra-service time. Dr. Aster completed the procedure and administered moderate conscious sedation. How should Dr. Aster report this procedure?

a) 31661, 99152, 99153
b) 31661
c) 31622, 31661-51, 99152, 99153-51
d) 31645, 31661-51, 99152, 99153-51

16) Darlene underwent (SRS/SBRT) thoracic target delineation for sterotactic body radiation therapy. Her course of treatment required four sessions. How should the surgeon report this procedure?
   a) 31626, 32701 x 4
   b) 32701, 77435
   c) 32701 x 4
   d) 32701

17) Harry, a neonate weighing 3 kg, underwent a complex aortic valvuloplasty with cardiopulmonary bypass using trans-ventricular dilation. During the same operative session, a trans-myocardial laser revascularization by thoracotomy was completed. How should you report this procedure?
   a) 33140, 33141
   b) 33390, 33141
   c) 33391, 33141
   d) 33140, 33390, 33141-51

18) Martin, a 54-year-old patient, underwent an insertion of a permanent pacemaker with transvenous electrodes placed in the right atrium and ventricle. The pacemaker device was evaluated and then placed in a subcutaneous pocket just below the ribcage. Dr. Gary completed this procedure, for Martin, under moderate conscious sedation and used fluoroscopic guidance to confirm lead placement. How should Dr. Gary report his professional services?
   a) 33208
   b) 33208, 76000-26, 93279-51
   c) 33217, 33213-51
   d) 33211, 76000-26, 93279-51

DIGESTIVE SYSTEM

19) A 26-year-old male patient had abnormal anal cytology on a screening exam. Today, the patient underwent a high-resolution anoscopy with four biopsies. How should you report today's service?
a) 46606
b) 46607
c) 46600, 46606 x 4
d) 46600, 46601, 46607 x 4

20) A 45-year-old male patient suffers from postprandial chest pain and abdominal pain. After workup and testing, he is diagnosed with a large paraesophageal hernia. Today, he undergoes a laparoscopic repair with implantation of mesh and a wedge gastroplasty. How should you report today's service?
a) 43282, 43283
b) 43281, 43282, 43283
c) 43332, 43283-51
d) 43280, 43283

21) Dr. Singh documents that a 57-year-old female patient presented to the office with rectal bleeding and watery diarrhea. The patient states these conditions have been ongoing for the past two weeks. The patient indicates she had noticed occasional rectal bleeding prior to the diarrhea. After clinical and diagnostic studies, Dr. Singh confirms a large tumor of the posterior rectal wall with the lower margin 5 cm from the anal verge. The patient undergoes a transanal full-thickness excision of the tumor. How should Dr. Singh report the procedure?
a) 45172, 0184T-59

b) 45190
c) 45172
d) 45160

22) A 61-year-old male patient has an unresectable carcinoma in the head of the pancreas. The patient agrees with treatment and undergoes the following procedure in the hospital. Dr. Cohn placed the patient under moderate sedation and then completed percutaneous placement of interstitial fiducial marker utilizing fluoroscopic guidance for visualization and confirmation of marker position. The patient was under sedation and for one hour as an independent observer monitored the patient's consciousness and physiological status. How should Dr. Cohn's report his professional services for this procedure?
a) 49411, 99152, 99153 x 2, 77002-26
b) 49411, 77002-26
c) 99152, 49411-59, 77002-26
d) 49411, 49412-51, 99156, 99157 x 2, 77002-26

23) Dr. Sanchez completed a harvest and transfer for an extra abdominal omental flap procedure for correction of chest wall defect in an 8-year-old patient. How should Dr. Sanchez report his procedure?
a) 49904
b) 44700, 49905
c) 49904, 20920-59
d) 44700, 49904-62, 20920-59

24) What codes should you report with the add-on code 49568?
a) 11004-11006
b) 49560-49566
c) Both A and B

d) None of the above

URINARY, MALE AND FEMALE REPRODUCTIVE SYSTEM

25) A patient underwent a complex cystometogram with bladder voiding pressure study and a urethral EMG. What codes should you use to report these services?
   a) 51728, 51784-51
   b) 51725, 51785-51
   c) 51726, 51797-59
   d) 51728, 51784-59

26) A 34-year-old patient gave birth to her third child via a cesarean delivery following an attempted vaginal delivery. Her two previous deliveries were vaginal without complications. She requested a tubal ligation be completed at the time of delivery. Dr. Milton followed this patient from the time of conception providing antepartum care, completed the delivery with tubal ligation, and will follow the patient through postpartum care. How should Dr. Milton report her services for this patient?
   a) 59510, 58611
   b) 59618, 58611
   c) 59510, 58605-59
   d) 59618, 58611-59

27) Lydia, a 25-year-old patient, was self-referred to Dr. Nedder for further examination and testing due to findings of severe dysplasia on her previous pap smear. Today, at the first visit with Dr. Nedder, he documented a comprehensive history, comprehensive examination, and moderate decision-making. He then performed a colposcopic examination with three biopsies of the cervix, endocervical curettage, and endometrial sampling. How should Dr. Nedder report his services?

a) 99213-25, 57455, 57456, 58110
b) 99244-25, 57454, 58110
c) 99204-25, 57454, 58110
d) 99204-25, 57455, 57456, 58110

28) Sandy, a 46-year-old patient, underwent anterior colporrhaphy, repair of a cystocele with repair of the urethrocele and inserted mesh. The procedure was completed via a vaginal approach. How should you report this surgery?
a) 57240, 57267
b) 57250, 57267
c) 57240, 57267-51
d) 57240, 49568-51

29) A patient underwent a surgical laparoscopy with ablation of four renal lesions. The surgeon used ultrasound guidance during the procedure. How should you report this service?
a) 50205, 77002-26
b) 50542
c) 50593
d) 50542, 77002-26

30) Jeannie, a 28-year-old female patient presented to the office with a concern that her IUD was "lost internally." Upon examination in the office, an attempt was made to remove the IUD but due to discomfort, the procedure was stopped. The next morning, Jeannie was taken to the outpatient surgical center and the IUD was removed, without complication, under general anesthesia. There was active bleeding at the end of the procedure. The patient tolerated the procedure well and was taken to recovery. How should Dr. Minor report the removal of the IUD?
a) 58300, 58301-59

b) 58301
c) 00840-P1, 58301
d) 58301-47

NERVOUS SYSTEM, EYE AND EAR

31) A patient with hydrocephalus required an aspiration and investigative nonvascular shuntogram completed via a puncture into a previously placed shunt to check for effective drainage. This procedure was completed in the emergency room. How should you report the physician's professional services for this procedure?
   a) 61070, 75809-26
   b) 62180, 75898-26
   c) 62220, 75809-26
   d) 62160, 75898-26

32) Which of the following statement(s) is correct when reporting cranial stereotactic radiosurgery?
   a) Report code 61796 when all lesions are simple
   b) Report code 61798 if treating multiple lesions and any single lesion treated is complex.
   c) Do not report codes 61796-61800 in conjunction with code 20660.
   d) All of the above.

33) With which code set or individual codes can add-on code 61781 be correctly reported?
   a) 61720-61791
   b) 62201 or 77432
   c) 77371-77373
   d) None of the above

34) Dr. Tubman completed and excision and repair to one-half of the margin of the left eyelid on Logan, a 42-year-old patient. During this procedure, Dr. Tubman completed preparation for skin grafts. Logan will undergo graft procedure when the lid margin is evaluated for proper healing. How should Dr. Tubman report her services?
   a) 67950-LT
   b) 67971-LT, 15120-59
   c) 67966-LT, 15120-59
   d) 67966-LT

35) Dr. Grant injected Mrs. Brown with two units of chemodenervation (Onabotulinumtoxin A) to treat her bilateral blepharospasm. How should Dr. Grant report his services?
   a) 67345-50, J0585x2
   b) 67345
   c) 64612-50, J0585x2
   d) 64612

36) Following an accident, a patient underwent a removal of the lens in his right eye via a pars plana approach without a vitrectomy. A McCannel suture technique was used to repair the ciliary body at the end of the procedure. How should you report these services?
   a) 66982-50, 66250-RT-59
   b) 66852-RT, 66682-RT-51
   c) 66840-E3, 66250-E3-59
   d) 66820, 66682-51, 66990-51

EVALUATION AND MANAGEMENT

37) Discharge note: Dr. Kara dictated and completed discharge

service in 26 minutes.

Mr. Davis, a 54-year-old male patient, is doing well following laparoscopic appendectomy completed at Calvin Hospital yesterday. He has been afebrile since the procedure, tolerating surgical soft diet, and ambulating with minimal assistance. He states he has "quality help" at home with his wife and son. Given his current improved condition and eagerness to leave the hospital, he will be discharged today. The nursing staff provided discharge instructions and review these with the patient and home health team (family). A follow-up office visit is set for 10 days. I have instructed the patient to notify me immediately if he experiences a fever, pain, or oozing from the operative site. It took 26 minutes in discharge management. How should Dr. Kara report today's service?

a) 99232-25, 99239

b) 99238

c) 99315

d) 99232-25, 99217

38) Dr. Martin admitted Mrs. Worth to Community Hospital for a laparoscopic cholecystectomy and cholangiograms. Dr. Martin's admission was documented as a comprehensive history, comprehensive examination, and moderate decision-making. Later that same day (10 hours later), after tolerating the procedures well, Mrs. Worth was discharged without complications. She was instructed to call Dr. Martin if she experienced any problems. Mrs. Worth's sister accompanied her home and will be her primary caregiver for the next few days. Mrs. Worth was instructed to call Dr. Martin's office and schedule a follow-up visit. How should Dr. Martin report her services for the admission?

a) 99222, 99238

b) 99225

c) 99235
d) 99219, 99217

39) What code range should you use if the same physician provides critical care services to a neonate or a pediatric patient in both the outpatient and inpatient settings on the same day?
a) 99460-99463
b) 99291-99292
c) 99468-99469
d) 99281-99285

40) Baby-boy Busch was evaluated in the birthing centre the morning of his birth. The documentation noted a comprehensive examination and a maternal/fetal/and newborn history, and decision making for discharge was straight-forward. Documentation revealed a normal newborn and decision was made to discharge later on the same day. How should you report this service?
a) 99463
b) 99460-25, 99463
c) 99221-25, 99238
d) 99234

41) Dr. South documented a comprehensive history, comprehensive examination, and high complexity decision making for this first visit with Burton, a 19-year-old patient. Burton has a complicated history of diabetes mellitus, which continues to be out of control, further complicated with current alcohol and drug abuse. Additionally, Burton brought tests results that he received three days ago from his visit to a free clinic. These test results were positive for a sexually transmitted disease. Dr. South spent two hours face- to-face talking with Burton.

How should Dr. South report her services for today?
a) 99354-25, 99355
b) 99245, 99356
c) 99205, 99354
d) 99215, 99354-51, 99355-51

42) Danielle, a 39-year-old established patient, was seen for her annual female examination. Documentation was completed related to a comprehensive female exam, including discussion of current birth control pills and a prescription for refill for the following year. During this visit, Danielle showed Dr. Bill a growth on her right arm. Dr. Bill completed a separate workup, including documentation of a problem-focused examination and straightforward medical decision-making. Dr. Bill completed an incisional biopsy of the lesion and noted a suspected benign lesion. Dr. Bill told Danielle that she would get a call with results from the biopsy the next day. Additionally, Dr. Bill instructed Danielle to watch the growth on her arm and to schedule a follow-up visit for reevaluation if any changes should occur. How should Dr. Bill report today's services?
a) 99395, 11106-57
b) 99213-25, 99385, 11106-57
c) 99214, 99395-25, 11106-25
d) 99395, 99212-25, 11106

ANESTHESIA

43) Dr. Sally, an anesthesiologist, provided general anesthesia for a 72-year-old patient with mild hypertension undergoing an open arthroscopy of the humeral neck. During this procedure, Dr. Sally was not supervising or monitoring any other cases. How should Dr. Sally report her

codes for this case?
a) 01630-AA-P2, 99100
b) 01620-AA-P2, 99100
c) 01630-P2
d) 01634-P2

44) James, a 74-year-old patient who has severe hypertension that is difficult to manage, cut his lower right leg while water skiing. He suffered a deep open wound of the right lower leg with exposed fibula due to the injury. He underwent an emergency muscle flap repair with grafts from his right thigh to the right lower leg to repair the open defect. This case required general endotracheal anesthesia with medical necessity for both an anesthesiologist and an independently acting CRNA. What anesthesia codes should Dr. Smith, the anesthesiologist, and Jane, the CRNA, report?
a) Dr. Smith: 01480-P3, 99100, 99140-51; Jane: 01480-P3, 99100, 99140-51
b) Dr. Smith: 01470-QZ-P3, 99100-51; Jane: 01470-AA-P3, 99100-51
c) Dr. Smith: 01480-AA-P3, 99100, 99140; Jane: 01480-QZ-P3, 99100, 99140
d) Dr. Smith: 01470-AA-P3, 99100, 99140; Jane: 01470-QZ-P3, 99100, 99140

45) Mark, a 45-year-old, mild diabetic patient, underwent an abdominal radical orchiectomy. Dr. Terry, the anesthesiologist, administered general anesthesia and an epidural infusion for control and management of postoperative pain. What codes should Dr. Terry report for this case?
a) 00928-51, 62322-P1
b) 00928-51, 62322-59
c) 00926-AA-P1
d) 00920-AA-59

46) Code 00940, anesthesia for vaginal procedures, has a base value of three (3) units. The patient was admitted under emergency circumstances, qualifying circumstance code 99140, which allows two (2) extra base units. A pre-anesthesia assessment was performed and signed at 2:00 a.m. Anesthesia start time is reported as 2:21 am, and the surgery began at 2:28 am. The surgery finished at 3:25 am and the patient was turned over to PACU at 3:36 am, which was reported as the ending anesthesia time. Using fifteen-minute time increments and a conversion factor of $100, what is the correct anesthesia charge?
   a) $800.00
   b) $900.00
   c) $1,000.00
   d) $1,200.00

RADIOLOGY

47) Jane, a 45-year-old asymptomatic female patient completed an annual screening mammogram on Monday, revealing a mass in the left breast. After reading the screening mammogram, the radiologist on Tuesday scheduled the patient for follow-up unilateral diagnostic mammogram with computer aided detection. The diagnostic mammogram showed a primary neoplasm of the lower outer quadrant. How should the radiologist report his professional services for Tuesday?
   a) 77065-26-LT
   b) 77067-26-50, 77065-26-LT
   c) 77065-26-RT
   d) 77066-26-LT

48) Dr. Levitt's office owns and operates the x-ray equipment he used to complete the reading of the films for this patient.

At the conclusion of the x-ray and his interpretation, he dictated the following report:

Patient: Mrs. Russell

X-ray left foot: Three views

Impressions: Fracture of distal phalanx, first digit Fractures of second and third digits (phalangeal). There is a fracture of the proximal portion of the first-digit phalanx. A comminuted fracture is noted in the middle phalanx of the second digit and an increased density is seen medially in the joint space of the middle phalanx of the third and fourth digits. Oblique films confirm displaced fragment of bone between the second and third digits. No other abnormalities present or noted. How should Dr. Levitt report his services?

a) 73630-LT
b) 73620-26-LT
c) 73650-LT
d) 73630-26-LT

49) A patient with a diagnosis of primary hyperparathyroidism underwent a parathyroid planar imaging with SPECT and concurrently acquired CT. How should you report this study and the diagnosis?

a) 78070, 70498, 78071, E21.0
b) 78072, E21.3
c) 78803, 78099, 78071, E21.0
d) 78072, E21.0

50) Ralph is a 52-year-old male undergoing treatment for a malignant tumor in his right lung. On Monday, he received his regularly scheduled radiation treatment with 10 MeV to a single treatment area. Today, on Wednesday, he received intracavitary hyperthermia treatment. How should you report Wednesday's service?

a) 77620

b) 77600
c) 77620, 77402
d) 77605, 77402-26

51) A patient underwent a thyroid imaging test with vascular flow and three uptakes on the same date of service. How would you report this study?
a) 78014x3
b) 78014
c) 78012, 78014x3
d) 78015, 78020x3

52) A patient underwent a single planar stress cardiac blood pool imaging study with gated equilibrium, wall motion and ejection fraction. In addition to the primary blood pool study, a first-pass technique at rest with right ventricular ejection fraction was completed. How should you report this service?
a) 78473, 78496
b) 78472, 78496
c) 78472, 78452, 78496
d) 78481, 78483

PATHOLOGY

53) Brent, a 37-year-old patient, had a comprehensive metabolic panel completed. In addition to the comprehensive metabolic panel, from the same single collection, a renal function panel was completed. How should you report these services?
a) 80053-22
b) 80069, 82247, 84075, 84155, 84460, 84450
c) 80053, 80069
d) 80053, 84100

54) Jason, a 17-year-old patient, arrived at the ER after taking drugs and drinking. He was semiconscious and told the ER staff that he took his cousin's Phenobarbital and another pill he could not identify. The laboratory completed a therapeutic assay for Phenobarbital, multiple drug class testing utilizing two nonchromatographic methods, and three confirmation procedures. How should you report the drug screening and confirmation in this case?
a) 80184, 80305
b) 80305 x2, 80184 x3
c) 80305, 80306, 80307
d) 80184, 80307

55) Patient required a C-section delivery during her early second trimester. Her placenta was submitted for gross and microscopic pathology examination following the C-section delivery. The placenta was submitted in two separate specimens and a decalcification procedure was utilized during pathology testing. How should you report this pathology service?
a) 88307 x 2, 88111
b) 88305 x 2, 88311
c) 88300 x 2, 88311-51
d) 88300, 88305 x 2, 88311-51

56) Dr. Garcia, a pathologist, was consulted during surgery on Mr. Barber. Dr. Garcia was provided with two tissue blocks and five frozen sections from Mr. Barber's gallbladder. Additional cytologic examination by squash prep was required on two separate sites of the gallbladder specimens (one squash prep completed on tissue without frozen section, one squash prep completed on tissue with frozen section). How should Dr. Garcia's professional services be reported?

a) 88329, 88332-26, 88334-26
b) 88304-26
c) 88331-26, 88334-26
d) 88331-26, 88332-26, 88333-26, 88334-26

57) What type of microorganism testing is identified in the CPT Professional Edition as: Colony morphology, growth on selective media, Gram stains or up to three tests (eg. catalase, oxidase, indole, urease)?
   a) Presumptive
   b) Definitive
   c) Molecular
   d) Compatibility

58) Sarah is being tested as a possible bone marrow donor for her brother. The laboratory completing the tests for HLA cross match used flow cytometry on two serum samples Sarah provided. How should you report these laboratory services?
   a) 86835, 86826
   b) 86829
   c) 86825, 86826
   d) 86831

MEDICINE

59) Which of the following must be included to report from code range 93040-93042?
   a)   A specific order for an electrocardiogram or rhythm strip followed by a separate, signed, written, and retrievable report
   b)   A verbal request for a consult including only a record review
   c)   A specific order for an electrocardiogram or rhythm

strip followed by a separate, signed, verbal, and non-retrievable report

d)   A written request for a consult including only a record review.

60) Cassidy, a 35-year-old patient, has a history of diabetes mellitus controlled with insulin. She was diagnosed with background diabetic retinopathy three years ago. Today, Cassidy was referred to Dr. Nelson for retinal images with fundus photography of both eyes. Upon completion of the images, Dr. Nelson reviewed the study and sent a detailed report back to the referring physician outlining the progression in Cassidy's condition. How should Dr. Nelson report, her services?
a)   99242-25, 92228, 92250-59
b)   92228
c)   99242-25, 92227, 92250-59
d)   92227

61) George, a 26-year-old patient, returned to Dr. Morris's office for his scheduled psychotherapy visit. In addition to the 45-minute psychotherapy session, Dr. Morris documented George's increased anxiety and depression, completed an expanded problem-focused history, expanded problem-focused examination, and documented low-complexity medical decision-making. Total time spent face-to- face with the patient was documented as 65 minutes. How should Dr. Morris report services for today's visit?
a)   99213, 90836
b)   99213, 90834
c)   99214, 90838
d)   99214, 90836

62) Brandi, a 14-year-old patient, underwent four daily end-stage renal dialysis services in the outpatient clinic prior to being hospitalized. A complete assessment was not provided before Brandi's hospitalization. How should you report the daily services?
a) 90957, 90969
b) 90965
c) 90957
d) 90969 x 4

63) Harper, a 55-year-old female patient is being tested for focal weakness and twitching of her lower extremity motor nerves. Today, she underwent three nerve conduction studies and a needle electromyography testing of three muscles. How should you report these services?
a) 95860, 95885
b) 95863, 95886
c) 95908, 95885
d) 95908, 95887

64) Dr. Risser treated a 44-year-old established patient with a history of CHF in the ER for acute shortness of breath and chest pain. After testing, Dr. Risser took the patient to the cardiac procedure suite with a diagnosis of an impending infarction. Dr. Risser completed a primary diagnostic PTCA to the left circumflex and left anterior descending artery. Following the PTCA, Dr. Risser determined that placement of three stents in the left anterior descending artery was indicated. He proceeded with placement of the stents during this same surgical session. How should Dr. Risser report his services for this procedure?
a) 99284-25, 92920, 92928 x 3
b) 92928, 92929 x 2
c) 92920, 92928-59, 92929-59

d) 92928, 92921

ANATOMY

65) Cushing's syndrome may be caused by prednisone therapy. This syndrome is considered a disorder of which gland(s)?
   a) Thymus
   b) Testes
   c) Ovarian
   d) Adrenal

66) Which of the following describes the location of the femur?
   a) Distal to the acetabulum and proximal to the patella
   b) Proximal to the acetabulum and distal to the patella
   c) Distal to the patella and proximal to the ischium
   d) Proximal to the ischium and distal patella

67) Which of the following terms best reflects the function of the growth plate?
   a) Longitudinal growth
   b) Blood cell formation
   c) Formation of synovial fluid
   d) Apoptosis fragmentation

68) What bones make up the axial skeleton?
   a) Spine, collar bone, arms
   b) Skull, rib cage, spine
   c) Shoulder bones, pelvic bones, arms and legs
   d) Coccyx, ulna, femur, tibia

MEDICAL TERMINOLOGY

69) What type of condition describes a patient diagnosed with oligospermia?
   a) Knots in the varicose vein
   b) Inflammation of the prostate gland
   c) Abnormally low number of sperms in the semen
   d) Failure to ovulate

70) Blepharoplasty describes what type of procedure?
   a)   Surgical reduction of the eyelids to remove excess fat, skin and muscle
   b)   Treatment for spider veins with injections of sclerotic solutions
   c) Replacement of damaged skin with healthy tissue taken from the donor
   d) Destruction of tissue by burning or freezing

71) Which term describes the death of a tissue resulting from interrupted blood flow to that area?
   a) Hypercirculation
   b) Agglutination
   c) Stenosis
   d) Infarction

72) A patient's complaint for painful menstrual bleeding will be documented in the medical record as which of the following?
   a) Amenorrhea
   b) Dysmenorrhea
   c) Menorrhagia
   d) Metrorrhagia

ICD-10 CM

73) Signs and symptoms that are associated routinely with a disease process should not be assigned as additional codes, unless otherwise instructed by classification.
   a) True
   b) False

74) Henry was playing baseball at the town's sports field and slid for home base where he collided with another player. He presents to the emergency department complaining of pain in the distal portion of his right middle finger. It is swollen and deformed. The physician orders an x-ray and diagnoses Henry with a displaced tuft fracture. He splints the finger, provides narcotics for pain, and instructs Henry to follow-up with his orthopedic in two weeks.
   a) S62.632A, Y93.64, W51.XXXA, Y92.320
   b) S62.662A, Y93.64, W03.XXXA, Y92.320
   c) S62.392A, Y93.64, W51.XXXA, Y92.320
   d) 562.632A, Y93.67, W03.XXXA, Y92.320

75) A newborn has been placed in NICU to treat herpetic vesicles on her torso and lower extremities. Tests have been ordered to rule out herpetic encephalitis, chorioretinitis and sepsis, and prophylactic protocols will be put in place to prevent spread of the infection from rupturing lesions. Code the patient's diagnosis.
   a) B00.9
   b) P35.2
   c) P37.8
   d) B00.0

76) Which of the following Z codes can be reported as a first listed code?
   a) Z37.0

b) Z89.621
c) Z87.710
d) Z00.129

77) A 36-year-old who is pregnant in her 38th week with her first child is admitted to the hospital. She experiences a prolonged labor during the first stage and eventually births a healthy baby boy.
a) O63.0, O09.519, Z37.0
b) O80, Z37.0
c) O80, O63.0, O09.519, Z37.0
d) O63.0, O09.513, Z37.0

HCPCS

78) During an emergency room visit, Sally was diagnosed with pneumonia. She was admitted to the hospital observation unit and treated with 500 mg of Zithromax through an IV route. How would you report the supply of this drug?
a) J0456
b) Q0144
c) J1190x2
d) J2020x2

79) Joe lost his ability to speak as a result of an accident. Today, he received a speech-generating synthesized device, which is activated by physical contact with the device. Which code would you report for supply of this device?
a) E2502
b) E2510
c) E2500
d) E2508

80) A patient has a home health aide come to his home to

clean and dress a burn on his lower leg. The aide used a special absorptive sterile dressing to cover a 20 sq. cm. area. She also covers a 15 sq. cm. area with a self-adhesive sterile gauze pad.

a) A6204, A6403
b) A6252, A6403
c) A6252, A6219
d) A6204, A6219

COMPLIANCE AND REGULATORY

81) What organization is responsible for updating CPT codes each year?
   a) American Health Information Management Association (AHIMA)
   b) American Academy of Professional Coders (AAPC)
   c) American Medical Association (AMA)
   d) Centre for Medicare and Medicaid Services (CMS)

82) Which of the following statements regarding advanced beneficiary notices (ABN) is TRUE?
   a) ABN must specify only the CPT® code that Medicare is expected to deny.
   b) Generic ABN which states that a Medicare denial of payment is possible or the internist is unaware whether Medicare will deny payment or not is acceptable.
   c) An ABN must be completed before delivery of items or services are provided.
   d) An ABN must be obtained from a patient even in a medical emergency when the services to be provided are not covered.

83) Which of the following is an example of fraud?
   a) Reporting the code for ultrasound guidance when used

to perform a liver biopsy.
b) Reporting a biopsy and excision performed on the same skin lesion during the same encounter.
c) Failing to append modifier 26 on an X-ray that is performed in the physician's office.
d) Failure to append modifier 57 on the EM service performed the day prior to a minor procedure.

CODING GUIDELINES

84) What is the time limit for reporting diagnosis codes for late effects?
a) Three months
b) Six months
c) One year
d) No limit

85) Which of the following statements regarding the ICD-10-CM coding conventions is TRUE?
a) If the same condition is described as both acute and chronic and separate subentries exist in the Alphabetic Index at the same indentation level, code only the acute condition.
b) Only assign a combination code when the Alphabetic Index explanation directs the coder to use it.
c) An ICD-10-CM code is still valid even if it has not been coded to the full number of digits required for that code.
d) Signs and symptoms that are integral to the disease process should not be assigned as additional codes, unless otherwise instructed.

86) When using the CPT index to locate procedures, which of the following are considered primary classes for main entries?

a)   Procedure or service; organ or other anatomic site; condition; synonyms, eponyms, and abbreviations
b)   Abbreviations; signs and symptoms, anatomic site; and code assignment
c)   Conventions; code ranges; modifying terms
d)   Procedure or service; modifiers; clinical examples; and definitions

87) Which of the following code and modifier combinations are correct?
a)   0165T-25
b)   15003-51
c)   93572-51
d)   None of the above

88) In which position should you sequence a manifestation code in brackets [ ]?
a)   Primary code
b)   Primary code in newborn cases
c)   Secondary code to an underlying condition
d)   Parenthesis

89) Which types of contrast administration alone do not qualify as a study "with contrast'?
a)   Oral and/or extravascular
b)   Oral and/or intrathecal
c)   Oral and/or intravascular
d)   Oral and/or rectal

90) Which of the following place of service codes is reported for fracture care performed by an orthopedic physician in the urgent care facility?
a)   11
b)   20
c)   22

d) 23

CASE STUDY

91) What codes should you report for Dr. West in this case?

Preoperative Diagnosis: Right knee medial meniscal tear.

Postoperative Diagnosis: Current, right knee medial meniscal tear with mild grade three chondral change in the medial femoral condyle.

Procedure: Right knee arthroscopy with medial meniscectomy.

Summary of procedures: A 52-year-old male patient signed consent forms and was taken to the surgical suite. After adequate anesthesia was obtained, a tourniquet was applied to the right thigh. Examination of the right knee under anesthesia showed full range of motion. No instability to provocative testing. The left lower extremity was placed in a well leg holder. The right lower extremity was then prepped and draped in usual sterile fashion.

Anteromedial and anterolateral portals were established after distention of soft tissues with 20 cc of 0.5% Marcaine with epinephrine. The arthroscope was inserted with a blunt trocar and the joint distended with lactated Ringer's. Examination of the medial compartment showed a tear in the posterior root of the medial meniscus right at the intersection which was unstable to probing. This area was debrided with punch, motorized shaver, and electrocautery unit until stable. There was a mild grade-three change on the medial lateral compartment that showed normal articular cartilage and a stable lateral meniscus to probing. The anterior compartment showed normal articular cartilage and no loose bodies. The joint was copiously irrigated with lactated Ringer's and the instruments were removed. The wounds were closed with 4-0 nylon suture in an interrupted fashion. The joint was injected with additional 10 cc of 0.5% Marcaine with epinephrine and 2 mg of estradiol. Sterile dressings were applied. The patient was awakened and brought to recovery room in stable condition. The tourniquet was applied but not inflated and blood loss was minimal. The patient tolerated the procedure well.

a) M23.205, 29880-RT
b) M23.205, 29881-RT
c) S83.232A, 29881-RT
d) S83.232A, 29880-RT

92) What codes should Dr. Field report for his service in the following case? Preoperative Diagnosis: Adenotonsillar hypertrophy and obstructive sleep apnea. Postoperative Diagnosis: Same.

Procedure: Tonsillectomy and Adenoidectomy

Anesthesia: General by endotracheal tube by Dr. Rush

Operative report: The patient is a 10-year-old female with a history of adenotonsillar hypertrophy as well as symptoms of sleep apnea. Informed consent was obtained from parents and the risks of surgery explained. The patient was taken to the operating room and placed in the supine position. Shoulder roll was placed. McIvor mouth retractor was used to retract the tongue inferiorly. Red rubber catheter was used to retract the palate superiorly. Adenoids were inspected and found to be enlarged and obstructed in the nasopharynx. They were removed with an adenoid curette. The area was then packed with tonsil sponges soaked in Marcaine. The right tonsil and then the left tonsil were grasped with curved Allis and removed with Bovie cautery. The regions were then further cauterized with suction cautery and 4 cc of 0.25% Marcaine was injected in the field. The patient tolerated the procedure well, and blood loss was minimal; patient was awakened and taken to recovery room in stable condition.

a) J35.1, J35.2, 42820
b) J35.3, 42821
c) J35.1, J35.2, 42820
d) J35.3, 42820

93) What codes should Dr. Stone report in the following case?
Brief history of present illness: 26-year-old female with a history of nephrolithiasis. She complains of left- sided flank discomfort with hematuria, dysuria, and passage of fragments. This morning she presented to ER with increased left and right-side flank pain. She underwent CT with contrast of the abdomen and pelvis showing approximately 8 right renal calculi ranging between 2 and 12 mm and 10 left renal calculi ranging between 5 and 8 mm with possible nephrocalcinosis based on the radiologist's interpretation. Dr. Stone, the urologist, consulted with patient, reviewed results of the CT scan, and discussed treatment options. The patient signed an informed consent for the following procedure.
Postoperative diagnosis: Bilateral nephrolithiasis
Procedure: Lithotripsy, extracorporeal shock wave. She was given 1 g Ancef, brought to the operating room, placed supine on the lithotropsy table. Using fluoroscopy, the right and left kidneys were evaluated with no overlying bowel gas, stool, or bowel contents; multiple stones were visualized (R. 8 and L. 10). The ureters were examined showing no stones or fragments present. Stones were targeted for treatment via extracorporeal shock wave with successful break down and flush. After treatment the patient was awoken in the operating room and extubated without difficulty. She was taken to recover in stable condition.
a) N20.1, N20.0, 50590
b) N20.0, 74177, 50590
c) N20.0, N20.1, R10.30, 50590

d) N20.0, 50590

94) What codes should Dr. Orange report in the following case?
Surgeon: Dr. Orange, Anesthesiologist: Dr. Mee
Preoperative Diagnosis: Prominent left spermatocele
Postoperative Diagnosis: Same
Procedure performed: Left spermatocystectomy with epididymectomy
Indications for procedure: The patient is a 66-year-old male with a progressively enlarging left-sided spermatocele causing discomfort in this area. This lesion is 4 times the size of the testicle. After careful explanation of the risks, benefits, and alternatives, he agreed to the procedure.
Operative report: The patient was taken to the operating room, prepped and draped in the usual fashion, and induced under general anesthesia. He was placed in a supine position. Midline raphe incision was made using a skin knife, Bovie electro-cautery was used to dissect through the subcutaneous tissues down to the level of the tunica vaginalis, which was incised. The testicle and spermatocele were exposed. A portion of the epididymis was overlying the spermatocele and I dissected this carefully with resection of a portion of the epididymis, which was tied off using a 3-0 Vicryl free tie. I proceeded to dissect circumferentially to free the spermatocele leaving adequate blood supply to the testicle. The testicle was placed back within the tunica vaginalis; proceeded to reapproximate this without difficulty using a 3-0 Vicryl stitch. Subcutaneous closure was performed using a 3-0 Vicryl in a running fashion, followed by closure of the skin using 3-0 chromic in a running horizontal mattress fashion. The patient tolerated the procedure well with no complications. He was taken to the recovery room in satisfactory condition.
a) Q52.8, 54860-LT, 54840-LT

   b) Q52.8, 54840-LT
   c) N43.40, 54860-LT
   d) N43.40, 54840-LT

95) What codes should Dr. Roger's report in the following case?
Preoperative Diagnosis: Cervical stenosis with left upper extremity radiculopathy Postoperative Diagnosis: Same
Procedure: Cervical epidural steroid injection at C4-C5 directed to the left midline with fluoroscopic guidance.
Anesthesia: Local
Indications: Fluoroscopy is utilized to confirm placement of the needle within the epidural spaces and rule out any vascular uptake. Epidural steroid injections performed to reduce swelling and inflammation as an adjunct to rehabilitation of the spine.
Procedure: Dr. Rogers explained the procedure and risks and benefits to her 42-year- old male patient. The patient agreed to the procedure and signed consent forms. The patient was escorted to the procedure suite and laid in a prone position on the procedure table. The skin of the cervicothoracic region was scrubbed and draped in the usual sterile fashion. C4-C5 interspace was identified. Overlying skin was anesthetized with 1% buffered lidocaine. An 18-guage 3 1/2-inch Tuohy epidural needle was slowly advanced through the aforementioned interspace until the ligamentum flavum was perforated with a loss-of-resistance technique. Aspiration was negative for CSF or blood, and contrast was slowly infiltrated, demonstrating appropriate epidural spread on PA and lateral views without vascular uptake or intrathecal flow in either view. Final aspiration was likewise negative and 9 mg of Betamethasone was slowly infiltrated through the needle. The needle was then removed. The patient tolerated the procedure well and was transported to the recovery room for postprocedural observation. He

experienced no complications and was discharged in stable and satisfactory condition in the company of a driver. He will follow up in the office in two weeks and by phone for any questions in the interim.

a) M48.02, M54.12, 62320, 77003-26
b) M48.02, M54.12, 62320
c) M50.00, M48.02, M54.12, 62324, 77003-26
d) M54.2, M48.02, 62320, 62322

96) Preoperative diagnosis: Left knee medial collateral ligament tear. Anterior cruciate ligament tear. Possible meniscus tear

Postoperative diagnosis: Same Procedures:

Left knee medial collateral ligament tear: Exam under anesthesia Anterior cruciate ligament tear: Diagnostic arthroscopy of left knee Possible meniscus tear: Left knee arthroscopic repair of lateral meniscus Tourniquet time: 2.5 hours

Procedure: The patient was taken to the operating room and positioned, and an epidural anesthetic was placed. Once the anesthetic had taken effect, the patient's left leg was examined under anesthesia and noted to have increased valgus laxity with end point, a positive Lachman test, and positive pivot-shift test. The patient was prepped and draped in the normal fashion, exsanguinated, and the tourniquet applied to a 350 mmHg. The knee was then insufflated and irrigated with fluid. Using the arthroscopic sheath, visualization of the knee joint began. Attention was turned to the lateral meniscus where the tear was debrided. Using the arthroscope, the lateral meniscus was sutured with two mattress-type sutures of non- absorbable 2-0 material. The sutures were then tied and visualized with arthroscopy to reveal the meniscus to be in excellent shape and stable position. The 3.5-cm wound was thoroughly irrigated and closed with intermediate subcutaneous sutures. A sterile compression dressing was applied. The patient was placed in a TED hose and Watco brace, setting the brace between 40º and 60º of free motion. He was then taken to the recovery room in stable condition. The instrument, sponge, and needle counts were correct.

a) 29882, 29877-52, 29870-51
b) 29866, 29868
c) 29870, 29882, 12032
d) 29882

97) Dr. Manning, a thoracic surgeon, was asked to consult with Nancy, a 66-year-old female with atherosclerotic heart disease. The patient, who requested the visit, is well known to Dr. Manning, who performed thoracic surgery on her two years ago. She was seen in his office Monday morning for a consultative visit with mild complaints of fatigue and shortness of breath. Dr. Manning dictated comprehensive history, comprehensive examination, and high-complexity decision-making. During this consultation, Dr. Manning made the decision to re operate on Nancy. He sent a written report back to her cardiologist, Dr. Shaw, regarding the need for another surgery to take place the following day. Monday evening, Nancy was admitted to the hospital to start the prep for the planned bypass surgery Tuesday morning.

Tuesday's operative report

Preoperative diagnosis: Atherosclerotic heart disease

Postoperative diagnosis: Same

Anesthesia: General

Procedure: The patient was brought to the operating room and placed in the supine position. With the patient under general intubation anesthesia, the anterior chest, abdomen, and legs were prepped and draped in the usual fashion. Review of a postoperative angiography showed severe, recurrent, two-vessel disease with normal ventricular function. A segment of the femoropopliteal artery was harvested using endoscopic vein-harvesting technique and prepared for grafting. The patient was heparinized and placed on cardiopulmonary bypass. The patient was cooled as necessary for the remainder of the procedure and an aortic cross-clamp was placed. The harvested vein was anastomosed to the aorta and brought down to the circumflex and anastomosed into place. An artery was anastomosed to the left subclavian artery and brought down to the left anterior descending and anastomosed into place. The aortic cross-clamp was removed after 55 minutes with spontaneous cardio version to a normal sinus rhythm. The patient was warmed and weaned from the bypass without difficulties after 104 minutes. The patient achieved homeostasis. The chest was drained and closed in layers in the usual fashion. The leg was closed in the usual fashion. Sterile dressings were applied and the patient returned to intensive care recovery in satisfactory condition.

How should Dr. Manning report his services for Monday and Tuesday in this case?

a) Monday: 99255-57; Tuesday: 33511, 33517, 35600
b)   Monday: 99215-57; Tuesday: 33533, 33517-51, 35572-80, 33530-51
c)   Monday: 99255-57; Tuesday: 33533, 33510, 33572, 33530
d)   Monday: 99215-57; Tuesday: 33533, 33517, 35572, 33530

98) How would the following case be coded?

Preoperative diagnosis: Lesion, buccal submucosa, right lower lip Postoperative diagnosis: Same

Procedure performed: Excision of lesion, buccal submucosa, and right lower lip

Anesthesia: Local

Procedure: The patient was placed in the supine position. A

measured 7x8 mm hard lesion is felt under the submucosa of the right lower lip. After application of 1% Xylocaine with 1:1000 epinephrine, the lesion was completely excised. The lesion does not extend into the muscle layer. The 8-cm wound was closed with complex mattress sutures to the submucosal level and dressed in typical sterile fashion. The patient tolerated the procedure well and returned to the recovery area in satisfactory condition.

a) 40816, D10.39
b) 40814, 40831-51, D10.39
c) 40814, K13.79
d) 40814, D10.39

99) What codes should be reported with the following case?
Preoperative Diagnosis: Total retinal detachment, right eye
Postoperative Diagnosis: Same
Procedure performed: Complex repair of retinal detachment with photocoagulation, scleral buckle, sclerotomy/vitrectomy
Anesthesia: Local
Procedure: The patient was placed, prepped, and draped in the usual manner. Adequate local anesthesia was administered. The operating microscope was used to visualize the retina, which has fallen into the posterior cavity. The vitreous was extracted using a VISC to complete the posterior sclerotomy. Minimal scar tissue was removed to release tension from the choroid. The retina was repositioned and attached using photocoagulation laser, a gas bubble, and a suture placement of a scleral buckle around the eye. The positioning of the retina was checked during the procedure to ensure proper alignment. Antibiotic ointment was applied to the eye prior to placement of a pressure patch. The patient tolerated the procedure well and returned to the recovery suite in satisfactory condition.

a) 67113-RT, 67107-51, 67145-51, 66990-51
b) 67113-RT, 69990-RT
c) 67113-RT, 66990-RT
d) 67107-51, 67145-51, 66990-51

100) What codes would the physician report for the following case?

Preoperative Diagnosis: Displaced impacted Colles fracture, left distal radius and ulna.

Postoperative Diagnosis: Same

Operative procedure: Reduction with application of internal fixator, left wrist fracture

FINDINGS: The patient is a 46-year-old right-hand-dominant female who fell off stairs 4 to 5 days ago sustaining an impacted distal radius fracture with possible intraarticular component and an associated ulnar styloid fracture. Today in surgery, fracture was reduced anatomically and an external fixator was applied.

PROCEDURE: Under satisfactory general anesthesia, the fracture was manipulated and C-arm images were checked. The left upper extremity was prepped and draped in the usual sterile orthopedic fashion. Two small incisions were made over the second metacarpal and after removing soft tissues including tendinous structures out of the way, frame was next placed and the site for the proximal pins was chosen. Small incision was drawing was carried out and blunt-tipped pins were placed for the EBI external fixator. The subcutaneous tissues were carried out of the way. The pin guide was placed and 2 drilled and blunt-tipped pins placed. Fixator was assembled. C-arm images were checked. Fracture reduction appeared to be anatomic. Suturing was carried out where needed with Vicryl interrupted subcutaneous and 4-0 nylon interrupted sutures. Sterile dressings were applied. Vascular supply was noted to be satisfactory. Final frame tightening was carried

out.
a) 25600-LT, 20692-51
b) 25605- LT, 20690-51
c) 25606-LT
d) 25607-LT

EXAM A ANSWERS AND RATIONALES

1. Answer C – The code description of 15828 is Rhytidectomy; cheek, chin, and neck and the code description of 15826 is Rhytidectomy; glabellar frown lines. Hence option B and D are incorrect. The code description of 15879 is Suction assisted lipectomy; lower extremity hence option A is also incorrect. The Coe description of 15878 is Suction assisted lipectomy; upper extremity which is in option c.

2. Answer A – The code description of 11104 is Punch biopsy of skin and hence option B and D are incorrect. The code description of 11303 is Shaving of epidermal or dermal lesion, single lesion, trunk, arms or legs; lesion diameter over 2.0 cm hence this option C is also incorrect. The code description of 11308 is Shaving of epidermal or dermal lesion, single lesion, scalp, neck, hands, feet, genitalia; lesion diameter over 2.0 cm and this s the correct code as per the scenario. We need to add modifier LT as the procedure done on left foot.

3. Answer B – The code 11422 is for the excision of benign lesion so option C is incorrect. As per the question the total excised diameter of lesion with margins

was 4.0 cm and code 11626 is for excised diameter over 4.0 cm hence option D is incorrect. "Excision —Malignant Lesions" guideline says that excision of malignant lesions requiring more than simple closure, it required intermediate or complex closure hence code 12032 used. The code 96372 can't be used as the description says Therapeutic, prophylactic, or diagnostic injection (specify substance or drug); subcutaneous or intramuscular. Hence B is the correct answer.

4. Answer A – The code 11602 is for Excision, malignant lesion including margins, trunk, arms, or legs; excised diameter 1.1 to 2.0 cm and in our Scenario the Benign Lesion excision is done so Option D is incorrect. Code 11423 says that Excision, benign lesion including margins, except skin tag (unless listed elsewhere), scalp, neck, hands, feet, genitalia; excised diameter 2.1 to 3.0 cm but in our scenario the final excised diameter for neck is 2.0 cm. hence option C is also incorrect. The code 11422 should be used. As defects were closed by simple suture technique hence code 12004 should not be used. Hence only option is correct.

5. Answer C – The code 11044 says Debridement, bone (includes epidermis, dermis, subcutaneous tissue, muscle and/or fascia, if performed), but in our scenario the debridement of bone is not done hence option B is incorrect. For debridement of skin [ie, epidermis and/or dermis only] and for active wound care management we use 97597, 97598 hence Option A and D is incorrect. The correct answer is C which fulfills all the requirements.

6. Answer D - CPT code 19083 describes a percutaneous needle biopsy of the breast using imaging guidance. This code includes all imaging guidance performed during the procedure. In this case, Dr. Linda performed

a percutaneous automated vacuum-assisted biopsy under ultrasonic guidance, which falls under code 19083.

Codes 19081 and 19085 also describe breast biopsy procedures but involve different techniques than what was used in this case. Code 19081 describes an open surgical biopsy of the breast, while code 19085 describes a percutaneous needle core biopsy using a spring-loaded device. These codes do not accurately describe the procedure performed in this case.

Code 76942 describes ultrasound guidance for needle placement and is commonly reported in conjunction with biopsy codes to indicate the use of imaging guidance during the procedure. The -26 modifier is used to indicate that only the professional component of the service was provided. However, code 76942 alone does not accurately describe the biopsy procedure performed in this case.

Therefore, the correct way to report Dr. Linda's professional services is with CPT code 19083, which includes the percutaneous automated vacuum-assisted biopsy and ultrasonic guidance.

7. Answer A - The correct answer is a) 24666-LT.

CPT code 24666-LT describes an open treatment of a radial shaft fracture with internal fixation, which includes the use of a plate, screw, or rod to stabilize the fracture site. This code is appropriate for Jack's procedure because it involved the replacement of the implant used for internal fixation of the radial shaft.

8. Answer A - The primary repair of the left ankle ligament is reported with code 27695-LT, which includes any exploration and repair of the ligament. The percutaneous tenotomy to lengthen the Achilles tendon is reported with code 27606-59-LT, which represents a distinct procedural service from the

primary repair and is appended with modifier 59 to indicate that it is a separate and distinct service. Modifier LT is used to indicate that the procedure was performed on the left ankle.

Therefore, the correct coding for this scenario is 27695-LT, 27606-59-LT.

9. Answer B - Answer b is the correct choice to report the procedure performed by Dr. Hewes.

The procedure described in the scenario involves an anterior lumbar fusion with allograft and instrumentation. The code for this procedure is 22558 (Arthrodesis, anterior interbody, including disc space preparation, discectomy, osteophytectomy, and decompression of spinal cord and/or nerve roots; lumbar below L5-S1).

Additionally, the procedure involved minimal discectomy at L1-2, L3-4, and L4-5 levels. For this, code 22585 (Arthrodesis, anterior interbody technique, including minimal discectomy to prepare interspace (other than for decompression); lumbar) can be used, with a total of 2 units to account for the multiple levels.

Since anterior instrumentation was required for stabilization of the entire lumbar region, code 22846 (Posterior non-segmental instrumentation [e.g., Harrington rod technique, pedicle fixation across one interspace, atlantoaxial transarticular screw fixation, sublaminar wiring] [List separately in addition to code for primary procedure]) should also be reported.

Finally, since allograft was used, code 20931 (Tissue grafts, other [e.g., paratenon, fat, dermis]) should be reported.

Therefore, the correct code sequence for the described procedure is: 22558, 22585 x 2, 20931, 22846.

10. Answer B - The correct answer is (b) 20103.

The code 20103 describes the repair of a wound in the arm that requires extensive cleaning and removal of foreign material. This code would be appropriate for the repair of a stab wound in the arm, as described in the scenario.

The code 24200, on the other hand, describes the exploration and removal of foreign bodies from a deep wound in the arm. While this code may be appropriate in some cases, it does not accurately reflect the services provided in the scenario, as the wound is not described as deep.

The codes 24000 and 24001 describe the closure of separate layers of muscle and fascia in a wound, and would not be appropriate in this scenario as the wound is described as being repaired with coagulation of minor blood vessels.

Therefore, the correct code to report for this service is 20103.

11. Answer C - The correct answer is c) 29914-RT.

In the given scenario, Dr. Stegman performed a surgical right hip arthroscopy with a femoroplasty to repair the cam lesion. The correct code for this procedure is 29914, which describes an arthroscopic femoroplasty. The -RT modifier is added to indicate that the procedure was performed on the right side.

The other codes, 29860-RT and 27130-RT, are not appropriate in this case. Code 29860-RT describes an arthroscopic meniscectomy, which is not the procedure performed in this case. Code 27130-RT describes an arthroplasty of the hip joint, which is a more extensive procedure than the arthroscopy with femoroplasty performed in this case.

Code 73525-26 is a radiological supervision and interpretation code for a hip x-ray with arthrography, which was performed prior to the arthroscopy. Code 73701-26 is a radiological supervision and interpretation code for a CT scan with contrast, which was also performed prior to the arthroscopy. However, since Dr. Stegman did not perform these imaging studies, he should not report these codes. These codes should be reported by the radiologist who performed the imaging studies.

12. Answer A - The correct CPT definition of external fixation is:

a) The usage of skeletal pins plus an attaching mechanism/device used for temporary or definitive treatment of acute or chronic bony deformity.

External fixation is a technique used in orthopedic surgery to treat fractures, dislocations, and other injuries by immobilizing bones and joints with the use of pins, wires, and external devices. It can be used for both temporary and definitive treatment of acute or chronic bony deformity.

13. Answer A - The correct answer is a) 31622, 31627.

In this scenario, the 20-year-old smoker has a single 8.2-mm lung nodule that is not amendable to biopsy by routine bronchoscopy. Therefore, the patient underwent a diagnostic bronchoscopy with computer-assisted navigation under moderate sedation to obtain a tissue sample for further analysis.

The CPT code for diagnostic bronchoscopy with transbronchial lung biopsy is 31622. The code for moderate sedation is 31627. Since Dr. Smith provided both services, she should report both codes. Modifier -51 is not necessary as there is no bundling issue between the two codes.

Codes 76376, 99152, and 99153 are not relevant in this scenario, as they are related to additional procedures such as CT guidance, prolonged services, and moderate sedation by a physician or other qualified health care professional.

Therefore, the correct answer is a) 31622, 31627.

14. Answer A - The correct answer is a) D14.30, 31770.

In this scenario, the patient has a benign neoplasm of the bronchus and lung and underwent a bronchoplasty with a cartilage autograft repair. The thoracotomy site was closed with layered closure and a chest tube left in place for drainage.

The diagnosis code for a benign neoplasm of the bronchus and lung is D14.30. The CPT code for bronchoplasty with cartilage autograft repair is 31770. This code describes the repair of a bronchus or bronchus-like structure using cartilage from the patient's own body.

Codes 31775 and 20910-51 are not appropriate in this scenario. Code 31775 is for a complex chest wall repair, which is not performed in this scenario. Code 20910 is for a tissue grafting procedure, which is also not performed in this scenario.

Code D3A.090 is not relevant in this scenario, as it is used to report a benign neoplasm of the bronchus, which is already represented by code D14.30. Code 31825 is for the thoracoscopy procedure, which is not performed in this scenario.

Therefore, the correct answer is a) D14.30, 31770.

15. Answer B - The correct answer is b) 31661. The Current Procedural Terminology (CPT) code 31661 is used to report bronchial thermoplasty performed during bronchoscopy. This code includes moderate sedation, so there is no need to report separate codes for sedation.

The other codes listed in options a), c), and d) are not appropriate for this procedure:

Option a) includes codes for observation and monitoring (99152 and 99153) that are not separately billable with a bronchoscopy procedure, as the monitoring is considered part of the primary service.

Option c) includes code 31622, which is used for a different type of bronchoscopy procedure (bronchoalveolar lavage) and would not be appropriate for this case.

Option d) includes code 31645, which is used for a different type of bronchoscopy procedure (removal of a foreign body) and would not be appropriate for this case.

Therefore, the correct code to report this procedure is 31661.

16. Answer D - The correct answer is d) 32701.

In this scenario, Darlene underwent stereotactic body radiation therapy (SBRT) for thoracic targets, and the surgeon performed target delineation, which is the process of identifying the specific area to be targeted for radiation therapy.

CPT code 32701 describes the SBRT treatment delivery for the thorax, and it includes all necessary steps, such as target delineation, simulation, imaging guidance, and treatment delivery.

The other codes listed in the options are as follows:

a) 31626 is a code for endoscopic bronchial ultrasound-guided transbronchial needle aspiration, which is not relevant to this scenario. Additionally, it is not appropriate to report this code multiple times for a single procedure.

b) 77435 is a code for three-dimensional radiotherapy planning, which is also not relevant to this scenario.

c) Reporting code 32701 four times would suggest that Darlene underwent four separate SBRT treatments, which is not accurate. She received a single course of treatment that required four sessions.

Therefore, the appropriate code to report for this procedure is 32701.

17. Answer C - The correct answer is c) 33391, 33141.

In this scenario, the neonate Harry underwent two procedures during the same operative session: a complex aortic valvuloplasty with cardiopulmonary bypass using trans-ventricular dilation and a trans-myocardial laser revascularization by thoracotomy.

CPT code 33391 describes a complex congenital heart procedure that involves major vessel repair, valve repair, or valve replacement. The complex aortic valvuloplasty with cardiopulmonary bypass using trans-ventricular dilation falls under this category and should be reported with this code.

CPT code 33141 describes a trans-myocardial laser revascularization, which was also performed during the same operative session. This code should be reported separately, as it is a different and distinct procedure from the complex aortic valvuloplasty.

The other codes listed in the options are as follows:

a) 33140 is a code for aortic valve replacement, which is not accurate for the procedure performed on Harry. Additionally, it is not appropriate to report this code in addition to the correct code for the complex aortic valvuloplasty.

b) 33390 is a code for a congenital heart procedure, which is not specific to the procedures performed on Harry.

d) Reporting code 33141 with a -51 modifier suggests that it is a reduced service, which is not accurate for the procedure performed on Harry.

Therefore, the appropriate codes to report for this procedure are 33391 and 33141.

18. Answer A - The correct answer is a) 33208.

The procedure described in the scenario is the insertion of a permanent pacemaker, which is reported with CPT code 33208 (Insertion or replacement of permanent pacemaker with transvenous electrode(s); atrial and ventricular). This code includes the placement of the transvenous electrodes in the right atrium and ventricle, the insertion of the pacemaker device, and the creation of a subcutaneous pocket below the ribcage for the device.

The use of moderate conscious sedation and fluoroscopic guidance are considered part of the main procedure and are not separately reported. Therefore, codes 76000-26 (Fluoroscopic guidance for needle placement (eg, biopsy, aspiration, injection, localization device), radiological supervision and interpretation (RS&I)) and 93279-51 (Programming device evaluation (in person) with iterative adjustment of the implantable device to test the function of the device and select optimal permanent programmed values with analysis, review and report by a physician or other qualified health care professional; multiple lead system) are not reported with code 33208.

Codes 33217 (Insertion of a pacing electrode, cardiac venous system, for left ventricular pacing, at time of insertion of pacing cardioverter-defibrillator or pacemaker pulse generator (eg, biventricular pacing system)) and 33213-51 (Insertion of pacing electrode, cardiac venous system) are also not reported because they describe the insertion of pacing electrodes in the cardiac venous system, which was not performed in this case.

Therefore, the correct code to report the professional services performed by Dr. Gary is 33208.

19. Answer B - The correct answer is b) 46607.

CPT code 46606 is used to report an anoscopy with biopsy. However, since the patient underwent a high-resolution anoscopy with four biopsies, the appropriate code to report this service is 46607. This code describes a high-resolution anoscopy with biopsy, single or multiple.

CPT code 46600 is used to report a proctosigmoidoscopy. CPT code 46601 is used to report a proctosigmoidoscopy with biopsy. These codes are not appropriate for reporting a high-resolution anoscopy with biopsies.

Therefore, the correct way to report this service is with CPT code 46607.

20. Answer A - The correct answer is a) 43282, 43283.

CPT code 43282 describes a laparoscopic repair of a paraesophageal hernia with implantation of mesh. This code is appropriate for reporting the laparoscopic repair of the paraesophageal hernia in this case.

CPT code 43283 describes a laparoscopic wedge gastroplasty. This code is also appropriate for reporting the wedge gastroplasty performed during the same surgical session.

Therefore, the correct way to report this service is with CPT codes 43282 and 43283.

CPT code 43281 is used to report a laparoscopic repair of a paraesophageal hernia without mesh implantation, which is not applicable in this case. CPT code 43332 is used to report a laparoscopic gastroplasty, which is not the same as a wedge gastroplasty. CPT code 43280 is used to report an open repair of a paraesophageal hernia, which is not applicable in this case since the repair was performed laparoscopically.

21. Answer C - The correct answer is c) 45172.

45172 is the correct CPT code for a "Proctectomy, transanal excision of rectal tumor(s), full thickness (ie, through muscularis propria) with or without perirectal or pelvic lymphadenectomy, single or multiple lesions" which is the procedure Dr. Singh performed.

0184T-59 is an add-on code used to report "Transanal excision of benign neoplasm(s), including margins, using any method, single or multiple lesions" which is not appropriate in this case since the tumor was not benign.

45190 is a code for a "Biopsy of rectum", which is not the same as the procedure Dr. Singh performed.

45160 is a code for "Hemorrhoidectomy, internal, by ligation other than rubber band; single hemorrhoid column/group", which is not the same procedure that was performed on this patient.

22. Answer B - The correct answer is b) 49411, 77002-26.

CPT code 49411 describes the percutaneous placement of interstitial device(s) for radiation therapy guidance. This is the primary procedure performed by Dr. Cohn.

CPT code 77002-26 is used for fluoroscopic guidance and is reported separately with modifier -26, indicating the professional component only.

CPT codes 99152, 99153, 99156, and 99157 are not applicable in this case, as they are codes for anesthesia services, and the patient was under moderate sedation, not general anesthesia.

Modifier -59 is also not applicable in this case, as it is used to indicate a distinct procedural service, which is not the case here.

23. Answer A - The correct answer is a) 49904.

The harvest and transfer of an extra abdominal omental flap is reported with CPT code 49904, which describes a procedure to harvest an omental flap from the abdomen and transfer it to another location. This code includes both the harvest and transfer of the flap.

Codes 44700 and 49905 are not appropriate for this procedure as they do not describe the specific procedure of harvesting and transferring an omental flap.

Code 20920 is also not appropriate as it describes a different procedure of tissue grafting or implantation, which is not the same as the harvest and transfer of an omental flap.

Therefore, the correct code to report the harvest and transfer of an extra abdominal omental flap for correction of chest wall defect in an 8-year-old patient is 49904.

24. Answer C - The add-on code 49568 is used to report an additional intra-abdominal procedure during a laparoscopic procedure. According to the American Medical Association (AMA) Current Procedural Terminology (CPT) guidelines, the code should be reported with the primary procedure code and any additional codes that describe the intra-abdominal procedure(s) being performed.

Therefore, the answer would be (c) Both A and B as

you would report the primary procedure code along with the codes that describe the additional intra-abdominal procedure(s) being performed. Option A lists codes for debridement procedures, and option B lists codes for laparoscopic procedures related to the gallbladder and liver.

25. Answer A - The correct answer is a) 51728, 51784-51. A complex cystometrogram (CMG) is a diagnostic test that measures bladder and urethral function. This test involves filling the bladder with sterile water and measuring pressure changes during filling and voiding. The bladder voiding pressure study is part of the CMG procedure and measures the pressure within the bladder during voiding.

A urethral EMG (electromyography) is a test that measures the electrical activity of the muscles in the urethra. This test helps to evaluate the strength and coordination of the muscles used during urination.

To report these services, you would use CPT codes 51728 and 51784-51. Code 51728 is used to report a complex cystometrogram, and code 51784 is used to report the bladder voiding pressure study that is part of the CMG. The -51 modifier is appended to indicate that multiple procedures were performed during the same session.

Therefore, option a) 51728, 51784-51 is the correct answer.

26. Answer A - The correct answer is a) 59510, 58611. The Current Procedural Terminology (CPT) code 59510 is used to report a cesarean delivery without any complicating factors. In this case, the patient had an attempted vaginal delivery before the cesarean delivery, but the question doesn't mention any complications, so we can assume that the cesarean delivery was without complications.

The CPT code 58611 is used to report a laparoscopic tubal ligation at the time of cesarean delivery.

Therefore, Dr. Milton should report CPT codes 59510 and

58611 for the services provided to this patient.

27. Answer C - The correct answer is c) 99204-25, 57454, 58110.

The evaluation and management (E/M) code for this visit should reflect a comprehensive history, comprehensive examination, and moderate decision-making, which is best represented by code 99204.

The colposcopic examination with three biopsies of the cervix is reported with code 57454, and the endometrial sampling is reported with code 58110.

The -25 modifier is appended to the E/M code to indicate that the visit was separately identifiable and significant from the other procedures performed on the same day.

Therefore, the correct coding for Dr. Nedder's services is 99204-25, 57454, and 58110. Code 57456, which is a biopsy of the endocervix, was not performed, so option a) and d) can be ruled out. Code 99244 in option b) represents a higher level of E/M service than what was documented, making it an incorrect choice.

28. Answer A - The correct answer is a) 57240, 57267.

The procedure performed in this case is an anterior colporrhaphy (57240) and repair of cystocele with repair of the urethrocele and inserted mesh (57267). These two procedures can be reported separately since they involve different anatomical areas and techniques.

Modifier 51 (multiple procedures) should not be appended to either code as they are not considered "multiple procedures" as defined by CPT guidelines. Similarly, modifier 51 is not appropriate for use with 57267 since it is a component code of the colporrhaphy and represents an integral part of the overall procedure.

Therefore, the correct way to report this surgery is with codes 57240 and 57267, without any modifiers.

29. Answer B - The correct answer is b) 50542.

In this scenario, the surgeon performed laparoscopic ablation of four renal lesions using ultrasound guidance during the procedure. The appropriate CPT code to report this service is 50542 (Laparoscopy, surgical; ablation of renal mass lesion(s), including intraoperative ultrasound guidance and monitoring).

CPT code 50205 (Renal biopsy, percutaneous, by trocar or needle; imaging guidance) would not be appropriate in this case because the procedure performed was not a renal biopsy.

CPT code 50593 (Laparoscopy, surgical; with partial nephrectomy) would also not be appropriate because the procedure performed was not a partial nephrectomy.

The -26 modifier appended to the CPT code 77002 (Fluoroscopic guidance for needle placement (e.g., biopsy, aspiration, injection, localization device)), indicates that only the professional component of the service was performed, meaning the physician only provided the interpretation and report of the ultrasound guidance. Since ultrasound guidance was integral to the laparoscopic ablation procedure, the -26 modifier should not be used.

Therefore, the correct CPT code to report this service is 50542.

30. Answer B - The correct answer is b) 58301.

In this scenario, the patient came to the office with a complaint that her IUD was lost internally, and an attempt was made to remove it. However, due to discomfort, the procedure was stopped, and the patient was taken to the outpatient surgical center the next day, where the IUD was successfully removed under general anesthesia. There was active bleeding noted at the end of the procedure, but no other complications were mentioned.

CPT code 58301 describes the removal of an intrauterine device (IUD), including a review of the IUD string and localization of the device. This code is appropriate in this scenario because the IUD was successfully removed during the outpatient surgical procedure.

Option a) 58300, 58301-59 would be incorrect because 58300 is used for the insertion of an IUD, not removal.

Option c) 00840-P1, 58301 would be incorrect because 00840-P1 is an anesthesia code, and it is not clear from the scenario that anesthesia was administered using this specific code.

Option d) 58301-47 would also be incorrect because -47 is a modifier used for anesthesia codes, and it is not appropriate to use it with a surgical procedure code like 58301.

Therefore, the correct answer is b) 58301.

31. Answer A - The correct answer is a) 61070, 75809-26. The procedure described in the question involves two distinct components: an aspiration and a shuntogram. Therefore, it requires two codes to report both services. Code 61070 describes the aspiration of fluid from a shunt reservoir or ventricular catheter, which is the first component of the procedure described in the question.

Code 75809 is used to report a nonvascular shuntogram, which is a radiologic examination used to assess the function and patency of a shunt. The -26 modifier is appended to indicate that the physician provided only the professional component of this service.

Therefore, the correct coding for the physician's professional services for this procedure is 61070, 75809-26.

32. Answer D - All of the above.

When reporting cranial stereotactic radiosurgery, it is important to follow the correct coding guidelines. Code 61796 should be reported when all lesions are simple, and code 61798 should be reported if treating multiple lesions and any single lesion treated is complex. Additionally, codes 61796-61800 should not be reported in conjunction with code 20660. Therefore, option d) is the correct statement as all of the above statements are true.

33. Answer D - The correct answer is indeed d) None of the above.

Add-on code 61781 is used to report stereotactic radiosurgery (SRS) delivery of radiation therapy to the head or neck. This code cannot be reported alone and must be reported with a primary code that describes the SRS treatment.

In the code sets provided in options a), b), and c), none of the codes accurately describe SRS treatment of the head or neck, which is what add-on code 61781 is used for. Therefore, none of the codes in these code sets can be used with add-on code 61781.

Therefore, the correct answer is d) None of the above.

34. Answer D - The correct answer is d) 67966-LT.

CPT code 67966 describes the excision and repair of the eyelid margin. The LT modifier is added to indicate that the procedure was performed on the left eyelid. This code includes preparation for skin grafts, so there is no need to report any additional codes for this.

Option a) is incorrect because it only reports the excision and repair of the eyelid margin and does not include the preparation for skin grafts.

Option b) is incorrect because code 67971 is used for flap procedures, not excision and repair. Additionally, code 15120 is not appropriate for this procedure as it is for skin grafting only.

Option c) is also incorrect because code 67966 already includes the preparation for skin grafts, so there is no need to report code 15120.

Therefore, the correct answer is d) 67966-LT.

35. Answer C - The correct answer is c) 64612-50, J0585x2.

CPT code 64612 is used to report Chemodenervation of the eyelid muscles. This code includes both the right and left sides, so it is reported only once.

However, the injection itself requires reporting with the HCPCS code J0585, which is used for Onabotulinumtoxin A. Since two units were injected, the code should be reported twice, as J0585x2.

The modifier -50 is used to indicate that the procedure was performed bilaterally, which is appropriate in this case since both sides were treated.

Therefore, the correct coding for this scenario would be 64612-50, J0585x2.

36. Answer B - The correct answer is option b) 66852-RT, 66682-RT-51.

Explanation:

The provided scenario describes a surgical procedure performed on the right eye to remove the lens and repair the ciliary body using a McCannel suture technique. To report these services, we need to identify the appropriate CPT codes that describe the procedure.

CPT code 66852 describes the removal of the lens by any method, including phacoemulsification, aspiration, or mechanical lens extraction, without an implant. This code is appropriate for the removal of the lens in the right eye.

CPT code 66682 describes the repair of the ciliary body, which involves suturing the ciliary body to the sclera or other tissue. The -RT modifier should be added to both codes to indicate that the procedure was performed on the right eye.

Finally, the -51 modifier should be added to code 66682 to indicate that this code is a secondary procedure to the primary procedure (i.e., the lens removal). The -51 modifier indicates that the second procedure is a reduced service.

Therefore, the correct codes to report the services performed in this scenario are 66852-RT and 66682-RT-51.

37. Answer B - The most appropriate code for Dr. Kara to report today's service would be option (b) 99238, which is for hospital discharge day management.

This code is used when the physician provides comprehensive discharge services to a patient who is leaving the hospital, including reviewing the patient's hospital stay, discussing the patient's discharge needs, and coordinating the patient's care with other healthcare providers. The fact that Dr. Kara spent 26 minutes on discharge management indicates that he provided comprehensive services to Mr. Davis.

Option (a) 99232-25, 99239 is incorrect because 99232-25 is for subsequent hospital care for a patient who requires a significant, separately identifiable E/M service on a day subsequent to the initial E/M service, and 99239 is for prolonged service in the office or other outpatient setting requiring direct patient contact beyond the usual service.

Option (c) 99315 is incorrect because it is for prolonged evaluation and management service in the inpatient setting, which does not seem to be the case here.

Option (d) 99232-25, 99217 is incorrect because 99232-25 is for subsequent hospital care, as mentioned above, and 99217 is for observation care discharge day management.

38. Answer C - The correct code to report Dr. Martin's services for the admission of Mrs. Worth would be 99235, which represents a hospital inpatient subsequent visit of moderate complexity. This code should be used since Mrs. Worth was discharged on the same day of admission but still received additional hospital care from Dr. Martin, such as post-procedure monitoring and instructions for follow-up care. The code 99222, which represents a comprehensive initial hospital visit, would not be appropriate since the patient was not hospitalized

for an extended period of time. The code 99225 would also not be appropriate since it represents a subsequent hospital visit of low complexity. The codes 99219 and 99217 would not be appropriate since they represent subsequent hospital visits of higher and lower complexity, respectively, than what was documented by Dr. Martin.

39. Answer C - The correct answer is c) 99468-99469. Initial inpatient neonatal critical care (99468) may only be reported once per hospital admission. If readmitted for neonatal critical care services during the same hospital stay, then report the subsequent inpatient neonatal critical care code (99469) for the first day of readmission to critical care, and 99469 for each day of critical care following readmission.

40. Answer A - The correct answer is A) 99463.
Code 99463 describes a discharge service provided to a newborn patient that includes a final exam, instructions for follow-up care, and preparation of discharge records. This code is appropriate for reporting the decision to discharge the newborn on the same day after a comprehensive evaluation.
Codes 99460 and 99234/99238 are not appropriate for reporting this service. Code 99460 describes initial newborn care provided in the delivery room or birthing center, and code 99234/99238 describe an evaluation and management service for an established patient in the hospital setting.
Code 99221-25 is an evaluation and management code for initial hospital care, and would not be appropriate for reporting a newborn discharge service.

41. Answer C - The correct answer is c) 99205, 99354.
In this scenario, Dr. South documented a comprehensive history, comprehensive examination, and high complexity

decision making for the first visit with the patient, which supports the level 5 new patient office visit code 99205. The key components of this code include a comprehensive history, comprehensive examination, and medical decision making of high complexity.

Additionally, Dr. South spent two hours face-to-face talking with the patient, which indicates prolonged services. However, there is no indication in the scenario that the prolonged service was performed on a different day, so 99354 (Prolonged service in the office or other outpatient setting requiring direct patient contact beyond the usual service; first hour) is the appropriate code to report the prolonged service.

Therefore, the correct way to report this service is by using the codes 99205 for the office visit and 99354 for the prolonged service.

42. Answer D - The correct answer is d) 99395, 99212-25, 11106.

In this scenario, Dr. Bill provided two separate and distinct services during the encounter: a comprehensive female exam and a problem-focused examination with incisional biopsy. To report these services correctly, the CPT codes should be selected based on the key components documented in the medical record.

The comprehensive female exam would be reported with code 99395, which describes an annual wellness visit for an established patient, including a comprehensive history, examination, and counseling/anticipatory guidance/risk factor reduction interventions. This code covers the evaluation and management (E/M) component of the visit.

The problem-focused examination with incisional biopsy would be reported with code 11106, which describes a biopsy of a skin lesion. The -57 modifier is appended to indicate that this service was separately identifiable from the E/M service provided.

Finally, because Dr. Bill provided an additional E/M service beyond the comprehensive female exam, a second E/M code should be reported with modifier -25 appended to indicate that it was a significant, separately identifiable service. In this case, the appropriate E/M code is 99212, which describes a problem-focused E/M service.

Therefore, the correct way to report today's services is 99395, 99212-25, 1110

43. Answer A - Answer A is correct. Dr. Sally should report the codes 01630-AA-P2 and 99100 for this case.

The CPT code 01630 is used to report anesthesia services for open or surgical arthroscopic procedures of the shoulder, wrist, elbow, or ankle. The -AA modifier indicates that the procedure was performed by the primary physician, in this case, Dr. Sally.

The -P2 modifier indicates that the patient is over 70 years of age and has a mild systemic disease, which in this case is mild hypertension. This modifier indicates that the patient has a higher risk of complications during anesthesia.

Finally, Dr. Sally should report the code 99100 for anesthesia care provided during the procedure. This code is used to report the routine monitoring of the patient's vital signs during anesthesia administration.

Therefore, the correct coding for this case is 01630-AA-P2 and 99100.

44. Answer D - The correct answer is d) Dr. Smith: 01470-AA-P3, 99100, 99140; Jane: 01470-QZ-P3, 99100, 99140.

In this case, James underwent an emergency muscle flap repair with grafts from his right thigh to the right lower leg to repair the open defect. The procedure required general endotracheal anesthesia with medical necessity for both an anesthesiologist and an independently acting CRNA.

The anesthesia codes used for reporting should reflect the type of anesthesia provided, the patient's condition, and the level of difficulty of the procedure. The primary anesthesia code for this case is 01470, which describes general anesthesia for an emergency procedure. The modifier AA indicates that the service was provided by an anesthesiologist and the modifier P3 indicates that the service was provided for an emergency.

In addition to the primary anesthesia code, both the anesthesiologist and the CRNA can report the anesthesia modifiers 99100 and 99140. Modifier 99100 indicates that anesthesia care was provided to a patient who has a severe systemic disease and 99140 indicates that anesthesia was performed by a qualified CRNA who was not medically directed.

Therefore, the correct anesthesia codes for Dr. Smith and Jane are:

Dr. Smith: 01470-AA-P3, 99100, 99140

Jane: 01470-QZ-P3, 99100, 99140

45. Answer B - The correct answer is b) 00928-51, 62322-59.

The anesthesia code for an abdominal radical orchiectomy is 00928-51 (Anesthesia for radical surgery of testis, unilateral or bilateral). The "-51" modifier is used to indicate that multiple procedures were performed during the same anesthesia session.

In addition, an epidural infusion was administered for control and management of postoperative pain. The code for this service is 62322 (Continuous infusion of analgesia, including needle or catheter placement, accessing an external reservoir and programming the pump). However, since this service is considered a component of the anesthesia service and was performed during the same anesthesia session, it should be reported with the "-59" modifier (Distinct procedural service) to indicate that it is a separate and distinct service from the anesthesia service.

The other code options provided are not correct for

this scenario. Code 00926-AA-P1 (Anesthesia for open or surgical arthroscopic procedures of knee joint; with continuous intraoperative neurophysiology monitoring) is not applicable to this case as it pertains to knee surgery. Code 00920-AA-59 (Anesthesia for procedure on lower anterior abdominal wall; not otherwise specified) is also not applicable as it does not specify the type of surgery performed.

46. Answer C - The correct answer is c) $1,000.00.
To calculate the correct anesthesia charge, we need to determine the total number of base units and time units for this service:

Base Units: The base value for anesthesia code 00940 is 3 units. Since the patient qualified for an additional two base units due to the emergency circumstances (using qualifying circumstance code 99140), the total number of base units for this service is 5.

Time Units: Anesthesia start time is reported as 2:21 am, and the surgery began at 2:28 am. This means that anesthesia was provided for a total of 57 minutes (from 2:21 am to 3:18 am). We round up to the next 15-minute increment, which is 60 minutes, and add one time unit for the additional time (3:18 am to 3:36 am). Therefore, the total time units for this service are 5.

To calculate the anesthesia charge, we multiply the total number of base units (5) by the conversion factor ($100) to get $500. We then add the total number of time units (5) multiplied by the conversion factor ($20) to get $100. This gives us a total anesthesia charge of $600.

However, we also need to take into account the pre-anesthesia assessment that was performed and signed at 2:00 am. Since this assessment was performed within 24 hours prior to the anesthesia service, it qualifies as a separately reportable service. We can report this service using code 01996 (Anesthesia for diagnostic or therapeutic nerve blocks and injections (when block or injection is performed by a different provider), which has a base value of 1 unit. We add this unit to the total base units for the anesthesia service, giving us a total of 6 base units.

Finally, we multiply the total number of base units (6) by the conversion factor ($100) to get $600. Adding the total time units (5) multiplied by the conversion factor ($20) gives us $100. Therefore, the correct anesthesia charge is $600 + $100 = $1,000.00.

Therefore, the correct answer is c) $1,000.00.

47. Answer A - The correct answer is (a) 77065-26-LT.

In this scenario, the radiologist performed a follow-up unilateral diagnostic mammogram with computer aided detection. The appropriate CPT code for this service is 77065 (Diagnostic mammography, including computer-aided detection (CAD) when performed; unilateral). The -26 modifier is used to indicate that only the professional component of the service was provided by the radiologist, and the LT modifier is used to indicate that the service was performed on the left breast.

Option (b) is incorrect because the 77067 code is used for bilateral mammography, but the scenario only mentions imaging of the left breast. The -50 modifier is also unnecessary because the scenario does not mention imaging of the right breast.

Option (c) is incorrect because the scenario states that the imaging was performed on the left breast, not the right.

Option (d) is incorrect because the 77066 code is used for a bilateral diagnostic mammogram with computer aided detection, which is not what was performed in this scenario.

48. Answer A - The correct answer is a) 73630-LT.

The CPT code 73630 (Radiologic examination, foot; minimum of 3 views) describes the radiologic examination of the foot with a minimum of three views, which includes anteroposterior, oblique, and lateral views. In this case, Dr. Levitt performed a radiologic examination of the left foot with three views and interpreted the images.

Modifier LT is used to indicate that the service was performed on the left side of the body. No other modifier is necessary in this case.

The other options are not appropriate because:

b) 73620-26-LT describes a radiologic examination, foot; two views, which is not sufficient for this case. Additionally, modifier 26 is used to indicate a professional component only, which is not necessary in this case.

c) 73650-LT describes a radiologic examination, foot; complete, minimum of 3 views, which is similar to 73630. However, modifier LT is used to indicate that the service was performed on the left side of the body, not that the service was complete.

d) 73630-26-LT is similar to option b but includes modifier 26, which is not necessary in this case.

49. Answer D - The patient has a diagnosis of primary hyperparathyroidism, and underwent a parathyroid planar imaging with SPECT and concurrently acquired CT. The appropriate way to report this study and diagnosis would be with code 78072 for the SPECT study and code E21.0 for the diagnosis of primary hyperparathyroidism. Code 78072 is used for the imaging of parathyroid with SPECT, and it includes the use of a concurrent CT. Code E21.0 is used to report the diagnosis of primary hyperparathyroidism.

Therefore, the correct way to report this study and diagnosis would be with code 78072 for the SPECT study and code E21.0 for the diagnosis of primary hyperparathyroidism, which is option d.

50. Answer A - The correct answer is (a) 77620.

CPT code 77620 is used to report the delivery of superficial or deep hyperthermia treatment. Intracavitary hyperthermia treatment involves the use of heat to treat cancer cells in body cavities. Therefore, CPT code 77620 is appropriate to report Wednesday's service.

CPT code 77402 is used to report radiation treatment delivery of 10 MeV photons or electrons. Ralph received radiation treatment on Monday, and this service was reported with CPT code 77402. Therefore, CPT code 77402 should not be reported again on Wednesday.

Option (b) is incorrect because CPT code 77600 is used to report a brachytherapy isotope source implantation, not hyperthermia treatment.

Option (c) is incorrect because CPT code 77402 should not be reported again, as it was already reported on Monday.

Option (d) is incorrect because CPT code 77605 is used to report interstitial or percutaneous hyperthermia treatment, not intracavitary hyperthermia treatment. Additionally, the -26 modifier should not be used with CPT code 77402, as it is not a professional component code.

51. Answer B - The correct answer is (b) 78014.

Thyroid imaging with vascular flow and three uptakes on the same date of service is reported with code 78014, which is a comprehensive code for thyroid imaging and uptake studies. This code includes both static and dynamic imaging, as well as the measurement of radioactive iodine uptake at multiple time points.

Option (a) 78014x3 is incorrect because it implies that the code 78014 should be reported three times, which is not necessary.

Option (c) 78012, 78014x3 is incorrect because code 78012 is not appropriate for this study. Code 78012 is used for thyroid uptake imaging only, without the vascular flow component, whereas the question specifically mentions that the study includes vascular flow imaging.

Option (d) 78015, 78020x3 is also incorrect because these codes do not accurately describe the comprehensive thyroid imaging and uptake study that was performed. Code 78015 is used for thyroid imaging without vascular flow, and code 78020 is used for radioactive iodine uptake imaging without other imaging components.

52. Answer B - The correct answer is option b) 78472, 78496.

In this scenario, the patient underwent a single planar stress cardiac blood pool imaging study with gated equilibrium, wall motion, and ejection fraction. Additionally, a first-pass technique at rest with right ventricular ejection fraction was completed.

According to CPT coding guidelines, code 78472 should be reported for a first-pass technique at rest with wall motion, ejection fraction, and ventricular volume measurement. Code 78496 is used for a planar cardiac blood pool imaging study with wall motion, ejection fraction, and ventricular volume measurements.

Therefore, the correct codes to report for this service are 78472 for the first-pass technique at rest with right ventricular ejection fraction, and 78496 for the single planar stress cardiac blood pool imaging study with gated equilibrium, wall motion, and ejection fraction. Option b) includes both of these codes and is, therefore, the correct answer.

53. Answer D - The correct answer is D) 80053, 84100.

The comprehensive metabolic panel (CMP) is reported with CPT code 80053. This panel includes tests such as glucose, electrolytes, kidney function tests (BUN and creatinine), liver function tests, and others.

The renal function panel includes tests such as BUN and

creatinine, which are also included in the CMP. Therefore, the renal function panel should be reported separately only if additional tests beyond the CMP were performed for the renal function panel.

In this scenario, both the CMP and renal function panel were completed from the same single collection, and no additional tests beyond the CMP were performed for the renal function panel. Therefore, the correct way to report these services is to use CPT code 80053 for the CMP and CPT code 84100 for the BUN test that is part of both panels.

54. Answer A - The correct answer is a) 80184, 80305.

In this case, the patient presented to the ER with a drug overdose, and the laboratory conducted a therapeutic assay for Phenobarbital, multiple drug class testing utilizing two nonchromatographic methods, and three confirmation procedures.

CPT code 80184 is for the drug assay, qualitative or semiquantitative, except immunoassays; multiple drug class procedures, by high complexity test methods (e.g., immunoassay, enzyme assay), per patient encounter. This code covers the multiple drug class testing utilizing two nonchromatographic methods.

CPT code 80305 is for the drug test, presumptive, any number of drug classes; any number of devices or procedures, (e.g., immunoassay) capable of being read by direct optical observation only (e.g., dipsticks, cups, cards, cartridges), includes sample validation when performed, per date of service. This code covers the initial drug screening.

Therefore, the appropriate codes to report the drug screening and confirmation in this case are 80184 and 80305.

55. Answer B - The correct answer is b) 88305 x 2, 88311.

When a placenta is submitted for pathology examination,

there are two main components that need to be evaluated - the gross examination and the microscopic examination. The gross examination involves examining the placenta with the naked eye to identify any abnormalities, while the microscopic examination involves looking at the tissue under a microscope to assess the cellular structure and identify any abnormalities.

In this case, the placenta was submitted in two separate specimens, which means that there were likely two separate portions of the placenta that needed to be evaluated. Additionally, a decalcification procedure was utilized during pathology testing, which is a separate service that involves removing calcium from bone or other hard tissues to allow for easier examination.

Therefore, the appropriate way to report this pathology service would be with code 88305 (Level IV - Surgical pathology, gross and microscopic examination) billed twice, once for each specimen, and code 88311 (Decalcification procedure [List separately in addition to the code for the primary procedure]) for the additional service of decalcification. This would accurately reflect the work performed during the pathology examination of the placenta.

56. Answer D - The correct answer is d) 88331-26, 88332-26, 88333-26, 88334-26.

In this scenario, Dr. Garcia performed a consultation during surgery and examined tissue samples from Mr. Barber's gallbladder. The examination involved both frozen sections and cytologic examination by squash prep.

CPT code 88331 is used for the interpretation and report of a frozen section, and code 88332 is used for each additional frozen section. Since there were five frozen sections, codes 88331 and 88332 (x4) should be reported with modifier -26 to indicate Dr. Garcia's professional service.

CPT code 88333 is used for the interpretation and report of

a cytologic preparation (e.g., squash prep), and code 88334 is used for each additional cytologic preparation. Since there were two cytologic examinations, codes 88333 and 88334 (x1) should be reported with modifier -26 to indicate Dr. Garcia's professional service.

Therefore, the correct way to report Dr. Garcia's professional services in this scenario is 88331-26, 88332-26, 88333-26, 88334-26.

57. Answer A - The type of microorganism testing identified in the CPT Professional Edition as: Colony morphology, growth on selective media, Gram stains or up to three tests (eg. catalase, oxidase, indole, urease) is known as "Presumptive" testing.

Presumptive testing is a preliminary or initial test used to identify the presence of a particular microorganism in a sample. It is called "presumptive" because the results of these tests are not always definitive and require further confirmation using more specific tests.

The tests mentioned in the question, such as colony morphology, growth on selective media, Gram stains, catalase, oxidase, indole, and urease are all examples of presumptive tests commonly used to identify bacteria in a clinical or research laboratory setting.

Therefore, the correct answer is (a) Presumptive.

58. Answer C - The correct answer is c) 86825, 86826.

Flow cytometry is a laboratory technique that is used to identify and quantify the characteristics of cells or particles in a fluid sample. In this case, the laboratory used flow cytometry to perform an HLA cross match on two serum samples provided by Sarah.

The American Medical Association's (AMA) Current Procedural Terminology (CPT) manual provides codes for the various laboratory services that may be used in testing and analyzing samples. The codes for flow cytometry include:

86825: Flow cytometry, interpretation, and report; technical component

86826: Flow cytometry, cell surface, cytoplasmic, or nuclear marker, technical component

Based on the information provided in the scenario, it would be appropriate to report both of these codes, as they reflect the services that were performed by the laboratory on Sarah's serum samples. Therefore, the correct answer is c) 86825, 86826.

59. Answer A - The correct answer is a) A specific order for an electrocardiogram or rhythm strip followed by a separate, signed, written, and retrievable report.

The Current Procedural Terminology (CPT) code range 93040-93042 describes various types of electrocardiogram (ECG or EKG) services, which involve the recording and interpretation of electrical activity of the heart. When reporting these services, it is essential to document the medical necessity for the ECG, as well as the provider's interpretation and report.

According to CPT guidelines, to report codes in the 93040-93042 range, a specific order for an ECG or rhythm strip must be documented, and the provider must generate a separate, signed, written, and retrievable report. This report should include the interpretation and medical decision-making related to the ECG service provided. This documentation helps to support the medical necessity of the service and ensures accurate billing and reimbursement.

Therefore, answer choice a) is the correct option that must be included to report from code range 93040-93042. The other options do not meet the documentation requirements for these services.

60. Answer B - The correct answer is (b) 92228.

Cassidy was referred to Dr. Nelson for retinal images with fundus photography of both eyes, which is a diagnostic test to assess the progression of diabetic retinopathy. The Current Procedural Terminology (CPT) code for this service is 92228, which describes the capture and interpretation of retinal images.

The other CPT codes listed are not appropriate for this scenario. Code 99242 is a consultation code, which is not applicable in this case. Code 92227 is used for electroretinography, which is a different type of diagnostic test that evaluates the function of the retina. Code 92250 is used for visual field testing, which is also not relevant to this situation.

Therefore, the appropriate CPT code for Dr. Nelson's service is 92228.

61. Answer A - The correct answer is a) 99213, 90836.

In this scenario, Dr. Morris spent a total of 65 minutes with the patient, including a 45-minute psychotherapy session, an expanded problem-focused history, and an expanded problem-focused examination. Dr. Morris also documented low-complexity medical decision-making.

For coding purposes, the time spent with the patient is the key factor in determining the appropriate E/M code. In this case, the total time spent with the patient is 65 minutes, which falls within the time range for a level 3 established patient visit (99213) that requires a minimum of 15 minutes of face-to-face time.

Additionally, Dr. Morris provided psychotherapy services during this visit. According to CPT guidelines, the appropriate code for a 45-minute psychotherapy session is 90836.

Therefore, the correct coding for this visit is 99213 for the evaluation and management services and 90836 for the psychotherapy services, making option a) the correct answer.

62. Answer D - The correct answer is d) 90969 x 4.

The Current Procedural Terminology (CPT) code 90969 is used to report end-stage renal disease (ESRD) related services provided on an outpatient basis. This code is used to report daily dialysis services that are provided to patients with ESRD, including the necessary equipment, supplies, and monitoring.

Since Brandi underwent four daily end-stage renal dialysis services in the outpatient clinic prior to being hospitalized, the correct way to report these services would be to use code 90969 four times, one for each service provided. Therefore, the correct answer is d) 90969 x 4.

Code 90957 is used to report the initial assessment and training of the patient and family for home dialysis therapy, and code 90965 is used to report hemodialysis performed in a hospital or facility setting, but these codes are not appropriate for reporting daily dialysis services provided on an outpatient basis. Code 90957 is also not appropriate in this scenario as it is mentioned that complete assessment was not provided before Brandi's hospitalization.

63. Answer C - The correct answer is c) 95908, 95885.

The given scenario describes a patient, Harper, who is being tested for focal weakness and twitching of her lower extremity motor nerves. The testing includes three nerve conduction studies and a needle electromyography (EMG) testing of three muscles.

CPT code 95908 describes the testing of three or more motor nerves, which includes both a nerve conduction study and needle EMG. This code would be appropriate to report for the testing of the motor nerves in Harper's lower extremity.

CPT code 95885 describes a needle electromyography (EMG) testing of each extremity. Since Harper underwent a needle EMG testing of three muscles, this code would be appropriate to report as well.

Therefore, the correct codes to report for the services provided to Harper would be 95908 for the testing of three or more motor nerves, which includes a nerve conduction study and needle EMG, and 95885 for the needle EMG testing of three muscles. The correct answer is c) 95908, 95885.

64. Answer D - The correct answer is D) 92928, 92921.

The given scenario describes a patient who presented to the emergency room with symptoms of acute shortness of breath and chest pain, and after testing, the patient was diagnosed with an impending infarction. Dr. Risser performed a primary diagnostic PTCA to the left circumflex and left anterior descending artery, and after the PTCA, he decided to place three stents in the left anterior descending artery during the same surgical session.

In this scenario, Dr. Risser performed two procedures: a primary diagnostic PTCA and stent placement. For the PTCA, Dr. Risser should report CPT code 92928 (Percutaneous transcatheter placement of intracoronary stent(s), with coronary angioplasty when performed; single major coronary artery or branch). For the stent placement in the left anterior descending artery, Dr. Risser should report CPT code 92921 (Percutaneous transcatheter placement of intracoronary stent(s), cervical or thoracic, single vessel).

Therefore, the correct answer is D) 92928, 92921.

65. Answer D - Adrenal gland(s)

Cushing's syndrome is a disorder that occurs when the body is exposed to high levels of the hormone cortisol over a long period of time. In most cases, this is caused by the overproduction of cortisol by the adrenal glands, which are located on top of the kidneys.

In some cases, Cushing's syndrome can also be caused by

the use of corticosteroid medications such as prednisone, which are used to treat a variety of medical conditions. In these cases, the excess cortisol is caused by the medication rather than by a problem with the adrenal glands themselves.

66. Answer A - The location of the femur is actually described as "distal to the acetabulum and proximal to the patella," which is answer choice a).

The femur is the bone in the upper leg that connects the hip joint to the knee joint. It is located proximal to the patella (kneecap) and distal to the acetabulum (the socket of the hip joint).

67. Answer A - Longitudinal growth best reflects the function of the growth plate. The growth plate, also known as the epiphyseal plate, is a layer of cartilage at the ends of long bones in children and adolescents. It is responsible for longitudinal bone growth, as the cartilage cells in the growth plate divide and differentiate, eventually being replaced by bone tissue. The growth plate is an important part of bone development and is essential for increasing height during childhood and adolescence. Blood cell formation occurs in the bone marrow, synovial fluid is produced by the synovial membrane, and apoptosis fragmentation refers to a process of cell death and fragmentation that occurs in some cells.

68. Answer B - The correct answer is b) Skull, rib cage, spine.

The axial skeleton consists of the bones that form the central axis of the body. It includes the skull, which protects the brain and supports the face; the rib cage, which protects the heart and lungs; and the spine, which houses and protects the spinal cord and provides support for the body. These bones work together to provide structure, protection, and support for the body's vital organs and tissues.

69. Answer C - The correct answer is c) Abnormally low number of sperms in the semen.

Oligospermia is a medical condition in which the male has a low sperm count, usually defined as less than 15 million sperm per milliliter of semen. This can make it difficult for a couple to conceive naturally.

Knots in the varicose vein (a) refers to varicocele, a condition in which the veins in the scrotum become enlarged and twisted, which can lead to reduced sperm count and quality.

Inflammation of the prostate gland (b) is known as prostatitis, which can cause pain during ejaculation, but it does not directly affect the sperm count.

Failure to ovulate (d) is a condition that affects women, not men, and is known as anovulation.

70. Answer A - The correct answer is a) Surgical reduction of the eyelids to remove excess fat, skin and muscle.

Blepharoplasty is a cosmetic surgical procedure that involves removing excess skin, fat, and muscle from the upper and/or lower eyelids to improve their appearance and reduce sagging or puffiness. The procedure is commonly performed for cosmetic reasons, but in some cases, it can also be done for medical reasons, such as to improve vision obstructed by sagging eyelids. Therefore, option a) is the correct answer.

Option b) refers to a treatment for spider veins, not related to Blepharoplasty. Option c) describes a skin grafting procedure, which is a different surgical procedure altogether. Option d) refers to a technique called cryotherapy, which is also not related to Blepharoplasty.

71. Answer D - The term that describes the death of a tissue resulting from interrupted blood flow to that

area is "infarction." Infarction occurs when a blood vessel that supplies a particular area of the body becomes blocked or obstructed, leading to ischemia (lack of oxygen and nutrients) of the tissue supplied by that vessel. If the obstruction is not relieved promptly, the affected tissue can become irreversibly damaged or die. This can happen in various organs such as the heart, brain, lungs, kidneys, and intestines.

Hypercirculation refers to increased blood flow to a specific area, whereas agglutination is the clumping together of cells or particles, and stenosis refers to the narrowing of a blood vessel or other tubular structure.

72. Answer B - The patient's complaint for painful menstrual bleeding will be documented in the medical record as "dysmenorrhea." Dysmenorrhea is a medical term that refers to painful menstruation or menstrual cramps that occur just before or during menstruation.

Amenorrhea, on the other hand, refers to the absence of menstruation, either temporarily or permanently. Menorrhagia refers to heavy menstrual bleeding that lasts for longer than seven days or involves passing large clots, while metrorrhagia refers to irregular bleeding between periods.

73. Answer A - Signs and symptoms that are associated routinely with a disease process should not be assigned as additional codes unless otherwise instructed by classification. The ICD-10-CM Official Guidelines for Coding and Reporting state that codes for signs and symptoms that are not integral to the disease process or are routinely associated with the disease process should not be assigned as additional codes, but rather, the underlying condition or disease

should be assigned as the principal diagnosis.

However, if the signs and symptoms are not routinely associated with the disease process or are not integral to the disease process, they can be assigned as additional codes. Additionally, certain guidelines may allow for the assignment of codes for associated signs and symptoms in specific situations.

74. Answer A - The correct answer is a) S62.632A, Y93.64, W51.XXXA, Y92.320.

The International Classification of Diseases, Tenth Revision, Clinical Modification (ICD-10-CM) codes used to document Henry's injury are:

S62.632A - Displaced fracture of distal phalanx of right middle finger, initial encounter for closed fracture.

This code indicates that Henry has a fracture of the distal phalanx (the tip) of his right middle finger that is displaced (meaning the bone fragments are not in their normal position) and that this is his first visit to receive treatment for this closed fracture.

Y93.64 - Activity, baseball.

This code indicates that the injury occurred during a baseball game.

W51.XXXA - Accidental striking against or struck by a sports equipment, initial encounter.

This code indicates that Henry's injury was caused by being struck by a piece of sports equipment (in this case, a baseball) during the game.

Y92.320 - Sports and athletic area as the place of occurrence of the external cause.

This code indicates that the injury occurred at the sports field where the baseball game was being played.

The other options are incorrect because:

b) S62.662A - Displaced fracture of distal phalanx of left middle finger, initial encounter for closed fracture.

This code is for a similar injury, but on the left hand instead of the right, so it is not correct.

c) S62.392A - Displaced fracture of distal phalanx of unspecified finger, initial encounter for closed fracture.

This code is not specific enough, as it does not indicate which finger is injured.

d) 562.632A - Diverticulitis of colon, acute, with perforation and abscess, without bleeding, unspecified as to episode of care or not applicable.

This code is not related to Henry's injury at all.

75. Answer B - The correct answer is b) P35.2.

The International Classification of Diseases, Tenth Revision, Clinical Modification (ICD-10-CM) code used to document the newborn's diagnosis is:

P35.2 - Congenital herpesviral [herpes simplex] infection.

This code describes a congenital infection with the herpes simplex virus, which has caused the vesicles on the newborn's torso and lower extremities.

Option a) B00.9 - Herpesviral infection, unspecified, is not specific enough to describe the newborn's condition.

Option c) P37.8 - Other specified congenital infectious and parasitic diseases, includes other congenital infections, but does not specifically mention herpesviral infection.

Option d) B00.0 - Herpesviral gingivostomatitis and pharyngotonsillitis, refers to an infection of the mouth and throat, which is not the same as the newborn's condition involving vesicles on the torso and lower extremities.

76. Answer D - The Z codes are used to report factors that influence health status and healthcare encounters but are not considered as a primary diagnosis. However, there are some circumstances where a Z code can be reported as the first-listed or principal diagnosis.

In this case, only Z00.129 can be reported as a first-listed code. Z00.129 is a code for an encounter for a general adult medical examination without abnormal findings. This code can be used as the first-listed code when a patient comes in for a routine medical exam or check-up and there are no abnormal findings or complaints.

The other codes listed are:

a) Z37.0 - Outcome of delivery, single liveborn

b) Z89.621 - Acquired absence of left ankle and foot

c) Z87.710 - Personal history of (corrected) congenital malformations of urinary system

These codes are not appropriate to be reported as first-listed codes as they describe outcomes, past medical history or physical characteristics of the patient rather than a current medical condition or reason for the encounter.

77. Answer D - The correct answer is option d) O63.0, O09.513, Z37.0.

Explanation:

The diagnosis codes in this case represent the following:

O63.0 - Prolonged first stage of labor

O09.513 - Supervision of pregnancy with history of in utero procedure, third trimester

Z37.0 - Single liveborn infant, born in hospital

The patient is 36 years old and in her 38th week of pregnancy. She experiences a prolonged first stage of labor, but eventually gives birth to a healthy baby boy in the hospital.

Option a) is incorrect because it includes O09.519 instead of O09.513, which is not appropriate in this case as there is no mention of complications in the patient's pregnancy.

Option b) is incorrect because it only includes the code for the delivery and does not include the code for the prolonged labor.

Option c) is incorrect because it includes O09.519 instead of O09.513, which is not appropriate in this case as there is no mention of complications in the patient's pregnancy.

Therefore, the correct answer is option d), which includes the codes for prolonged labor, supervision of pregnancy with history of in utero procedure, and delivery of a single liveborn infant in the hospital.

78. Answer A - The correct answer is a) J0456.
J0456 is the Healthcare Common Procedure Coding System (HCPCS) code for Azithromycin, 500 mg, injection. Azithromycin is the generic name for Zithromax, which was administered to Sally via intravenous (IV) route during her hospital stay.

HCPCS codes are used to report medical procedures, supplies, and equipment for billing purposes. In this case, J0456 is the appropriate code to report the supply of the drug Azithromycin.

Option b) Q0144 is the HCPCS code for Injection, Adalimumab, 20 mg. Adalimumab is a different medication used to treat autoimmune disorders and is not related to the treatment of pneumonia.

Option c) J1190x2 is incorrect because J1190 is the HCPCS code for Injection, Dexamethasone Sodium Phosphate, 1 mg. Dexamethasone is a steroid used to reduce inflammation, but it is not the same as Azithromycin, which was administered to Sally.

Option d) J2020x2 is incorrect because J2020 is the HCPCS code for Injection, Linezolid, 200 mg. Linezolid is an antibiotic used to treat bacterial infections, but it is not the same as Azithromycin, which was administered to Sally.

79. Answer D - The correct answer is D) E2508.
E2508 is the Healthcare Common Procedure Coding System (HCPCS) code for "Speech generating device, synthesized speech, requiring message formulation by spelling and access by physical contact with the device". This code is used to report the supply of a speech-generating device that requires physical contact with the device and message formulation by spelling.

In this scenario, Joe has lost his ability to speak as a

result of an accident and has received a speech-generating synthesized device that is activated by physical contact with the device. Therefore, the appropriate code to report the supply of this device would be E2508.

It's worth noting that the other codes listed are also HCPCS codes related to speech-generating devices, but they are not as specific to the device's features as E2508. For example, E2502 is used for "Speech generating device, digitized speech, using pre-recorded messages", and E2510 is used for "Speech generating device, synthesized speech, requiring message formulation by the device with dynamic display communication device". These codes may be used for different types of speech-generating devices with different features, but in this scenario, the device requires message formulation by spelling and access by physical contact with the device, so E2508 is the most appropriate code to use.

80. Answer C - The correct answer is c) A6252, A6219.
A6252 describes a self-adhesive, non-elastic, non-woven, sterile gauze pad, which was used to cover the 15 sq. cm. area.

A6219 describes a specialty absorptive dressing, sterile, pad size more than 16 sq. in. but less than or equal to 48 sq. in. (i.e., 103 sq. cm. to 310 sq. cm.). This code is used to report the dressing used for the 20 sq. cm. area.

Therefore, both A6252 and A6219 are the correct codes to report the dressings used by the home health aide to clean and dress the patient's burn on his lower leg.

81. Answer C - The correct answer is (c) American Medical Association (AMA).
CPT codes, or Current Procedural Terminology codes, are a set of five-digit codes used by healthcare providers to describe medical, surgical, and diagnostic services. These codes are used for billing purposes, and they help ensure

that healthcare providers are reimbursed accurately for the services they provide.

The American Medical Association (AMA) is responsible for updating the CPT codes each year. The AMA CPT Editorial Panel is a group of experts in healthcare and healthcare coding who meet regularly to review and update the codes. They consider input from healthcare providers, payers, and other stakeholders to ensure that the codes reflect the most current and accurate descriptions of medical services. Once the codes are updated, they are published in the CPT manual, which is used by healthcare providers and coders across the United States.

While the other organizations listed (AHIMA, AAPC, and CMS) may also play a role in healthcare coding and billing, they are not responsible for updating the CPT codes.

82. Answer C - The statement that is true regarding advanced beneficiary notices (ABN) is (c) "An ABN must be completed before delivery of items or services are provided."

An ABN is a notice given to a Medicare beneficiary before receiving services or items that are likely to be denied by Medicare. The purpose of the ABN is to inform the patient that they may be responsible for payment if Medicare denies coverage.

The ABN form must be completed and signed by the patient or their representative before the delivery of the items or services. The form must clearly state the reason why Medicare may not pay and provide an estimate of the cost of the service or item.

Option (a) is incorrect because the ABN must specify all items or services that Medicare is expected to deny, not just the CPT® code. Option (b) is incorrect because a generic ABN is not acceptable. The ABN must be specific to the patient and the item or service being provided. Option (d) is incorrect because an ABN is not required in a medical emergency, and the patient cannot be held responsible for payment in such situations.

83. Answer B - Answer b is not an example of fraud. Reporting a biopsy and excision performed on the same skin lesion during the same encounter is an example of unbundling, which is a type of billing error where multiple services that are typically billed together are billed separately in order to increase reimbursement. While this practice is not appropriate and may result in overpayment, it is not necessarily fraudulent.

Fraud involves intentional misrepresentation or deception that is intended to result in financial gain. In contrast, unbundling is typically the result of errors or ignorance of billing guidelines.

Answer a could be an example of fraud if the ultrasound guidance code was reported with the intent to obtain additional reimbursement, even though it was not used during the liver biopsy procedure. Answer c could also be an example of fraud if the failure to append modifier 26 was intentional and resulted in higher reimbursement than would have been allowed without the modifier. Answer d could be an example of fraud if the failure to append modifier 57 was intentional and resulted in the physician receiving payment for both the EM service and the minor procedure, which may not have been appropriate.

84. Answer D - The time limit for reporting diagnosis codes for late effects is not specified by any official coding guidelines. Therefore, the correct answer is (d) No limit.

Late effects are defined as residual conditions that arise from a previous injury or illness, and they may develop months or even years after the initial event. As such, there may not be a specific time limit for reporting these conditions as they can occur at any time in the future.

However, it is important to note that timely and accurate documentation of these late effects is essential for appropriate patient care and reimbursement. So, it is advisable to report the diagnosis codes as soon as they are discovered or diagnosed, regardless of the amount of time that has passed since the initial event.

85. Answer D - Answer (d) is true. According to the ICD-10-CM coding conventions, signs and symptoms that are integral to the disease process should not be assigned as additional codes, unless otherwise instructed.

This means that when a patient has a disease or condition that is known to cause specific signs and symptoms, those signs and symptoms should not be coded separately unless there is a specific instruction in the coding guidelines to do so.

For example, if a patient has pneumonia, which commonly causes cough, fever, and chest pain, the coder should not assign codes for cough, fever, and chest pain unless there is a specific instruction in the guidelines to do so. Instead, the coder should only assign the code for pneumonia, which includes the signs and symptoms as part of the disease process.

This convention helps to ensure that the codes assigned accurately reflect the patient's condition and prevent unnecessary duplication of codes.

86. Answer A - The correct answer is a) Procedure or service; organ or other anatomic site; condition; synonyms, eponyms, and abbreviations.

The Current Procedural Terminology (CPT) index is a tool used in medical coding to find the appropriate code for a specific medical procedure or service. It is organized into several primary classes, including:

Procedure or service: This class includes a list of medical procedures and services that are performed on a patient.

Organ or other anatomic site: This class includes the specific location on the body where the procedure or service is performed.

Condition: This class includes the reason for the procedure or service, such as a diagnosis or medical condition.

Synonyms, eponyms, and abbreviations: This class includes alternative names or abbreviations for the procedure or service.

These four primary classes are considered the main entries in the CPT index, and they are used to help locate the appropriate code for a specific procedure or service. Therefore, option a) is the correct answer.

87. Answer D - The correct answer is indeed d) None of the above. Here's why:

CPT codes are used to report medical procedures and services performed by healthcare professionals, and they follow a specific format that consists of five digits. The first digit represents the category of the service or procedure, the second digit represents the body system, and the third, fourth, and fifth digits represent the specific service or procedure. The format of CPT codes also includes modifiers, which are two-digit codes that provide additional information about the service or procedure performed.

In the options given, only option c) 93572-51 follows the correct format of a CPT code and a modifier. However, upon further research, I found that the correct modifier for code 93572 is actually -26, not -51. Modifier -26 is used to indicate that the healthcare professional provided only the professional component of the service, such as the interpretation of the test results, while the technical component, such as the equipment used to perform the test, was provided by another healthcare professional or facility.

Option a) 0165T-25 and option b) 15003-51 are not correct

because they do not follow the correct format of a CPT code and a modifier. Option a) has a letter in the first position, which is not valid for CPT codes, and option b) has only one set of five digits and no modifier.

Therefore, the correct answer is d) None of the above.

88. Answer C - Manifestation codes are used to indicate a particular symptom or manifestation of a disease or condition. These codes are always secondary codes, meaning they are used in conjunction with a primary code that identifies the underlying condition being manifested.

When coding for a manifestation, the manifestation code should be sequenced after the primary code for the underlying condition. The manifestation code should be enclosed in square brackets [ ] to indicate that it is a manifestation code.

For example, if a patient has hypertension (primary code I10) and presents with chest pain due to the hypertension, the chest pain code (manifestation code R07.9) would be listed second, enclosed in square brackets: I10 [R07.9].

Therefore, the correct answer is c) Secondary code to an underlying condition.

89. Answer D - The correct answer is d) Oral and/or rectal. In medical imaging, a "study with contrast" refers to the use of contrast agents, which are substances that are administered to highlight specific areas or structures in the body during imaging procedures such as computed tomography (CT) scans or magnetic resonance imaging (MRI) scans.

Oral contrast agents are commonly used to enhance visualization of the gastrointestinal tract, and extravascular contrast agents may be used for imaging of the urinary system or other organs. Intravascular contrast agents, on the other hand, are administered directly into the bloodstream, typically through an intravenous (IV) injection, and are used to visualize blood vessels, organs, or other structures within the body.

Intrathecal contrast agents are injected into the spinal canal for imaging of the spinal cord and surrounding structures.

However, oral and rectal contrast agents are not typically used for intravascular or intrathecal imaging studies. Instead, they are used to enhance visualization of the gastrointestinal tract or rectum during imaging studies such as CT scans or MRI scans. Therefore, oral and/or rectal contrast administration alone does not qualify as a study "with contrast" for the purpose of intravascular or intrathecal imaging.

90. Answer B - The correct answer is b) 20.

Place of service codes indicate where healthcare services were provided. In this scenario, the orthopedic physician performed fracture care in an urgent care facility, which is considered an outpatient setting.

Place of service code 20 indicates that the service was provided in an Urgent Care Facility. Place of service codes 11, 22, and 23 are not appropriate in this scenario.

Code 11 indicates that the service was performed in an office setting.

Code 22 indicates that the service was performed in an outpatient hospital setting.

Code 23 indicates that the service was performed in an emergency room setting.

Therefore, the most appropriate place of service code for fracture care performed by an orthopedic physician in an urgent care facility is 20.

91. Answer C - The correct answer is c) S83.232A, 29881-RT.

The ICD-10-CM code for the postoperative diagnosis of

"right knee medial meniscal tear with mild grade three chondral change in the medial femoral condyle" is S83.232A. The CPT code for the procedure performed, "right knee arthroscopy with medial meniscectomy," is 29881-RT.

Option a) is incorrect because M23.205 is the ICD-10-CM code for unspecified tear of the meniscus, which is not specific enough to describe the patient's condition.

Option b) is incorrect because 29881-RT is the correct CPT code for the procedure performed, but the ICD-10-CM code provided (M23.205) is not specific enough to describe the patient's condition.

Option d) is incorrect because 29880-RT is the CPT code for a different procedure, "arthroscopy, knee, surgical; with meniscectomy (medial or lateral, including any meniscal shaving) including debridement/shaving of articular cartilage (chondroplasty), same or separate compartment(s)," which is not specific to the medial meniscus.

Therefore, the correct answer is c) S83.232A, 29881-RT.

92. Answer D - The appropriate codes to report for Dr. Field's service in this case are J35.3 and 42820.

J35.3 represents the diagnosis of adenotonsillar hypertrophy and obstructive sleep apnea. This code is used to indicate a hypertrophy or enlargement of the adenoids and tonsils, which can obstruct the airway during sleep and cause breathing difficulties.

42820 represents the procedure code for tonsillectomy and adenoidectomy. This code is used to report the surgical removal of the tonsils and adenoids.

Therefore, the correct answer is d) J35.3, 42820.

93. Answer D - The correct answer is d) N20.0, 50590.

Nephrolithiasis, or kidney stones, is indicated by the ICD-10 code N20.0, which is included in answer choices a, b, and

c. However, the postoperative diagnosis listed is bilateral nephrolithiasis, indicating that the condition is affecting both kidneys. Therefore, only N20.0 would be appropriate to report.

The CPT code 50590 is used to report the extracorporeal shock wave lithotripsy (ESWL) procedure, which is a non-invasive way of breaking up kidney stones using sound waves. This code is correctly included in all answer choices. Therefore, the correct answer is d) N20.0, 50590.

94. Answer D - The correct answer is d) N43.40, 54840-LT.

The preoperative and postoperative diagnosis is a prominent left spermatocele, which is a type of cyst that forms on the epididymis. The appropriate ICD-10 code for this condition is N43.40.

The procedure performed was a left spermatocystectomy with epididymectomy, which involves removal of the spermatocele as well as a portion of the epididymis. The appropriate CPT code for this procedure is 54840-LT.

Therefore, the correct answer is d) N43.40, 54840-LT. The LT modifier is used to indicate that the procedure was performed on the left side

95. Answer B - The correct answer is b) M48.02, M54.12, 62320.

In this case, the primary diagnosis is cervical stenosis with left upper extremity radiculopathy, which is reported with code M48.02. The secondary diagnosis is also reported, which is the cervical disc displacement with radiculopathy, coded as M54.12.

The procedure performed is a cervical epidural steroid injection at C4-C5, which is reported with code 62320. Fluoroscopic guidance was used during the procedure, which is reported with modifier -26 appended to code 77003. Anesthesia was local, but no specific anesthesia code is reported for this procedure.

Therefore, the correct codes for this case are M48.02, M54.12, 62320, and 77003-26.

96. Answer D - The correct answer is d) 29882.

The operative report describes arthroscopic repair of a torn lateral meniscus in the left knee. The correct CPT code for this procedure is 29882, which is a bundled code that includes all necessary arthroscopic procedures performed during the surgery, including debridement and repair of the meniscus.

The other codes listed in the answer choices are not appropriate for this procedure. Code 29877 is used for arthroscopic debridement of the medial or lateral meniscus, but it does not include repair. Code 29870 is used for removal of loose or foreign bodies from the knee joint, and code 29866 is used for arthroscopy with synovial biopsy.

Therefore, the correct code to report for this procedure is 29882.

97. Answer D - The correct answer is d) Monday: 99215-57; Tuesday: 33533, 33517, 35572, 33530.

On Monday, Dr. Manning performed a comprehensive evaluation and management (E/M) service for Nancy. The documentation indicates that he conducted a comprehensive history, comprehensive examination, and high-complexity decision-making. Therefore, the appropriate E/M code would be 99215-57, indicating that this was a high-complexity service that resulted in a decision to perform surgery.

On Tuesday, Dr. Manning performed a coronary artery bypass graft (CABG) procedure. The appropriate CPT codes for this procedure are 33533 (Harvest of vein(s) for coronary artery bypass graft, open), 33517 (Coronary artery bypass, vein only; one coronary venous graft), 35572

(Anastomosis, artery, by vein(s); each additional artery [List separately in addition to code for primary procedure]), and 33530 (Cardiopulmonary bypass, without pump oxygenator, any age). Therefore, the correct code sequence for Tuesday's services would be 33533, 33517, 35572, and 33530.

Therefore, the correct answer is d) Monday: 99215-57; Tuesday: 33533, 33517, 35572, 33530.

98. Answer C - Based on the information provided, the correct code for this case is option c) 40814, K13.79.

The code 40814 describes the excision of a lesion in the oral cavity, and the additional code K13.79 indicates that the lesion is in the buccal submucosa of the right lower lip. The code D10.39 is not necessary since it represents a malignant neoplasm of the mouth, which is not indicated in this case.

The procedure was performed under local anesthesia, and no additional anesthesia code is necessary. The code 40831-51 is not necessary either, as it represents a separate procedure that was not performed in this case.

Therefore, the correct coding for this case is 40814 (excision of lesion, oral cavity) with the additional code K13.79 (lesion in buccal submucosa of right lower lip).

99. Answer B - The correct answer is b) 67113-RT, 69990-RT.

In this case, a complex repair of retinal detachment was performed with photocoagulation, scleral buckle, sclerotomy/vitrectomy under local anesthesia. The following codes should be reported:

67113-RT - Repair of retinal detachment; with vitrectomy, any method, including, when performed, air or gas tamponade, focal endolaser photocoagulation, cryotherapy, drainage of subretinal fluid, scleral buckling, and/or removal of lens by same technique

69990-RT - Microsurgical techniques, requiring use of

operating microscope (List separately in addition to code for primary procedure)

Code 67113-RT includes all the procedures that were performed to repair the retinal detachment, such as photocoagulation, scleral buckle, and vitrectomy. Code 69990-RT should also be reported since the operating microscope was used during the procedure.

Codes 67107-51, 67145-51, and 66990-51 are not appropriate for this case because they do not accurately describe the procedures performed. Code 67107-51 is for repair of retinal detachment with vitrectomy and air or gas tamponade, but does not include the other procedures performed in this case. Code 67145-51 is for cryotherapy to the retina, which was not performed in this case. Code 66990-51 is for an extraocular procedure, which was not performed in this case.

100.   Answer B - The correct answer is option b) 25605-LT, 20690-51.

Explanation:

In this case, the physician performed an anatomical reduction of a displaced impacted Colles fracture, left distal radius and ulna, with the application of an external fixator. The postoperative diagnosis is the same as the preoperative diagnosis.

The appropriate CPT codes for this procedure are:

25605 - Open treatment of distal radial extra-articular fracture or epiphyseal separation, with or without internal or external fixation.

LT - Left side.

20690 - Application of a multiplane (pins or wires in more than one plane), unilateral external fixation system (eg, Hoffmann II, Hybrid, or Ilizarov type).

51 - Modifier indicating that multiple procedures were performed during the same operative session.

Therefore, the correct CPT codes to report for this

procedure are 25605-LT for the anatomical reduction of the distal radius fracture with an external fixator and 20690-51 to indicate that multiple procedures were performed during the same operative session.

EXAM B

1) This term means the surgical removal of the fallopian tube:
   a) Ligation
   b) Hysterectomy
   c) Salpingostomy
   d) Salpingectomy

2) This combining form means thirst:
   a) Dips/o
   b) Acr/o
   c) Cortic/o
   d) Somat/o

3) This term is also known as a homograft:
   a) Autograft
   b) Allograft
   c) Xenograft
   d) Zenograft

4) Which of the following terms does NOT describe a receptor of the body?

a) Mechanoreceptor
b) Proprioceptor
c) Thermoreceptor
d) Endoreceptor

5) This is the first portion of the small intestine:
   a) Jejunum
   b) Ileum
   c) Duodenum
   d) Cecum

6) This is a part of the inner ear:
   a) Vestibule
   b) Malleus
   c) Incus
   d) Stapes

7) This is the area behind the cornea:
   a) Anterior chamber
   b) Choroid layer
   c) Ciliary body
   d) Fundus

8) This is the collarbone:
   a) Patella
   b) Tibia
   c) Scapula
   d) Clavicle

9) Admission for hemodialysis because of acute renal failure.
   a) N17.8, Z91.15
   b) N17.0, Z49.01
   c) N17.9, Z99.2
   d) N19, Z49.0

10) Sarcoidosis with cardiomyopathy.
   a) D86.85
   b) D86.87
   c) I43, D86.9
   d) D86.9, I42.9

11) Laceration of left hand.
   a) S61.402A
   b) S61.412A
   c) S61.412D
   d) S61.422A

12) Fracture of the right patella with abrasion.
   a) S02.80XA
   b) S82.001A
   c) S82.009A
   d) S82.001D

13) Mr. Hallberger is 62 and has multiple problems. I am examining him in the intensive critical care unit. I understand he has fluid overload with acute renal failure and was started on ultrafiltration by the nephrologist on duty. He has an abnormal chest x-ray. He has preexisting type II diabetes mellitus and sepsis. We are left with a patient now who is still sedated and, on a ventilator, because of respiratory failure. Code the diagnoses only.
   a) A41.9, R65.20, N17.9, J96.90, E11.9
   b) E87.70, A41.9, R65.20, N17.9, J96.90, E11.9
   c) A41.9, N17.9, J96.90, R93.89, E11.9
   d) A41.9, R65.20, N17.9, J96.90, E11.9, R93.89

14) A patient is issued a 22-inch seat cushion for his wheelchair.
   a) E2601

b) E0950
c) E0190
d) E2602

15) A patient with chronic lumbar pain previously purchased a TENS and now needs replacement batteries.
   a) E1592
   b) A5082
   c) A4772
   d) A4630

16) Which HCPCS modifier indicates the great toe of the right foot?
   a) T1
   b) T3
   c) T4
   d) T5

17) This entity develops and publishes an annual plan that outlines the Medicare monitoring program.
   a) MACS
   b) FIS
   c) OIG
   d) CMS

18) This program was developed by CMS to promote national correct coding methods and to control inappropriate payment of Part B claims and hospital outpatient claims.
   a) NCCI
   b) NFS
   c) HIPAA
   d) MA-PA

19) What is NPI?
   a) National Payer Incentive
   b) National Provider Identifier
   c) National Provider Index
   d) National Payer Identification

20) This document is a notification in advance of services that Medicare probably will not pay for and the estimated cost to the patient.
   a) Wavier of Liability
   b) Coordination of Benefits
   c) Advanced Beneficiary Notice
   d) UPIN

21) Specific coding guidelines in the CPT manual are located in:
   a) The index.
   b) The introduction
   c) The beginning of each section.
   d) Appendix A.

22) Which punctuation mark between codes in the index of the CPT manual indicates a range of codes is available?
   a) Period
   b) Comma
   c) Semicolon
   d) Hyphen

23) The term that indicates this is the type of code for which the full code description can be known only if the common part of the code (the description preceding the semicolon) of a preceding entry is referenced:
   a) Stand-alone
   b) Indented
   c) Independent

d) Add-on

24) The symbol that indicates an add-on code is:
   a) #
   b) *
   c) +
   d) O

25) When you see the symbol ►◄ next to a code in the CPT manual, you know that:
   a) The code is a new code.
   b) The code contains new or revised text
   c) Code is a modifier -51 exempt code.
   d) FDA approval is pending.

26) Which of the following is most accurately about the designation "Separate procedure". The procedure is:
   a) Incidental to another procedure
   b) Reported if it is the only procedure performed
   c) Reported if the procedure is unrelated to a more major procedure performed at the same time on the same site
   d) All of the above

27) **OPERATIVE REPORT**
   OPERATIVE PROCEDURE: Excision of back lesion.
   INDICATIONS FOR SURGERY: The patient has an enlarging lesion on the upper midback. FINDINGS AT SURGERY: There was a 5-cm, upper midback lesion.
   OPERATIVE PROCEDURE: With the patient prone, the back was prepped and draped in the usual sterile fashion. The skin and underlying tissues were anesthetized with 30 ml of 1% lidocaine with epinephrine.
   Through a 5-cm transverse skin incision, the lesion was excised. Hemostasis was ensured. The incision was closed

using 3-0 Vicryl for the deep layers and running 3-0 Prolene subcuticular stitchwith Steri-Strips for the skin.

The patient was returned to the same-day surgery center in stable postoperative condition. All sponge, needle, and instrument counts were correct. Estimated blood loss is 0 ml.

PATHOLOGY REPORT LATER INDICATED: Dermatofibroma, skin of back. Assign code(s) for the physician service only.

a) 11406, 12002, D21.9
b) 11424, D21.1
c) 11406, 12032, D21.6
d) 11606, D21.22

28) EMERGENCY DEPARTMENT REPORT

CHIEF COMPLAINT: Nasal bridge laceration

SUBJECTIVE: The patient is a 74-year-old male who presents to the emergency department with a laceration to the bridge of his nose. He fell in the bathroom tonight. He recalls the incident. He just sort of lost his balance. He denies any vertigo. He denies any chest pain or shortness of breath. He denies any head pain or neck pain. There was no loss of consciousness. He slipped on a wet floor in the bathroom and lost his balance; that is how it happened. He has not had any blood from the nose or mouth.

PAST MEDICAL HISTORY:

Parkinson's.

Back pain.

Constipation.

MEDICATIONS: See the patient record for a complete list of medications.

ALLERGIES: NKDA.

REVIEW OF SYSTEMS: Per HPI. Otherwise, negative.

PHYSICAL EXAMINATION: The exam showed a 74-year-old male in no acute distress. Examination of the HEAD showed no obvious trauma other than the bridge of the nose, where there is approximately a 1.5- to 2-cm laceration. He had no bony tenderness under this. Pupils were equal, round, and reactive. EARS and NOSE: OROPHARYNX was unremarkable. NECK was soft and supple. HEART was regular. LUNGS were clear but slightly diminished in the bases. PROCEDURE: The wound was draped in a sterile fashion and anesthetized with 1% Xylocaine with sodium bicarbonate. It was cleansed with sterile saline and then repaired using interrupted 6-0 Ethilon sutures (Dr. Barney Teller, first-year resident, assisted with the suturing).

ASSESSMENT: Nasal bridge laceration, status post fall.

PLAN: Keep clean. Sutures out in 5 to 7 days. Watch for signs of infection.

a) 12051, S012.1XA, G20, W01.XXXA, Y92.091
b) 12011, S012.1XA, G20, W01.0XXA, Y92.091
c) 12011, S012.1XA, G20, W18.39XA, Y92.094
d) 12011, S012.1XA, G20, W18.42XA, Y92.091

29) SAME-DAY SURGERY

DIAGNOSIS: Inverted nipple with mammary duct ectasia, left.

OPERATION: Excision of mass deep to left nipple.

With the patient under general anesthesia, a circumareolar incision was made with sharp dissection and carried down into the breast tissue. The nipple complex was raised up using a small retractor. Wegently dissected underneath to free up the nipple entirely. Once this was done, we had the nipple fully unfolded, and there was some evident mammary duct ectasis. An area 3 × 4 cm was excised using electrocautery. Hemostasis was maintained with the electrocautery, and then the breast tissue deep to the nipple was reconstructed using sutures of 3-0 chromic. Subcutaneous tissue was closed using 3-0 chromic, and then the skin was closed using 4-0 Vicryl. Steri-Strips were applied. The patient tolerated the procedure well and was returned to the recovery area in stable condition. At the end of the procedure, all sponges and instruments were accounted for.

a) 19120-RT
b) 11404-LT
c) 19112
d) 19120-LT

30) This patient returns today for palliative care to her feet. Her toenails have become elongated and thickened, and she is unable to trim them on her own. She states that she has had no problems and no acute signs of any infection or otherwise to her feet. She returns today strictly for trimming of her toenails.

EXAMINATION: Her pedal pulses are palpable bilaterally. The nails are mycotic, 1 through 4 on the left, and 1 through 3 on the right.

ASSESSMENT: Onychomycosis, 1 through 4 on the left and 1 through 3 on the right.

PLAN: Mild debridement of mycotic nails × 7. This patient is to return to the clinic in 3 to 4 months for follow-up palliative care.

a) 11721 × 7, B35.1
b) 99212, 11721, B49
c) 11719, B35.1
d) 11721, B35.1

31) OPERATIVE REPORT

With the patient having had a wire localization performed by radiology, she was taken to the operating room and, under local anesthesia of the left breast, was prepped and draped in a sterile manner. A breast line incision was made through the entry point of the wire, and a core of tissue surrounding the wire (approximately 1 × 2 cm) was removed using electrocautery for hemostasis.

The specimen, including the wire, was then submitted to radiology, and the presence of the lesion within the specimen was confirmed. The wound was checked for hemostasis, and this was maintained with electrocautery. The breast tissue was reapproximated using 2-0 and 3-0 chromic. The skin was closed using 4-0 Vicryl in a subcuticular manner. Steri-Strips were applied. The patient tolerated the procedure well and was discharged from the operating room in stable condition. At the end of the procedure, all sponges and instruments were accounted for. Pathology report later indicated: Benign lesion.

a) 11602-LT, D24.2
b) 11400-LT, D24.9
c) 19125-LT, D24.2
d) 19125-LT, D49.3

32) What CPT and ICD-10-CM codes would be used to code a split-thickness skin graft, both thighs to the abdomen, measuring 45 × 21 cm performed on a patient who has third-degree burns of the abdomen. Documentation stated 20% of the body surface was burned, with 9% third degree. The patient also sustained second-degree burns of the lower back.

a) 15100 × 2, T21.62XA, T22.119XA, T31.22
b) 15100, 15101 × 9, T21.32XA, T21.24XA, T31.20
c) 15100, 15101 × 9-51, T31.20, T21.32XA, T21.24XA
d) 15100, 15101 × 8, T21.32XA, T21.24XA, T31.20

33) Libby was thrown from a horse while riding in the ditch; a truck that honked the horn as it passed her startled her horse. The horse reared up, and Libby was thrown to the ground. Her left tibia was fractured and required insertion of multiple pins to stabilize the defect area. A Monticelli multiplane external fixation system was then attached to the pins. Code the placement of the fixation device and

diagnosis only.
a) 20661-LT, S82.221A, V80.41XA
b) 20692-LT, S82.202A, V80.010A
c) 20692-LT, S82.232A, V80.41XA
d) 20690-LT, S82.42XA, V80.41XA

34) A small incision was made over the left proximal tibia, and a traction pin was inserted through the bone to the opposite side. Weights were then affixed to the pins to stabilize the closed tibial fracture temporarily until fracture repair could be performed. Assign codes for the physician service.
a) 20650-LT, S82.102A
b) 20663-LT, S82.142A
c) 20690-LT, S82.231A
d) 20692-LT, S82.156A

35) Mary tells her physician that she has been having pain in her left wrist for several weeks. The physician examines the area and palpates a ganglion cyst of the tendon sheath. He marks the injection sites, sterilizes the area, and injects corticosteroid into two areas.
a) 20550-LT × 2, M67.849
b) 20551-LT, M67.52
c) 20551-LT × 2, M67.469
d) 20612-LT, 20612-59-LT, M67.432

36) The physician applies a Minerva-type fiberglass body cast from the hips to the shoulders and to the head. Before application, a stockinette is stretched over the patient's torso, and further padding of the bony areas with felt padding was done. The patient was diagnosed with Morquio-Brailsford kyphosis. Assign codes for the physician service only.
a) 29040

b) 29015
c) 29035
d) 29000

37) OPERATIVE REPORT

PREOPERATIVE DIAGNOSIS: Compound fracture, left humerus, with possible loss of left radial pulse.

PROCEDURE PERFORMED: Open reduction internal fixation, left compound humerus fracture. PROCEDURE: While under a general anesthetic, the patient's left arm was prepped with Betadine and raped in sterile fashion. We then created a longitudinal incision over the anterolateral aspect of his left arm and carried the dissection through the subcutaneous tissue. We attempted to identify the lateral intermuscular septum and progressed to the fracture site, which was actually fairly easy to do because there was some significant tearing and rupturing of the biceps and brachialis muscles. These were partial ruptures, but the bone was relatively easy to expose through this. We then identified the fracture site and thoroughly irrigated it with several liters of saline. We also noted that the radial nerve was easily visible, crossing along the posterolateral aspect of the fracture site. It was intact. We carefully detected it throughout the remainder of the procedure. We then were able to strip the periosteum away from the lateral side of the shaft of the humerus both proximally and distally from the fracture site. We did this just enough to apply a 6-hole plate, which we eventually held in place with six cortical screws. We did attempt to compress the fracture site. Due to some comminution, the fracture was not quite anatomically aligned, but certainly it was felt to be very acceptable. Once we had applied the plate, we then checked the radial pulse with a Doppler. We found that theradial pulse was present using the Doppler, but not with palpation. We then applied Xeroform dressings to the wounds and the incision. After padding the arm thoroughly, we applied a long-arm splint with the elbow flexed about 75 degrees. He tolerated the procedure well, and the radial pulsewas again present on Doppler examination at the end of the procedure.

a) 24515-RT
b) 24500-LT
c) 24515-LT
d) 24505-LT

38) OPERATIVE REPORT

PREOPERATIVE DIAGNOSIS: Left thigh abscess.

PROCEDURE PERFORMED: Incision and drainage of left thigh abscess.

OPERATIVE NOTE: With the patient under general anesthesia, he was placed in the lithotomy position. The area around the anus was carefully inspected, and we saw no evidence of communication with the perirectal space. This appears to have risen in the crease at the top of the leg, extending from the posterior buttocks' region up toward the side of the base of the penis. In any event, the area was prepped and draped in a sterile manner. Then we incised the area in fluctuation. We obtained a lot of very foul-smelling, almost stool-like material (it was not stool, but it was brown and very foul-smelling material). This was not the typical pus one sees with a Staphylococcus aureus–type infection. The incision was widened to allow us to probe the cavity fully. Again, I could see no evidence of communication to the rectum, but there was extension down the thigh and extension up into the groin crease. The fascia was darkened from the purulent material. I opened some of the fasciato make sure the underlying muscle was viable. This appeared viable. No gas was present. There was nothing to suggest a necrotizing fasciitis. The patient did have a very extensive inflammation within this abscess cavity. The abscess cavity was irrigated with peroxide and saline and packed with gauze vaginal packing. The patient tolerated the procedure well and was discharged from the operating room in stable condition.

a) 26990-LT, L03.119
b) 27301-LT, L02.416
c) 27301-LT, L02.419
d) 27025-LT, L03.229

39) OPERATIVE REPORT

Code only the operative procedure and diagnosis(es).
PREOPERATIVE DIAGNOSIS: Hypoxia, Pneumothorax
POSTOPERATIVE DIAGNOSIS: Hypoxia, Pneumothorax
PROCEDURE: Chest tube placement.
DESCRIPTION OF PROCEDURE: The patient was previously sedated with Versed and paralyzed with Nimbex. Lidocaine was used to numb the incision area in the mid lateral left chest at about nipple level. After the lidocaine, an incision was made, and we bluntly dissected to the area of the pleural space, making sure we were superior to the rib. On entrance to the pleural space, there was immediate release of air noted. An 18-gauge chest tube was subsequently placed and sutured to the skin. There were no complications for the procedure, and blood loss was minimal.
DISPOSITION: Follow-up, single-view, chest x-ray showed significant resolution of the pneumothorax except for a small apical pneumothorax that was noted.

a) 32422, J94.2, R04.81
b) 32551, J92.9, R09.02
c) 32551, J93.9, R09.02
d) 32422, J93.81, R07.2

40) OPERATIVE PROCEDURE

PREOPERATIVE DIAGNOSIS: 68-year-old male in a coma.

POSTOPERATIVE DIAGNOSIS: 68-year-old male in a coma
PROCEDURE PERFORMED: Placement of a triple lumen central line in right subclavian vein. With the usual Betadine scrub to the right subclavian vein area and with a second attempt, the subclavian vein was cannulated and the wire was threaded. The first time the wire did not thread right, and so the attempt was aborted to make sure we had good identification of structures. Once the wire was in place, the needle was removed and a tissue dilator was pushed into position over the wire. Once that was removed, then the central lumen catheter was pushed into position at 17 cm and the wire removed. All three ports were flushed. The catheter was sewn into position, and a dressing applied.

a) 36011, R40.0
b) 36011, R40.1
c) 36556, R40.24
d) 36556, R40.20

41) OPERATIVE REPORT: The patient is in for a bone marrow biopsy. The patient was sterilized by standard procedure. Bone marrow core biopsies were obtained from the left posterior iliac crest with minimal discomfort. At the end of the procedure, the patient denied discomfort, without evidence of complications. The patient has diffuse, malignant lymphoma. Assign codes for the physician service only.

a) 20225, C83.70
b) 38221, C83.50
c) 38230, C83.50
d) 38220, C84.17

42) What CPT and ICD-10-CM codes report a percutaneous insertion of a dual-chamber pacemaker by means of the subclavian vein? The diagnosis was sick sinus syndrome,

tachy-brady.
a) 33249, I50.1
b) 33217, I49.5
c) 33208, I49.5
d) 33240, I47.2

43) Patient is a 40-year-old male who was involved in a motor vehicle crash. He is having some pulmonary insufficiency.

PROCEDURE: Bronchoscope was inserted through the accessory point on the end of the ET tube and was then advanced through the ET tube. The ET tube came pretty close down to the carina. We selectively intubated the right mainstem bronchus with the bronchoscope. There were some secretions here, and these were aspirated. We then advanced this selectively into first the lower and then the middle and upper lobes. Secretions were present, more so in the middle and lower lobes. No mucous plug was identified. We then went into the left mainstem and looked at the upper and lower lobes. There was really not much in the way of secretions present. We did inject some saline and aspirated this out. We then removed the bronchoscope and put the patient back on the supplemental O2. We waited a few minutes. The oxygen level actually stayed pretty good during this time. We then reinserted the bronchoscope and went down to the right side again. We aspirated out all secretions and made sure everything was clear. We then removed the bronchoscope and pulled back on the ET tube about 1.5 cm. We then again placed the patient on supplemental oxygenation.

FINDINGS: No mucous plug was identified. Secretions were found mainly in the right lung and were aspirated. The left side looked pretty clear.

a) 31646, J91.8,
b) 32654, J95.89
c) 31645-50, J95.2

d) 31645-RT, 31622-51-LT, J95.2, V89.0XXA

44) This 52-year-old male has undergone several attempts at extubation, all of which failed. He also has morbid obesity and significant subcutaneous fat in his neck. The patient is now in for a flap tracheostomy and cervical lipectomy. The cervical lipectomy is necessary for adequate exposure and access to the trachea and also to secure tracheotomy tube placement. Assign code(s) for the physician service only.
a) 31610, 15839-51
b) 31610
c) 31610, 15838
d) 31603, 15839-51

45) The physician is using an abdominal approach to perform a proctopexy combined with a sigmoidresection; the patient was diagnosed with colon cancer, primary site sigmoid flexure of the colon.
a) 45540, C18.7, C80.0
b) 45541, C18.2, C80.0
c) 45550, C18.7, C79.9
d) 45342, C05.0, C79.9

46) OPERATIVE REPORT
PREOPERATIVE DIAGNOSIS: Abdominal pain
POSTOPERATIVE DIAGNOSIS: Normal endoscopy.
PROCEDURE: The video therapeutic endoscope was passed without difficulty into the oropharynx. The gastroesophageal junction was seen at 40 cm. Inspection of the esophagus revealed no erythema, ulceration, varices, or other mucosal abnormalities. The stomach was entered and the endoscope advanced to the second duodenum. Inspection of the second duodenum, first duodenum, duodenal bulb, and pylorus revealed no abnormalities. Retroflexion revealed no lesions along the curvature.

Inspection of the antrum, body, and fundus of the stomach revealed no abnormalities. The patient tolerated the procedure well. The patient complained of abdominal pain and weight loss.

a) 45378, R10.9, R63.4
b) 43235, R10.9, R63.4
c) 49320, R63.0, R10.9
d) 43255, R10.32, E66.01

47) This 70-year-old male is brought to the operating room for a biopsy of the pancreas. A wedge biopsy is taken and sent to pathology. The report comes back immediately indicating that primary malignant cells were present in the specimen. The decision was made to perform a total pancreatectomy. Code the operative procedure(s) and diagnosis only.

a) 48100-57, C32.3
b) 48155, C26.0
c) 48155, 48100-51, C25.9
d) 48155, 48100-51, 88309, C25.9

48) The patient was taken to the operating room for a repair of a strangulated inguinal hernia. This hernia was previously repaired 4 months ago.

a) 49521, K40.40
b) 49520, K40.11
c) 49492, K40.10
d) 49521-78, K41.30

49) This 43-year-old female comes in with a peritonsillar abscess. The patient is brought to same-day surgery and given general anesthetic. On examination of the peritonsillar abscess, an incision was made and fluid was drained. The area was examined again, saline was applied,

and then the area was packed with gauze. The patient tolerated the procedure well.

a) 42825, J36
b) 42700, J36
c) 42825, J32.4
d) 42700, J31.1

50) What code would you use to report a rigid proctosigmoidoscopy with removal of two non-adenomatous polyps of the rectum by snare technique?

a) 45320, K63.1
b) 45384, K61.2
c) 45309 × 2, K62.1
d) 45315, K62.1

51) OPERATIVE REPORT

PREOPERATIVE DIAGNOSIS: Missed abortion with fetal demise, 11 weeks. POSTOPERATIVEDIAGNOSIS: Missed abortion with fetal demise, 11 weeks.

PROCEDURE: Suction D&C.

The patient was prepped and draped in a lithotomy position under general mask anesthesia, and the bladder was straight catheterized; a weighted speculum was placed in the vagina. The anterior lip of the cervix was grasped with a single-tooth tenaculum. The uterus was then sounded to a depth of 8 cm. The cervical OS was then serially dilated to allow passage of a size 10 curved suction curette. A size 10 curved suction curette was then used to evacuate the intrauterine contents. Sharp curette was used to gently palpate the uterine wall with negative return of tissue, and the suction curette was again used with negative return of tissue. The tenaculum was removed from the cervix. The speculum was removed from the vagina. All sponges and needles were accounted for at completion of the procedure. The patient left the operating room in apparent good condition having tolerated the procedure well.

a) 59812, O03.9
b) 59812, O03.2
c) 59820, O02.1
d) 59856, O02.1

52) OPERATIVE REPORT

PREOPERATIVE DIAGNOSIS: Right ureteral stricture.

POSTOPERATIVE DIAGNOSIS: Right ureteral stricture.

PROCEDURE PERFORMED: Cystoscopy, right ureteral stent change.

PROCEDURE NOTE: The patient was placed in the lithotomy position after receiving IV sedation. He was prepped and draped in the lithotomy position. The 21-French cystoscope was passed into the bladder, and urine was collected for culture. Inspection of the bladder demonstrated findings consistent with radiation cystitis, which has been previously diagnosed. There is no frank neoplasia. The right ureteral stent was grasped and removed through the urethral meatus; under fluoroscopic control, a guidewire was advanced up the stent, and the stent was exchanged for a 7-French 26-cm stent under fluoroscopic control in the usual fashion. The patient tolerated the procedure well.

a) 51702-LT, N13.5
b) 52005-RT, N22
c) 52332-RT, N21.1
d) 52332-RT, N13.5

53) This patient is a 42-year-old female who has been having prolonged and heavy bleeding during menstruation. SURGICAL FINDINGS: On pelvic exam under anesthesia, the uterus was normal size and firm. The examination revealed no masses. She had a few small endometrial polyps in the lower uterine segment.

DESCRIPTION OF PROCEDURE: After induction of general anesthesia, the patient was placed in the dorsolithotomy position, after which the perineum and vagina were prepped, the bladder straight catheterized, and the patient draped. After bimanual exam was performed, a weighted speculum was placed in the vagina and the anterior lip of the cervix was grasped with a single toothed tenaculum. An endocervical curettage was then done with a Kevorkian curet. The uterus was then sounded to 8.5 cm. The endocervical canal was dilated to 7 mm with Hegar dilators. A 5.5-mm Olympus hysteroscope was introduced using a distention medium. The cavity was systematically inspected, and the preceding findings noted. The hysteroscope was withdrawn and the cervix further dilated to 10 mm. Polyp forceps was introduced, and a few small polyps were removed. These were sent separately. Sharp endometrial curettage was then done. The hysteroscope was then reinserted, and the polyps had essentially been removed. The patient tolerated the procedure well and returned to the recovery room in stable condition. Pathology confirmed benign endometrial polyps.

a) 58558, 57460-51, N82.5, N92.3
b) 58558, N92.0, N84.0
c) 58558, 57558-51, N84.1, N92.1
d) 58558, N92.0, N84.0

54) This patient is 35 years old at 35 weeks' gestation. She presented in spontaneous labor. Because of her prior cesarean section, she is taken to the operating room to have a repeat lower-segment transverse cesarean section performed. The patient also desires sterilization, and so a bilateral tubal ligation will also be performed. A single, liveborn infant was the outcome of the delivery.

a) 59510, 58600-51, Z30.2
b) 59620, 58611, O60.14X0, Z37.0

c) 59514, 58605-51, Z37.0, O60.14X0

d) 59514, 58611, O60.14X0, O34.21, Z37.0, Z30.2

55) OPERATIVE REPORT

PREOPERATIVE DIAGNOSIS: Possible recurrent transitional cell carcinoma of the bladder. POSTOPERATIVE DIAGNOSIS: No evidence of recurrence.

PROCEDURE PERFORMED: Cystoscopy with multiple bladder biopsies.

PROCEDURE NOTE: The patient was given a general mask anesthetic, prepped, and draped in the lithotomy position. The 21-French cystoscope was passed into the bladder. There was a hyperemic area on the posterior wall of the bladder, and a biopsy was taken. Random biopsies of the bladder were also performed. This area was fulgurated. A total of 7 sq cm of bladder was fulgurated. A catheter was left at the end of the procedure. The patient tolerated the procedure well and was transferred to the recovery room in good condition. The pathology report indicated no evidence of recurrence.

a) 52224, Z85.51

b) 51020, 52204, Z80.52

c) 52234, D41.4, Z85.51

d) 52224 × 4, D41.4

56) This 41-year-old female presented with a right labial lesion. A biopsy was taken, and the results were reported as VIN III, cannot rule out invasion. The decision was therefore made to proceed with wide local excision of the right vulva. PROCEDURE: The patient was taken to the operating room, and general anesthesia was administered. The patient was then prepped and draped in the usual manner in lithotomy position, and the bladder was emptied with a straight catheter. The vulva was then inspected. On the right labium minora at approximately the 11 o'clock

position, there was a multifocal lesion. A marking pen was then used to mark out an elliptical incision, leaving a 1-cm border on all sides. The skin ellipse was then excised using a knife. Bleeders were cauterized with electrocautery. A running locked suture of 2-0 Vicryl was then placed in the deeper tissue. The skin was finally reapproximated with 4-0 Vicryl in an interrupted fashion. Good hemostasis was thereby achieved. The patient tolerated this procedure well. There were no complications.

a) 56605, C51.9
b) 56625, D07.1
c) 56620, D07.1
d) 11620, C50.8

57) OPERATIVE REPORT

PREOPERATIVE DIAGNOSIS: Brain tumor versus abscess

PROCEDURE: Craniotomy

DESCRIPTION OF PROCEDURE: Under general anesthesia, the patient's head was prepped and draped in the usual manner. It was placed in Mayfield pins. We then proceeded with a craniotomy. An inverted U-shaped incision was made over the posterior right occipital area. The flap was turned down. Three burr holes were made. Having done this, I then localized the tumor through the burr holes and dura. We then made an incision in the dura in an inverted U-shaped fashion. The cortex looked a little swollen but normal. We then used the localizer to locate the cavity. I separated the gyrus and got right into the cavity and saw pus, which was removed. Cultures were taken and sent for pathology report, which came back later describing the presence of clusters of gram-positive cocci, confirming that this was an abscess. We cleaned out the abscessed cavity using irrigation and suction. The bed of the abscessed cavity was cauterized. Then a small piece of Gelfoam was used for hemostasis. Satisfied that it was dry, I closed the dura. I approximated the scalp. A dressing was applied. The patient was discharged to the recovery room.

a) 61154, D49.6
b) 61154, G11.0
c) 61320, G06.0
d) 61150, C24.0

58) This patient came in with an obstructed ventriculoperitoneal shunt. The procedure performed was to be a revision of shunt. After inspecting the shunt system, the entire cerebrospinal fluid shunt system was removed and a similar replacement shunt system was placed. Patient has normal pressure hydrocephalus (NPH).

a) 62180, T85.192D
b) 62258, T85.09XD
c) 62256, T85.09XA
d) 62190, T85.199A

59) This patient is in for a recurrent herniated disc at L5-S1 on the left. The procedure performed is a repeat laminotomy and foraminotomy at the L5-S1 interspace.

a) 63030-LT, M46.45
b) 63030-LT, M30.62
c) 63042-LT, M51.25
d) 63042-LT, M51.27

60) What CPT and ICD-10-CM codes would you assign to report the removal of 30% of the left thyroid lobe, with isthmusectomy? The diagnosis was benign growth of the thyroid.

a) 60210, D34
b) 60220, D44.0
c) 60212, D49.7
d) 60225, D44.0, D49.7

61) OPERATIVE REPORT

PREOPERATIVE DIAGNOSIS: Paralytic ectropion, left eye
PROCEDURE PERFORMED: Medial tarsorrhaphy, left eye
In the operating room, after intravenous sedation, the patient was given a total of about 0.5 ml of local infiltrative anesthetic. The skin surfaces on the medial area of the lid, medial to the punctum, were denuded. A bolster had been prepared and double 5-0 silk suture was passed through the bolster, which was passed through the inferior skin and raw lid margin, then through the superior margin, and out through the skin. A superior bolster was then applied. The puncta were probed with wire instrument and found not to be obstructed. The suture was then fully tied and trimmed. Bacitracin ointment was placed on the surface of the skin. The patient left the operating room in stable condition, without complications, having tolerated the procedure well.

a)   67875-LT, H02.236
b)   67710-LT, H02.129
c)   67882-LT, H02.146
d)   67880-LT, H02.156

62) This 66-year-old male has been diagnosed with a senile cataract of the posterior extracapsular and is scheduled for a cataract extraction by phacoemulsification of the right eye. The physician has taken the patient to the operating room to perform a posterior extracapsular cataract extraction with IOL placement, diffuse of the right eye.

a)   66982-RT
b)   66984-RT
c)   66983-RT
d)   66830-RT

63) Bill, a retired U.S. Air Force pilot, was on observation status

12 hours to assess the outcome of a fall from the back of a parked pickup truck into a gravel pit.

History of Present Illness: The patient is a 42-year-old gentleman who works at the local garden shop. He explained that yesterday he fell from his pickup truck as he was loading gravel for a landscaping project. He lost his footing when attempting to climb from the pickup bed and fell approximately 4 feet and landed on a rock that was protruding from the ground 4 inches, striking his head on the rock. He did not lose consciousness, but was dizzy. He subsequently developed a throbbing headache (8/10) and swelling at the point of impact. The duration of the dizziness was approximately 10 minutes. The headache persisted for 26 hours after the fall. He did take ibuprofen without significant improvement in the pain level. Review of Systems: Constitutional, eyes, ears, nose, throat, lungs, cardiovascular, gastrointestinal, skin, neurologic, lymphatic, and immunologic negative except for HPI statements.

PFSH: He is married and has 2 children. He has been working at the garden shop for 4 years. He currently smokes one pack of cigarettes a day and has smoked for 10 years. His father died of heart disease when he was 52. He has one brother with ankylosing spondylitis and one sister who is healthy as far as he knows. His mother died when he was 14 years old. He is currently on no prescribed medications. A comprehensive exam is documented and rendered. The medical decision making is of low complexity.

The physician discharged Bill from observation that same day after 10 hours, after determining that no further monitoring of his condition was necessary. The physician provided a detailed examination and indicated that the medical decision making was of a low complexity.

a) 99218, W18.39XA, R42

b) 99234, Z04.3, W17.89XA, R42, R51

c) 99217, W14.XXXA, R51
d) 99234, 99217, W20.XXA, Z04.3

64) Dr. Martin admits a 65-year-old female patient to the hospital to rule out acute pericarditis following a severe viral infection. The patient has complained of retrosternal, sharp, intermittent pain of 2 days' duration that is reduced by sitting up and leaning forward, accompanied by tachypnea.

ROS: She does not currently have chest pain but is complaining of shortness of breath. She states that her legs and feet have been swollen of late. She reports no change in her vision or her hearing, and she has not had a rash. No dyspnea stated.

PFSH: She states that she has had and echocardiogram in the past when she complained of chest tightness and her family physician gave her some medication, but she is not certain what it was. She has three adult children, all healthy. Her husband is deceased. She does not smoke or consume alcohol. Her father died at age 69 from congestive heart failure and her mother died of influenza at 70. Refer to the admission form for a list of current medications. The examination was detailed. The medical decision making was of low complexity.

a) 99236, R06.82, R06.02
b) 99223, I20.0, K22.9
c) 99245, I20.0, I30.0
d) 99221, R07.2, R06.82

65) A gynecologist admits an established patient, a 35-year-old female with dysfunctional uterine bleeding, after seeing her in the clinic that day. During the course of the history, the physician notes that the patient has a history of infrequent periods of heavy flow. She has had irregular heavy periods and intermittent

spotting for 4 years. The patient has been on a 3-month course of oral contraceptives for symptoms with no relief. The patient states that she has occasional headaches. A complete ROS was performed, consisting of constitutional factors, ophthalmologic, otolaryngologic, cardiovascular, respiratory, gastrointestinal, genitourinary, musculoskeletal, integumentary, neurologic, psychiatric, endocrine, hematologic, lymphatic, allergic, and immunologic which were all negative, except for the symptoms described above. The family history is positive for endometrial cancer, with mother, two aunts, and two sisters who had endometrial cancer. The patient has a personal history of cervical and endometrial polyp removal 3 years prior to admission. The patients states that she does not smoke and only drinks socially. As a part of the comprehensive examination, the physician notes the patient has alarge amount of blood in the vault and an enlarged uterus. The prolonged hemorrhaging has resulted in a very thin and friable endometrial lining. The physician orders the patient to be started on intravenous Premarin and orders a full laboratory workup. The medical decision making is of moderate complexity.

a) 99215, 99222, N93.8, Z87.42
b) 99222, N93.8, Z87.42, Z80.49
c) 99215, 99222, N89.8, Z87.42
d) 99222, N91.5, Z80.49

66) Dr. Black admits a patient with an 8-day history of a low-grade fever, tachycardia, tachypnea, and radiologic evidence of basal consolidation of the lung and limited pleural effusion on the left side, per patient as seen at outside clinic several days prior. The patient has also been experiencing swelling of the extremities. The pulse is rapid and thready, as checked by patient on her own during the past couple days. A complete ROS

of constitutional factors, ophthalmologic, otolaryngologic, cardiovascular, respiratory, gastrointestinal, genitourinary, musculoskeletal, integumentary, neurologic, psychiatric, endocrine, hematologic, lymphatic, allergic, and immunologic was performed and negative except for the symptoms described above. Past history includes tachycardia and pneumonia. Family history includes heart disease, hypertension and high cholesterol in both parents. The patient drinks only occasionally and quit smoking four years ago. The comprehensive examination was performed and diminished bowel sounds were noted. The physician orders laboratory tests and radiographic studies, including a follow-up chest x-ray as he considers the extensive diagnostic options and the medical decision-making complexity is high for this patient.

a) 99234
b) 99213
c) 99236
d) 99223

67) Dr. Stephanopolis makes subsequent hospital visits to Salanda Ortez, who has been in the hospital for primary viral pneumonia. She was experiencing severe dyspnea, rales, fever, and chest pain for over a week. The patient states that this morning she had nausea and her heart was racing while she was experiencing some dyspnea and SOB. The chest radiography showed patchy bilateral infiltrates and basilar streaking. Sputum microbiology was positive for a secondary bacterial pneumonia. An expanded problem-focused physical examination was performed. The medical decision making was moderate. The patient was given intravenous antibiotic as treatment for the bacterial pneumonia.

a) 99233, J15.8, J12.2
b) 99232, J15.9, J12.9

c) 99221, J11.0, J10.82

d) 99234, J14, J15.9

68) A 57-year-old male was sent by his family physician to a urologist for an office consultation due to hematuria. The patient has had bright red blood in his urine sporadically for the past 3 weeks. His family physician gave him a dose of antibiotic therapy for urinary tract infection; however, the symptom still persists. The patient states that he does experience some lower back discomfort when urinating, with no fever, chills or nausea. The patient is currently taking Lotrel 10/20 for his hypertension which is stable at this time and has allergies to Sulfa. The urologist performs a detailed history and physical examination. The urologist recommends a cystoscopy to be scheduled for the following day and discusses the procedure and risks with the patient. The urologist also contacted the family physician with the recommendations and is requested to proceed with the cystoscopy and any further follow-up required. The medical decision making is of moderate complexity. A report was sent to attending physician. Report only the office service.

a) 99243, R31.9, M54.5

b) 99244-57, 52000, R33, M54.9

c) 99253, R35, M53.2

d) 99221, R39.8, M50.9

69) Which HCPCS modifier indicates an anesthesia service in which the anesthesiologist medically directs one CRNA?

a) QX

b) QY

c) QZ

d) QK

70) Anesthesia service for a pneumocentesis for lung aspiration, 32420.
   a) 00522
   b) 00500
   c) 00520
   d) 00524

71) This type of anesthesia is also known as a nerve block.
   a) Local
   b) Epidural
   c) Regional
   d) MAC

72) This is the anesthesia formula:
   a) B + M + P
   b) B + P + M
   c) B + T + M
   d) B + T + N

73) This 69-year-old female is in for a magnetic resonance examination of the brain because of new seizure activity. After imaging without contrast, contrast was administered and further sequences were performed. Examination results indicated no apparent neoplasm or vascular malformation.
   a) 70543-26, R56.00
   b) 70543-26, R53.81
   c) 70553-26, R56.00
   d) 70553, R49.0

74) This patient undergoes a gallbladder sonogram due to epigastric pain. The report indicates that the visualized portions of the liver are normal. No free fluid noted within

Morison's pouch. The gallbladder is identified and is empty. No evidence of wall thickening or surrounding fluid is seen. There is no ductal dilatation. The common hepatic duct and common bile duct measure 0.4 and 0.8cm, respectively. The common bile duct measurement is at the upper limits of normal.

a) 76700-26, R10.84
b) 76705-26, R10.13
c) 76775-26, R10.33
d) 76705, R10.81

75) EXAMINATION OF: Chest.
CLINICAL SYMPTOMS: Pneumonia. PA AND LATERAL CHEST X-RAY WITH FLUOROSCOPY.
CONCLUSION: Ventilation within the lung fields has improved compared with previous study.

a) 71020-26, J15.8
b) 71034, J15.6
c) 71046-26, J18.9
d) 71023, J11.1

76) EXAMINATION OF: Abdomen and pelvis. CLINICAL SYMPTOMS: Ascites.
CT OF ABDOMEN AND PELVIS: Technique: CT of the abdomen and pelvis was performed without oral or IV contrast material per physician request. No previous CT scans for comparison.
FINDINGS: No ascites. Moderate-sized pleural effusion on the right.

a) 74176
b) 74176-26
c) 74150, 72192
d) 74177

77) EXAMINATION OF: Brain

CLINICAL FINDING: Headache

COMPUTED TOMOGRAPHY OF THE BRAIN was performed without contrast material. FINDINGS: There is blood within the third ventricle. The lateral ventricles show mild dilatation with small amounts of blood.

IMPRESSION: Acute subarachnoid hemorrhage.

a) 70460-26, G44.1

b) 70250, I74.1

c) 70450, I60.9

d) 70450-26, I73.8

78) Report both the technical and professional components of the following service: This 68year-old male is seen in Radiation Oncology Department for prostate cancer. The oncologist performs a complex clinical treatment planning, dosimetry calculation, complex isodose plan; treatment devices include blocks, special shields, wedges, and treatment management. The patient had 5 days of radiation treatments for 2 weeks, a total of 10 days of treatment.

a) 77263, 77300, 77307, 77334, C61

b) 77300, 77307, 77334, 77427 X 2, C61

c) 77263, 77307, 77427 X 2, C61

d) 77263, 77427 X 2, C61

79) CLINICAL HISTORY: Necrotic soleus muscle, right leg

SPECIMEN RECEIVED: Soleus muscle, right leg

GROSS DESCRIPTION: Submitted in formalin, labeled with the patient's name and "soleus muscle right leg," are multiple irregular fragments of tan, gray, brown soft tissue measuring 8 × 8 × 2.5 cm inaggregate. Multiple representative fragments are submitted in four cassettes.

MICROSCOPIC DESCRIPTION: The slides show multiple

sections of skeletal muscle showing severe coagulative and liquefactive necrosis. Patchy neutrophilic infiltrates are present within the necrotic tissue.

DIAGNOSIS: Soft tissue, soleus muscle, right leg debridement; necrosis and patchy acute inflammation, skeletal muscle— infective myositis.

a) 88305-26, M62.50
b) 88304-26, I96
c) 88307-26, I96
d) 88304-26, M46.98

80) This 34-year-old established female patient is in for her yearly physical and lab. The physician orders a comprehensive metabolic panel, hemogram automated and manual differential WBC count (CBC), and a thyroid-stimulating hormone. Code the lab only.

a) 99395, 80050
b) 80050-52
c) 80069, 80050
d) 80050

81) This is a patient with atrial fibrillation who comes to the clinic laboratory routinely for a quantitative digoxin level.

a) 80305, Z46.1, Z82.61, I34.0
b) 80306, Z44.2, Z83.42, I50.3
c) 80162, Z51.81, Z79.899, I48.91
d) 80162, Z41.8, Z80.52, I63.1

82) This patient presented to the laboratory yesterday for a creatine measurement. The results came back at higher-than-normal levels; therefore, the patient was asked to return to the laboratory today for a repeat creatine test before the nephrologist is consulted. Report the second day of test only.

a) 82540 × 2, R78.89

b) 82550, R79.0
c) 82550, R79.81
d) 82540, R79.89

83) Code a pregnancy test, urine.
   a) 84702
   b) 84703
   c) 81025
   d) 84702 × 2

84) What CPT code would you use to code a bilirubin, total (transcutaneous)?
   a) 82252
   b) 82247
   c) 82248
   d) 88720

85) DIALYSIS INPATIENT NOTE: This 24-year-old male patient is on continuous ambulatory peritoneal dialysis (CAPD) using 1.5%. He drains more than 600 ml. He is tolerating dialysis well. He continues to have some abdominal pain, but his abdomen is not distended. He has some diarrhea. His abdomen does not look like acute abdomen. His vitals, other than blood pressure in the 190s over 100s, are fine. He is afebrile. At this time, I will continue with 1.5% dialysate. I gave him labetalol IV for blood pressure. Because of diarrhea, I am going to check stool for white cells, culture. Next, we will see what the primary physician says today. His HIDA scan was normal. The patient suffers from ESRD.
   a) 90947, 90960, N13.7, R10.3
   b) 90945, N18.6, R19.7
   c) 90960, N17.2, R19.5
   d) 90945, N15.8, R18.8

86) INDICATION: Hypertension with newly diagnosed acute myocardial infarction

PROCEDURE PERFORMED: Insertion of Swan-Ganz catheter

DESCRIPTION OF PROCEDURE: The right internal jugular and subclavian area was prepped with antiseptic solution. Sterile drapes were applied. Under usual sterile precautions, the right internal jugular vein was cannulated. A 9-French introducer was inserted, and a 7-French Swan-Ganz catheter was inserted without difficulty. Right atrial pressures were 2 to 3, right ventricular pressures 24/0, and pulmonary artery 26/9 with a wedge pressure of 5. This is a Trendelenburg position. The patient tolerated the procedure well.

a) 93501, 93503-51, I26.0, I25.7
b) 93508, I34.0
c) 93503, 93539, I25.9, I30
d) 93503, I21.9, I11.9

87) DIAGNOSIS: Atrial flutter

PROCEDURE PERFORMED: Electrical cardioversion

DESCRIPTION OF PROCEDURE: The patient was sedated with Versed and morphine. She was given a total of 5 mg of Versed. She was cardioverted with 50 joules into sinus tachycardia.

The patient was given a 20-mg Cardizem IV push. Her heart rate went down to the 110s, and she was definitely in sinus tachycardia.

CONCLUSION: Successful electrical cardioversion of atrial flutter into sinus tachycardia.

a) 92961, I49.1
b) 92960, I48.92
c) 92960, 92973, I46.9
d) 92960, I49.8

88) A patient presents for a pleural cavity chemotherapy

session with 10 mg doxorubicin hcl that requires a thoracentesis to be performed.
a) 96446, J9000
b) 96440, 32554, J9000
c) 96440, J9000
d) 96446, 32554, J9000

89) What CPT code would be used to report a home visit for a respiratory patient to care for the mechanical ventilation?
a) 99503
b) 99504
c) 99505
d) 99509

90) What CPT code would be used to code the technical aspect of an evaluation of swallowing by video recording using a flexible fiberoptic endoscope?
a) 92611
b) 92612
c) 92610
d) 92613

91) A patient saw an Orthopedist on a consultation basis 18 months ago for symptoms of lower back pain. The patient non returns to see the Orthopedist after being referred by his primary care physician again for symptoms of lower back pain. The patient is considered as:
a) New patient
b) Established patient
c) Inpatient
d) Out patient

92) The patient is brought to surgery room for repair of an accidentally inflicted open wound of the left thigh, the total

extent measuring approximately 40 x 35 cm. DESCRIPTION OF PROCEDURE: The legs were prepped with Betadine scrub and solution and then draped in a routine sterile fashion. Split- thickness skin grafts measuring about a 10,000th inch thick were taken from both thighs, meshed with a 3:1 ratio mesher, and stapled to the wounds. The donor sites were dressed with scarlet red, and the recipient sites were dressed with Xeroform, Kerlix fluffs, and Kerlix roll, and a few ABD pads were used for absorption. Estimated blood loss was negligible. The patient tolerated the procedure well and left surgery in good condition.

What type of graft is used for the procedure?

a) Allograft
b) Split thickness graft
c) Autograft
d) None of the above

93) John, an 84-year-old male, tripped while on his morning walk. He stated he was thinking about something else when he inadvertently tripped over the sidewalk curb and fell to his knees. X-ray indicated a comminuted fracture of his right patella. With the patient under general anesthesia, the area was opened and extensively irrigated. The left aspect of the patella was severely fragmented, and a portion of the patella was subsequently removed. The remaining patella fractures were wired. The surrounding tissue was repaired, thoroughly irrigated, and closed in the usual manner.

What type of anesthesia procedure for the operation?

a) General Anesthesia
b) Regional Anesthesia
c) Local anesthesia
d) Sedation

94) PREOPERATIVE DIAGNOSIS: Leaking from intestinal

anastomosis.

POSTOPERATIVE DIAGNOSIS: Leaking from intestinal anastomosis. PROCEDURE PERFORMED: Proximal ileostomy for diversion of colon. Overview of right colonic fistula.

OPERATIVE NOTE: This patient was taken back to the operating room from the intensive care unit. She was having acute signs of leakage from an anastomosis I performed 3 days previously. We took down some of the sutures holding the wound together. We basically exposed all of this patient's intestine. It was evident that she was leaking from the small bowel as well as from the right colon. I thought the only thing we could do would be to repair the right colon. This was done in two layers, and then we freed up enough bowel to try to make an ileostomy proximal to the area of leakage. We were able to do this with great difficulty, and there was only a small amount of bowel to be brought out. We brought this out as an ileostomy stoma, realizing that it was of questionable viability and that it should be watched closely. With that accomplished, we then packed the wound and returned the patient to the intensive care unit. Code For colon diversion the doctor performed?

a) Proximal ileostomy
b) Colonoscopy
c) Deodenectomy
d) Esophageal hiatus

95) OPERATIVE REPORT PREOPERATIVE DIAGNOSIS: Fever of unknown origin PROCEDURE PERFORMED: Lumbar puncture.

DESCRIPTION OF PROCEDURE: The patient was placed in the lateral decubitus position with the left side up. The legs and hips were flexed into the fetal position. The lumbosacral area was sterilely prepped. It was then numbed with 1% Xylocaine. I then placed a 22-gauge spinal needle on the first pass into the intrathecal space between the LA and L5 spinous processes. The fluid was minimally xanthochromic I sent the fluid for cell count for differential, protein, glucose, Gram stain, and culture. The patient tolerated the procedure well without apparent complication. The needle was removed at the end of the procedure. The area was cleansed, and a Band-Aid was placed.

In which area was sterile prepped?
a) Thoraco cavity
b) Lumbo sacral
c) Supine position
d) Lamellar region

96) A 32-year-old woman complained of irritation and deposits on the eyelids. Visualization by slit lamp revealed multiple eggs attached to eyelashes and a mobile foreign body. What is the diagnosis?
a) Preorbital cellulitis
b) Blepharitis
c) Pediculosis
d) Chalazion

97) A 51-year-old patient with a history of type 2 diabetes presented with brown-to-black, poorly defined, velvety hyper-pigmentation of the skin. Can you name the medical sign?
a) Keratosis nigricans
b) Cyanosis
c) Vitiligo
d) None of these

98) A 47-year-old male with no significant past medical

history presents to the office complaining of a new rash in his armpits. He first noticed it 1 month ago, and since then it has grown "darker, thicker, and larger". He reports that it is occasionally mildly pruritic. His vital signs are normal. Upon examination he has hyper-pigmented tick plaque in both axillae. Which of the following is the most appropriate laboratory test to order?

a) Thyroid stimulating hormone
b) Fasting blood glucose
c) Fasting lipid panel
d) Serum electrolytes

99) A child was born with the failure of the spine to close over into a proper canal. The lump is a combination of nerves and skin exposed to the air. The baby's spinal cord fails to develop properly.
This birth defect is known as

a) Spina bifida
b) Lordosis
c) Kyphosis
d) Scoliosis

100)   A neurological consultation in the emergency department of the local hospital is requested by the ED physician for a 25-year-old male with suspected closed head trauma. The neurologist saw the patient in the ED. The patient had a loss of consciousness this morning after receiving a blow to the head in a basketball game. He presents to the emergency department with a headache, dizziness, and confusion During the course of the history, the patient relates that he has been very irritable, confused, and has had a bit of nausea since the incident. All other systems reviewed and are negative: Constitutional, ophthalmologic, otolaryngologic, cardiovascular, respiratory, genitourinary,

musculoskeletal, integumentary, psychiatric, endocrine, hematologic, lymphatic, allergic, and immunologic. The patients states that he does have a history of headaches and that both parents have hypertension, also a grandfather with heart disease. He also states that he does drink beer on the weekends and does not smoke. Physical examination reveals the patient to be unsteady and exhibiting difficulty in concentration when stating months in reverse. The pupils dilate unequally. The physician continues with a complete comprehensive examination involving an extensive review of neurological function. The neurologist orders a stat CT and MRI. The physician suspects a subdural hematoma or an epidural hematoma and the medical decision-making complexity is high. The neurologist admits the patient to the hospital. Assign codes for the neurologist's services only. Which radiology tests are ordered by the neurologist?

a) Comprehensive Testing and Memory Resonance imaging
b) Computed tomography and Magnetic Resonance Imaging
c) Continues Testing and Micro Resonance Imaging
d) Compress Testing and Mini Resonance Imaging

EXAM B ANSWERS AND RATIONALES

1)   Answer D – Salpingectomy is a surgical procedure in which one or both of the fallopian tubes are removed. The fallopian tubes are part of the female reproductive system and are responsible for transporting the egg from the ovary to the uterus. A salpingectomy may be performed for various reasons, including to treat an ectopic pregnancy, to prevent ovarian cancer or to sterilize a woman. It is usually performed using laparoscopic surgery, which involves making small incisions in the abdomen and using a camera and specialized instruments to remove the fallopian tubes.

2) Answer A – The combining form that means thirst is "dips/o". Therefore, option (a) is the correct answer.

3) Answer B - The term that is also known as a homograft is "allograft".
An autograft is a tissue or organ that is transplanted from one part of a person's body to another part in the same person. A xenograft is a tissue or organ that is transplanted from a different species, while a zenograft is not a commonly used medical term.
An allograft is a tissue or organ that is transplanted from one individual to another of the same species, but who are not identical twins.

4)   Answer D - The term that does NOT describe a receptor of the body is d) Endoreceptor. This term is not commonly

used in biology or anatomy, and does not refer to any known type of receptor in the human body.

Mechanoreceptors are sensory receptors that respond to mechanical stimuli such as touch, pressure, vibration, or stretch.

Proprioceptors are sensory receptors that provide information about body position, movement, and orientation.

Thermoreceptors are sensory receptors that respond to changes in temperature.

5) Answer C - Duodenum is the first portion of the small intestine.

6) Answer A - Vestibule is a part of the inner ear.

7) Answer A - Anterior chamber is the area behind the cornea.

8) Answer D - Clavicle is the collarbone.

9) Answer C - The correct ICD-10-CM codes for admission for hemodialysis because of acute renal failure are N17.9 - Acute kidney failure, unspecified, Z99.2 - Dependence on renal dialysis. The N17.9 code is used to indicate acute kidney failure without further specification, while the Z99.2 code indicates that the patient is dependent on renal dialysis, which means that the patient is undergoing regular dialysis treatment to replace the function of their kidneys. These codes may be used in conjunction with each other if a patient with acute kidney failure requires renal dialysis.

10) Answer A - Sarcoidosis is a multisystem granulomatous disorder that can affect different organs, including the heart. Cardiac sarcoidosis is characterized by the presence of non-caseating granulomas within the myocardium, and it can lead to various cardiac manifestations, including arrhythmias, heart failure, and cardiomyopathy. Option A has the combination code for the Sarcoidosis with

cardiomyopathy. Option B, D86.87 is incorrect because it refers to sarcoidosis of other and multiple sites, but does not specify the presence of cardiomyopathy. Option D, D86.9, I42.9 is incorrect because it lists the codes in the wrong order, and I42.9 is the code for unspecified cardiomyopathy, which is not specific enough to describe the cardiac manifestation of sarcoidosis.

11) Answer B - The correct answer is S61.412A.

S61.402A is for a laceration of the right hand, without damage to the nail, initial encounter.

S61.412D is for a laceration of the left hand, with damage to the nail, subsequent encounter.

S61.422A is for a laceration of the left hand, with foreign body, initial encounter.

S61.412A is for a laceration of the left hand, without damage to the nail, initial encounter, which is the most appropriate code for the given scenario.

12) Answer B - S82.001A

The patella is a bone located in the knee joint. A fracture of the patella is represented by the ICD-10 code S82.001. The letter "A" at the end of the code indicates that it is the initial encounter, which means the patient is receiving active treatment for the fracture.

The abrasion is a secondary diagnosis and would be coded separately. However, since the focus of the question is on the fracture, the primary code to report is S82.001A.

13) Answer D - The correct answer is option D:

A41.9 - Sepsis, unspecified organism
R65.20 - Severe sepsis without septic shock
N17.9 - Acute kidney failure, unspecified
J96.90 - Respiratory failure, unspecified, not elsewhere classified
E11.9 - Type 2 diabetes mellitus without complications
R93.89 - Abnormal findings on diagnostic imaging of other

specified body structures

These codes capture all the diagnoses mentioned in the patient's case: sepsis with acute renal failure, respiratory failure, type II diabetes mellitus, and an abnormal chest x-ray. The code for severe sepsis without septic shock (R65.20) is also included as the patient has multiple problems and is in a critical care unit.

14) Answer D – E2602 is for General use wheelchair seat cushion, width 22 inches or greater, any depth hence this is the correct answer.

15) Answer D - The correct HCPCS code for replacement batteries for a TENS unit is A4630.

16) Answer D – T5

TA	Left foot, great toe
T1	Left foot, second digit
T2	Left foot, third digit
T3	Left foot, fourth digit
T4	Left foot, fifth digit
T5	Right foot, great toe
T6	Right foot, second digit
T7	Right foot, third digit
T8	Right foot, fourth digit
T9	Right foot, fifth digit

17) Answer C – OIG (Office of Inspector General) develops and publishes an annual plan that outlines the Medicare monitoring program.

18) Answer A - NCCI (National Correct Coding Initiative) is the program developed by CMS (Centers for Medicare & Medicaid Services) to promote national correct coding methods and to control inappropriate payment of Part B claims and hospital outpatient claims. The NCCI is a set of edits that identify pairs of HCPCS/CPT codes that should not be billed together in certain circumstances, or that require a modifier to indicate that both codes are being billed for distinct and separate services. The NCCI edits help to prevent improper payments due to incorrect coding, billing, or documentation errors.

19) Answer B - National Provider Identifier (NPI) is a unique identification number for healthcare providers that is used in standard transactions such as insurance claims. The Centers for Medicare & Medicaid Services (CMS) developed the NPI as a way to simplify healthcare transactions and reduce fraud and abuse in the healthcare industry. The NPI is a 10-digit number that is assigned to healthcare providers by the National Plan and Provider Enumeration System (NPPES).

20) Answer C - Advanced Beneficiary Notice (ABN) is a document that notifies Medicare beneficiaries in advance of services that Medicare may not pay for and estimates the cost that the patient may have to pay. The ABN is intended to help the patient make an informed decision about whether to receive the service and assume financial responsibility or to decline the service.

21) Answer C - The specific coding guidelines in the CPT manual are located in option (c), which is the beginning of each section. Each section of the CPT manual contains

introductory guidelines that explain how to use the codes in that particular section. These guidelines are essential to properly assign the correct codes and ensure accurate reporting of medical services. The introduction and appendix of the CPT manual provide additional information, but the specific coding guidelines for each section are found at the beginning of that section. The index is a helpful tool for finding codes, but it does not provide specific coding guidelines.

22) Answer D - The punctuation mark between codes in the index of the CPT manual that indicates a range of codes is available is option (d), a hyphen. A hyphen is used to indicate a range of codes that fall between the two codes listed. For example, if the index lists "10021-10022," it indicates that the range of codes available is from 10021 to 10022. This allows the user to quickly identify a range of codes that may be relevant to a particular medical service. It is important to note that the use of a hyphen does not necessarily mean that all codes within the range are appropriate for the particular service being coded, and the coder must still review each code individually to ensure accuracy.

23) Answer B - The term that indicates this is the type of code for which the full code description can be known only if the common part of the code (the description preceding the semicolon) of a preceding entry is referenced is "Indented".

24) Answer C - The symbol that indicates an add-on code is "+".

25) Answer B - The symbol ►◄ next to a code in the CPT manual indicates that the code contains new or revised text.

26) Answer D - The designation "Separate procedure" indicates that the procedure is reported if it is an additional procedure performed at the same session, and it is unrelated to a more major procedure performed on the

same site. It is important to note that a separate procedure may or may not be incidental to another procedure, and it may or may not be the only procedure performed. The designation "Separate procedure" is intended to help coders and billers identify procedures that may require special coding rules and may affect reimbursement.

27) Answer C - ICD-10-CM Code: D21.6 - Other benign neoplasm of connective and other soft tissue of trunk, unspecified, Also, says that Benign neoplasm of connective and other soft tissue of back NOS hence This code accurately describes the pathology result of dermatofibroma, which is a benign neoplasm of connective tissue. CPT Code: 11406 - Excision, benign lesion, except skin tag (unless listed elsewhere), trunk, arms or legs; lesion diameter 4.1 to 6.0 cm. This code accurately describes the excision of the 5 cm lesion from the upper midback. CPT Code: 12032 - Closure, intermediate, wounds of scalp, axillae, trunk and/or extremities (excluding hands and feet); 2.6 cm to 7.5 cm, This code accurately describes the closure of the 5 cm skin incision used to remove the lesion.

28) Answer B - The CPT code 12011 is for simple repair of superficial wounds of the scalp, neck, axillae, external genitalia, trunk, and/or extremities (including hands and feet) that measures 2.6 cm to 7.5 cm. In this case, the laceration is approximately 1.5-2 cm, which falls within this range. The ICD-10-CM code S012.1XA represents a laceration of the bridge of the nose. The code G20 represents Parkinson's disease in the history, The code W01.0XXA is an external cause code represents a fall on the same level from slipping, tripping, or stumbling while engaged in activities. Y92.091 represents a place of occurrence code for an injury that occurred in a bathroom within a residence.

29) Answer D - The correct code for this procedure would be (d) 19120-LT, which is Excision of mammary duct ectasia, left, with or without biopsy, any method.

Explanation:

The operative report describes the excision of a mass deep to the left nipple, which was associated with mammary duct ectasia. The procedure involved the removal of an area of tissue using electrocautery and subsequent reconstruction of breast tissue using sutures. The code that best describes this procedure is 19120, which specifically involves the excision of mammary duct ectasia, with or without biopsy, using any method. The modifier LT is added to indicate that the procedure was performed on the left side.

30) Answer D - 11721, B35.1

The correct CPT code for the mild debridement of mycotic nails is 11721. The ICD-10 code for onychomycosis is B35.1. The patient is returning for palliative care, and there are no acute signs of infection or other issues, so an evaluation and management (E/M) code is not necessary. Option a) is incorrect because it includes the incorrect ICD-10 code. Option b) is incorrect because it includes an E/M code that is not necessary for this visit. Option c) is incorrect because it only includes the code for debridement, and not the code for onychomycosis.

31) Answer C - The correct CPT code for the procedure described is 19125 for a biopsy of the breast under stereotactic guidance. The LT modifier should be added to indicate that the procedure was performed on the left breast. The correct ICD-10 code to indicate the reason for the procedure is D24.2, which indicates a benign neoplasm of the breast. Option a) is incorrect because it includes the incorrect CPT code. Option b) is incorrect because it only includes a simple wound closure code, which is

not appropriate for this procedure. Option d) is incorrect because it includes an incorrect ICD-10 code.

32) Answer B - Explanation:

For the split-thickness skin graft procedure, we would use CPT codes 15100 and 15101. Code 15100 represents the first 100 square centimeters of the graft or donor site, and code 15101 represents each additional 100 square centimeters or part thereof.

ICD-10-CM codes T31.20 (third-degree burns of 20-29% of body surface), T21.32XA (second-degree burns of back, initial encounter), and T21.24XA (second-degree burns of abdomen, initial encounter) would be used to code the patient's burns.

Therefore, the correct code assignment is:

15100, 15101 × 9

T31.20 (burns of 20-29% of body surface)

T21.32XA (second-degree burns of back, initial encounter)

T21.24XA (second-degree burns of abdomen, initial encounter)

33) Answer B - The correct code for the placement of the fixation device and diagnosis is 20692-LT: This code is for the placement of the Monticelli multiplane external fixation system, which was attached to the pins in Libby's left tibia.

S82.202A This code is for the fracture of the left tibia that resulted from the fall from the horse.

V80.010A Animal-rider injured by fall from or being thrown from horse in non-collision accident

We can't use code , V80.41XA as it is for the Animal-rider injured in collision with car, pick-up truck, van, heavy transport vehicle or bus hence option A, C and D is incorrect.

34) Answer A - 20650-LT: This code describes the insertion of traction pins for temporary skeletal traction, which is what

was done in this scenario.

S82.102A: This code is for the closed fracture of the left proximal tibia, which was stabilized with traction pins.

35) Answer D – For Ganglion cyst we use code 20612 hence the option d is correct.

> 20612   Aspiration and/or injection of ganglion cyst(s) any location
>
> ⟳ *CPT Changes: An Insider's View* 2003
>
> (To report multiple ganglion cyst aspirations/injections, use 20612 and append modifier 59)

36) Answer A – The code 29040 states that Application of body cast, shoulder to hips; including head, Minerva type hence this is the correct answer.

37) Answer C - Based on the operative report provided, the correct CPT code for this procedure would be 24515-LT (Open treatment of humeral shaft fracture with plate/screws, with or without cerclage).

The code 24515 describes the open reduction and internal fixation of a humeral shaft fracture using a plate and screws, which is the procedure that was performed in this case. The "LT" modifier indicates that the procedure was performed on the left arm.

38) Answer B - 27301-LT, L02.416

The operative note describes the incision and drainage of a left thigh abscess located in the crease at the top of the leg, extending from the posterior buttocks' region up toward the side of the base of the penis. The appropriate CPT code for incision and drainage of an abscess of the skin and subcutaneous tissue, such as this one, is 27301. The ICD-10 code for a thigh abscess is L02.416. The LT modifier indicates that the procedure was performed on the left side. Therefore, the correct code is 27301-LT, L02.416.

39) Answer C - The procedure performed was chest tube

placement for hypoxia and pneumothorax. The CPT code for chest tube placement is 32551.

The ICD-10 diagnosis code for pneumothorax is J93.9 and for hypoxia is R09.02.

Therefore, the correct code combination is 32551 for the procedure, and J93.9 and R09.02 for the diagnoses.

40) Answer D - Explanation:

36556 is the CPT code for "Insertion of non-tunneled centrally inserted central venous catheter; age 5 years or older". This code describes the placement of a central venous catheter in a patient who is 5 years or older, without the use of a tunnel.

R40.20 is the ICD-10-CM code for "Unspecified coma". This code is used to indicate that the patient is in a coma, but the underlying cause is not specified or known.

The other options are not correct because:

36011 is the CPT code for "Introduction of needle or intracatheter, vein", which does not accurately describe the procedure performed.

R40.0 is the ICD-10-CM code for "Somnolence, stupor and coma, unspecified", which does not provide enough detail about the patient's condition.

R40.1 is the ICD-10-CM code for "Coma scale, eyes open, spontaneous", which is not relevant to the procedure performed.

R40.24 is the ICD-10-CM code for "Coma scale, motor response, none", which is not relevant to the procedure performed.

41) Answer B – The code 38221 states that Diagnostic bone marrow; biopsy(ies) hence only b option is correct. The diagnosis code C83.50 (Diffuse large B-cell lymphoma, unspecified site) is reported for the patient's condition of diffuse malignant lymphoma.

42) Answer C - 33208, I49.5.

Explanation:

CPT code 33208 is used to report the insertion of a pacemaker with dual leads through the subclavian vein. This code is appropriate for the described procedure of percutaneous insertion of a dual-chamber pacemaker by means of the subclavian vein.

ICD-10-CM code I49.5 is used to report sick sinus syndrome. This code also covers tachy-brady syndrome, which involves both rapid and slow heart rhythms.

Therefore, the correct codes to report the procedure of percutaneous insertion of a dual-chamber pacemaker in a patient with sick sinus syndrome, tachy-brady, are 33208 (CPT code) and I49.5 (ICD-10-CM code).

43) Answer D - The procedure described in the report is a bronchoscopy with selective intubation of the right mainstem bronchus and inspection of both lungs. Secretions were found mainly in the right lung and were aspirated. No mucous plug was identified. The code best describe is 31645-RT (Bronchoscopy, rigid or flexible, including fluoroscopic guidance, when performed diagnostic, with cell washing, when performed (separate procedure), with therapeutic aspiration of tracheobronchial tree, initial (eg. Drainage of lung abscess) 31622-51-LT (Bronchoscopy, rigid or flexible, including fluoroscopic guidance, when performed diagnostic, with cell washing, when performed (separate procedure), V89.0XXA (Person injured in unspecified motor-vehicle accident, nontraffic, initial encounter.)

44) Answer C - 31610, 15838
Explanation:
The patient is undergoing a flap tracheostomy, which is reported with CPT code 31610. Additionally, the physician is performing a cervical lipectomy to access the trachea and secure the tracheotomy tube placement, which is reported with CPT code 15838. The modifier -51 is not necessary since the procedures are performed during the same

operative session and are considered distinct procedures. Therefore, the correct code(s) for the physician service only are 31610 and 15838. Option a) includes modifier -51 which is not needed, and option d) includes an incorrect code 31603.

45) Answer C – Code 45550 states that Proctopexy (eg, for prolapse); with sigmoid resection, abdominal approach and this is the correct code to describe the procedure. Hence option c is correct.

46) Answer B - 43235, R10.9, R63.4
Explanation:
The procedure performed was a diagnostic endoscopy of the upper gastrointestinal tract, which involves passing a video endoscope through the oropharynx, esophagus, stomach, and duodenum to visually inspect the mucosal lining and structures for any abnormalities.
The preoperative diagnosis was abdominal pain, which suggests that the endoscopy was done to investigate the cause of the pain.
The postoperative diagnosis was normal endoscopy, indicating that no abnormalities were found during the procedure.
The ICD-10 codes that best capture the preoperative and postoperative diagnoses are R10.9 (Unspecified abdominal pain) and R63.4 (Abnormal weight loss).
The CPT code for the procedure performed is 43235 (Upper gastrointestinal endoscopy including esophagus, stomach, and either the duodenum and/or jejunum as appropriate; diagnostic, with or without collection of specimen(s) by brushing or washing, with or without colonoscopy).

47) Answer C - 48155, 48100-51, C25.9
Explanation:
The operative procedure performed in this case is a total pancreatectomy (48155), as stated in the scenario.

However, before performing the total pancreatectomy, a wedge biopsy of the pancreas was taken (48100), which was sent to pathology for immediate analysis. Therefore, code 48100 with modifier -51 (multiple procedures) should be added to the code for the total pancreatectomy.

The final diagnosis is primary malignant neoplasm of the pancreas (C25.9

48) Answer A - 49521, K40.40.

Explanation:

The CPT code for the repair of a strangulated inguinal hernia is 49521. The modifier -78 is used to indicate a return to the operating room for a related procedure during the postoperative period of the initial surgery, but in this case, the hernia was previously repaired four months ago, so it is not considered to be within the global period of the initial surgery. Therefore, modifier -78 is not applicable.

The ICD-10 code for a bilateral inguinal hernia without obstruction or gangrene is K40.40. Since the documentation does not mention whether the hernia is bilateral or not, it is safe to assume it is unilateral, so the correct ICD-10 code is K40.11 (unilateral inguinal hernia, without obstruction or gangrene). However, the documentation mentions that this hernia was previously repaired four months ago, so it is now considered to be a recurrent hernia. The correct ICD-10 code for a recurrent inguinal hernia without obstruction or gangrene is K40.40. Therefore, the correct codes for this scenario are 49521 (Repair initial inguinal hernia; strangulated) and K40.40 (Bilateral inguinal hernia, with gangrene).

49) Answer B - The correct code for this scenario would be option (b) 42700, J36.

42700 refers to the procedure code for incision and drainage of a peritonsillar abscess. J36 is the ICD-10 diagnosis code for peritonsillar abscess.

Option (a) 42825 is a procedure code for excision of a tonsil, which is not the procedure performed in this case. J32.4 in option (c) is an ICD-10 code for chronic sinusitis, which is not the correct diagnosis in this case. Option (d) 42700 is the correct procedure code but J31.1 is an ICD-10 code for chronic rhinitis, which is not the correct diagnosis for a peritonsillar abscess.

50) Answer D - Explanation:

Code 45320 is for flexible colonoscopy with removal of polyps by snare technique. Rigid proctosigmoidoscopy is a different procedure.

Code 45384 is for flexible colonoscopy with ablation of tumor(s), polyp(s) or other lesion(s) by any method. Ablation is not the same as removal by snare technique.

Code 45309 is for the removal of a single polyp by snare technique during a flexible or rigid colonoscopy. However, since two polyps were removed, this code should be reported twice, resulting in code 45309 × 2.

Code 45315 is for rigid proctosigmoidoscopy with removal of tumors, polyps, or other lesion(s) by any method. This code is appropriate for the procedure described in the question. The additional code K62.1 is used to report non-neoplastic polyps of the rectum.

Therefore, the correct code to report a rigid proctosigmoidoscopy with removal of two non-adenomatous polyps of the rectum by snare technique is 45315, K62.1.

51) Answer C - 59820, O02.1.

The procedure described is a suction dilation and curettage (D&C) for a missed abortion with fetal demise at 11 weeks. The code for this procedure is 59820, which describes a "suction curettage with intrauterine instillation" and includes dilation of the cervix. The diagnosis code for missed abortion with fetal demise is O02.1.

Option a) 59812, O03.9 describes a "suction curettage following spontaneous abortion" without specifying fetal demise and does not accurately capture the diagnosis.

Option b) 59812, O03.2 describes a "suction curettage following incomplete spontaneous abortion" without specifying fetal demise and does not accurately capture the diagnosis.

Option d) 59856, O02.1 describes a "combined antepartum and postpartum curettage" and is not appropriate for this scenario.

52) Answer D - 52332-RT, N13.5.

The procedure performed was a cystoscopy and right ureteral stent change. The code for this procedure is 52332. The modifier RT is used to indicate that the procedure was performed on the right side. The diagnosis codes should reflect the reason for the procedure. In this case, the preoperative and postoperative diagnosis is a right ureteral stricture, which should be coded with N13.5. Therefore, the correct code combination is 52332-RT for the procedure and N13.5 for the diagnosis.

53) Answer B - Explanation:

The surgical report describes a hysteroscopy with polypectomy, endocervical curettage, and sharp curettage of the endometrium. The codes that describe this procedure are:

58558 - Hysteroscopy, surgical; with sampling (biopsy) of endometrium and/or polypectomy, with or without D & C

N92.0 - Excessive and frequent menstruation with regular cycle

N84.0 - Polyp of corpus uteri

The "-51" modifier is not required as these are not distinct procedures. Additionally, N82.5 is not applicable as there is no mention of prolapse in the report. N92.3 and N84.1 are not applicable as the report does not mention adenomyosis or other specified types of uterine polyps. Therefore, the correct answer is B) 58558, N92.0, N84.0.

54) Answer D - Explanation:

59514: Cesarean delivery only, with or without antepartum care

58611: Bilateral surgical ligation of fallopian tubes (postpartum)

O60.14X0: Pre-existing hypertension complicating childbirth, antepartum condition or complication, unspecified trimester, not applicable or unspecified

O34.21: Maternal care for scar from previous cesarean delivery

Z37.0: Outcome of delivery, single liveborn

The code 58605 is not correct because it is for unilateral surgical ligation of fallopian tubes, and the scenario mentions bilateral ligation. The code 58600-51 is not correct because it is for unilateral or bilateral ligation, and the scenario clearly states bilateral ligation. The code 59620 is not correct because it is for implantation of intraceptive device (IUD), which is not mentioned in the scenario.

55) Answer A - The primary procedure performed was cystoscopy with multiple bladder biopsies (52224). The code Z85.51 represents the history of malignant neoplasm of the urinary bladder, which is the reason for the cystoscopy and biopsies.

The other codes listed in the answer choices are not appropriate for this procedure. 51020 is a code for a different type of bladder procedure, 52234 is a code for a different type of cystoscopy procedure, and 52204 and D41.4 are not relevant to this specific case.

56) Answer C - 56620, D07.1

Explanation:

The procedure described is a wide local excision of the vulva, which involves the removal of a portion of tissue from the vulva to treat a lesion. The code for this procedure is 56620.

The biopsy result was VIN III, which stands for vulvar intraepithelial neoplasia grade III, a precancerous condition of the vulva. The lesion cannot rule out invasion, meaning that it is not clear whether the lesion has invaded deeper tissues. The diagnosis code for VIN III is D07.1.

Therefore, the correct codes to report this procedure and diagnosis are 56620 for the procedure and D07.1 for the diagnosis.

57) Answer C - 61320, G06.0

The procedure performed was a craniotomy with removal of an abscess. The correct CPT code for this procedure is 61320 (Craniotomy for excision of brain lesion, supratentorial), and the correct ICD-10 diagnosis code is G06.0 (Intracranial abscess and granuloma). Therefore, the correct answer is c) 61320, G06.0.

58) Answer B - 62258, T85.09XD

Explanation:

The procedure performed was a revision of shunt, which involves the removal of the obstructed ventriculoperitoneal shunt and replacement with a similar shunt system. The correct code for this procedure is 62258, which describes "removal of cerebrospinal fluid shunt; with replacement of valve and proximal or distal catheter" (Current Procedural Terminology (CPT) code).

The diagnosis code would be T85.09XD, which describes a complication of a cerebrospinal fluid shunt, specifically "mechanical complication of other specified cerebrospinal fluid shunt and implant, initial encounter" (International Classification of Diseases, Tenth Revision, Clinical Modification (ICD-10-CM) code).

The other options provided are:

a) 62180, T85.192D - This code describes "revision or replacement of ventriculostomy catheter" and is not specific to a ventriculoperitoneal shunt.

c) 62256, T85.09XA - This code describes "removal of

cerebrospinal fluid shunt; without replacement" and does not include the replacement of a similar shunt system.

d) 62190, T85.199A - This code describes "revision or replacement of other cerebrospinal fluid shunt" and is not specific to a ventriculoperitoneal shunt

59) Answer D - 63042-LT, M51.27

Explanation:

63030: This code describes a laminotomy, which involves the removal of a portion of the vertebral lamina to gain access to the spinal canal. While this is part of the procedure being performed, it is not the only aspect of it.

63042: This code describes a laminotomy with facetectomy and foraminotomy, which involves the removal of part of the facet joint and the foramen to decompress the nerve root. This is the correct code for the procedure being performed.

LT modifier: This modifier indicates that the procedure was performed on the left side of the body.

M51.27: This is the ICD-10 code for recurrent disc herniation at the L5-S1 level on the left side.

60) Answer A – Code 60210 states that Partial thyroid lobectomy, unilateral; with or without

Isthmusectomy which is correct as only 30% removal was done in question. Hence only option a is correct, all other answers are incorrect.

61) Answer D - 67880-LT, H02.156.

Explanation:

The procedure performed is medial tarsorrhaphy, which involves the partial thickness closure of the eyelid.

The code for partial thickness closure of the eyelid is 67880.

The modifier LT is appended to indicate that the procedure was performed on the left eye.

The diagnosis is paralytic ectropion, left eye, which has the ICD-10-CM code H02.156.

The code 67875 can be ruled out as it is specifically for partial thickness closure of the eyelid and not the medial tarsorrhaphy procedure that was performed.

The code 67710 is for reconstruction of the eyelid margin, and is not the correct code for this procedure.

The code 67882 is for total tarsorrhaphy, which was not performed in this case as a superior bolster was applied instead.

62) Answer B - The correct CPT code for a posterior extracapsular cataract extraction with IOL placement of the right eye by phacoemulsification is 66984-RT.

Explanation:

66982-RT is used for an extracapsular cataract removal of the lens by manual technique, not phacoemulsification.

66984-RT is used for a posterior extracapsular cataract extraction with IOL placement, by phacoemulsification. This is the correct code for this scenario.

66983-RT is used for an extracapsular cataract removal with insertion of an intraocular lens prosthesis using an endoscope.

66830-RT is used for a partial removal of the lens by aspiration or mechanical disruption, not a complete cataract extraction with IOL placement.

Note that the "RT" modifier is used to indicate that the procedure was performed on the right eye.

63) Answer B - Explanation: In this case, Bill presented with a fall from a height, resulting in head trauma and persistent headache. The physician evaluated him and determined that observation was necessary for 12 hours. After the observation period, the physician discharged Bill and documented a detailed examination and low complexity medical decision making.

The appropriate codes to use for this encounter are:

99234: This code describes Hospital inpatient or observation care, for the evaluation and management of a patient including admission and discharge on the same date, which requires a medically appropriate history and/or examination and straightforward or low level of medical decision making. This code is appropriate because the physician provided a detailed examination and low complexity medical decision making after 12 hours of observation.

Z04.3: This code is used to indicate the reason for the encounter, which in this case is a general examination following an injury.

W17.89XA: This code is used to describe the external cause of the injury, which in this case is a fall from a height. The "A" at the end indicates that this is the initial encounter for the injury.

R42: This code is used to describe the headache Bill experienced following the fall.

R51: This code is used to describe the dizziness Bill experienced following the fall.

Therefore, the correct answer is b) 99234, Z04.3, W17.89XA, R42, R51.

64) Answer D - 99221, R07.2, R06.82, as the medical decision making is described as of low complexity in the scenario.

The CPT code 99221 represents an initial hospital encounter for a patient with a low to moderate severity of illness. The ICD-10 codes R07.2 (Precordial pain) and R06.82 (Shortness of breath) are specific to the patient's symptoms and medical history.

65) Answer B - The physician admitted an established patient for evaluation and management of dysfunctional uterine bleeding, which is a complex problem. The history of infrequent periods of heavy flow and irregular heavy periods and intermittent spotting for 4 years indicate a chronic condition. The fact that the patient has been on a 3-month course of oral contraceptives for symptoms with no relief and has a personal history of cervical and

endometrial polyp removal 3 years prior to admission indicate a need for a more comprehensive evaluation. Additionally, the family history of endometrial cancer is significant and requires consideration in the medical decision-making process.

The physician noted an enlarged uterus and a very thin and friable endometrial lining, which suggests that the patient may have endometrial hyperplasia or cancer. Therefore, the physician ordered a full laboratory workup, which may include imaging studies, endometrial biopsy, and blood tests to evaluate for anemia and other potential causes of dysfunctional uterine bleeding. Intravenous Premarin is also ordered to help control the bleeding and stabilize the endometrial lining.

The medical decision making is of moderate complexity, as there are multiple factors that need to be considered, including the patient's chronic condition, personal and family history, and the potential for endometrial hyperplasia or cancer.

The appropriate codes for this encounter are:

99222: Initial hospital care, moderate complexity, for the comprehensive evaluation and management of the patient's chronic condition.

N93.8: Other specified abnormal uterine and vaginal bleeding, to indicate the patient's chief complaint and reason for admission.

Z87.42: Personal history of diseases of the female genital organs, to indicate the patient's history of cervical and endometrial polyp removal.

Z80.49: Family history of other malignant neoplasms of lymphoid, hematopoietic and related tissues, to indicate the patient's family history of endometrial cancer.

66) Answer D - Code 99223 is a level 3 hospital admission code in the Evaluation and Management (E/M) section of the Current Procedural Terminology (CPT) manual. This code

is appropriate for patients who require a comprehensive history and physical examination, as well as medical decision-making of high complexity.

In this scenario, the patient's history and physical examination findings indicate a high level of complexity. The patient has been experiencing symptoms such as fever, tachycardia, and tachypnea, and has radiologic evidence of lung consolidation and pleural effusion. The patient's family history of heart disease and hypertension also adds to the complexity of the case.

Additionally, the physician notes that there are multiple diagnostic options available for this patient, which adds to the complexity of the medical decision-making required. Given these factors, code 99223 is the most appropriate code to use for this patient encounter

67) Answer B - In this scenario, the patient has primary viral pneumonia that has led to secondary bacterial pneumonia. The patient has been experiencing severe dyspnea, rales, fever, and chest pain for over a week. This morning, the patient had nausea, her heart was racing, and she was experiencing dyspnea and SOB.

The chest radiography showed patchy bilateral infiltrates and basilar streaking, and sputum microbiology was positive for a secondary bacterial pneumonia. The physician performed an expanded problem-focused physical examination, and the medical decision making was moderate. The patient was given intravenous antibiotics to treat the bacterial pneumonia.

Based on the above information, the appropriate level of evaluation and management (E/M) service would be a level 3 hospital progress note (99232). The reason being that the patient has moderate medical decision making, and the physician performed an expanded problem-focused examination. The appropriate ICD-10 codes for this scenario are J15.9 (bacterial pneumonia, unspecified) and

J12.9 (viral pneumonia, unspecified).

68) Answer B - The patient presented with hematuria, which is a concerning symptom that requires further evaluation by a urologist. The urologist performed a detailed history and physical examination, and recommended a cystoscopy to be scheduled for the following day to visualize the inside of the bladder and check for any abnormalities.

The medical decision making is of moderate complexity since the patient's symptom is not responding to the antibiotic therapy, and a cystoscopy is being recommended to rule out any underlying pathology.

The appropriate office service code for this encounter is 99244-57, which represents a comprehensive consultation that requires the physician to obtain a detailed history, perform a comprehensive examination, and provide a medical decision-making of moderate complexity.

In addition, the urologist performed a cystoscopy (52000) to evaluate the patient's bladder and urethra, and diagnosed the patient with hematuria (R33) and unspecified dorsalgia (M54.9).

Therefore, the correct code for this encounter is:
99244-57, 52000, R33, M54.9.

69) Answer B - Modifier QY is used to indicate that an anesthesiologist medically directed one CRNA during the administration of anesthesia in a single operative session. This means that the anesthesiologist was physically present during the entire anesthesia service and medically directed the anesthesia care provided by the CRNA.

70) Answer D - Code 00524 describes "Anesthesia for procedures on the posterior thorax; not otherwise specified," which would be the most appropriate code to use for anesthesia services for a pneumocentesis (lung aspiration) procedure (CPT code 32420) since the procedure involves accessing the lung through the back of the chest.

Code 00522 is for anesthesia for a procedure on the lower anterior abdominal wall, and code 00500 is for anesthesia for a procedure on the head or neck. Code 00520 is for anesthesia for procedures on the upper anterior abdominal wall, and would not be the most appropriate code for a pneumocentesis procedure.

71) Answer A - A nerve block is an injection of a local anaesthetic to numb the nerves supplying a particular part of the body, such as the hand, arm or leg. It may be used so an operation can be carried out without needing a general anaesthetic, or to prevent pain afterwards.

72) Answer C - AD = ([Base Unit Value + Time Units + Modifying Units] x Conversion Factor) x Modifier Percentage. For anesthesiologists or CRNAs:
(Base Factor + Total Time Units) x Anesthesia Conversion Factor x Modifier Adjustment = Allowance
For anesthesia performed under medical direction:
[(Base Factor + Total Time Units) x Anesthesia Conversion Factor] x Modifier Adjustment = Allowance for each provider

73) Answer C - Based on the given information, the most appropriate CPT code for the magnetic resonance examination of the brain with contrast would be 70553-26. This code describes a comprehensive examination of the brain with contrast, including pre- and post-contrast imaging sequences.
As for the ICD-10 codes, the appropriate code would depend on the reason for the seizure activity. Based on the information given, there is no apparent neoplasm or vascular malformation, so the most appropriate code would be R56.00, which describes an unspecified convulsions.

74) Answer B - The reason for this is that the report indicates that the examination was focused on the gallbladder

and visualized portions of the liver were normal, which suggests a limited examination. Therefore, the appropriate CPT code would be 76705-26, which describes a limited examination of the gallbladder, including a transabdominal approach.

The most appropriate ICD-10 code is R10.13, which describes right upper quadrant pain. Although the report mentions epigastric pain, the location of the pain is more specific to the right upper quadrant, which is reflected in the ICD-10 code.

75) Answer C - 71046 - Radiologic examination, chest; two views and J18.9 for Pneumonia, unspecified organism

76) Answer B – The CPT code for the CT of the abdomen and pelvis without contrast is 74176. The "-26" modifier is used to indicate that only the professional component of the service was provided, meaning the interpretation and report of the imaging study.

In this case, the clinical symptoms indicated the presence of ascites, but the CT scan did not show it. However, a moderate-sized pleural effusion on the right was identified. The CPT code 74150 is used for a CT scan with contrast for the abdomen and pelvis, and 72192 is a code for an additional computer-aided detection (CAD) for a radiologic examination. The code 74177 is used for a CT scan with contrast of the abdomen only. None of these codes accurately describe the service provided. Therefore, the correct CPT code for this scenario is 74176-26.

Stand Alone Code	74150 CT Abdomen WO Contrast	74160 CT Abdomen W Contrast	74170 CT Abdomen WO/W Contrast
72192 CT Pelvis WO Contrast	74176	74178	74178
72193 CT Pelvis W Contrast	74178	74177	74178
72194 CT Pelvis WO/W Contrast	74178	74178	74178

74176   Computed tomography, abdomen and pelvis; without contrast material

> ● *CPT Changes: An Insider's View* 2011

> ● *CPT Assistant* Nov 11:6

> ● *Clinical Examples in Radiology* Winter 11:9, Fall 11:8, Spring 16:10, Spring 17:7, Spring 20:13

77) Answer C - 70450, I60.9

The clinical finding of headache, along with the CT findings of blood within the third ventricle and mild dilatation of the lateral ventricles with small amounts of blood, suggest an acute subarachnoid hemorrhage. The appropriate CPT code for a non-contrast CT of the brain is 70450, and the appropriate ICD-10 code for acute subarachnoid hemorrhage is I60.9.

78) Answer C - The service provided in this case involved the treatment of prostate cancer in a 68-year-old male through a combination of radiation oncology techniques. The technical component of the service includes:

77263: Radiation treatment delivery, complex, which refers to the use of complicated treatment delivery methods, such as irregular treatment fields, to deliver radiation therapy

77307: Radiation treatment management, which involves

the management of radiation therapy for 5 treatments

77427: Radiation treatment management, which involves the management of radiation therapy for an additional 5 treatments using complex treatment devices

C61: Malignant neoplasm of prostate, which represents the professional component of the service

Additionally, the service included the performance of complex clinical treatment planning, dosimetry calculation, and the creation of a complex isodose plan. The treatment devices used included blocks, special shields, and wedges, and treatment management was required throughout the 10 days of treatment provided over the course of 2 weeks.

Overall, the service provided involved a complex and comprehensive approach to the treatment of prostate cancer in this patient, utilizing advanced radiation oncology techniques to achieve optimal results. The correct code choice for this service is (c) 77263, 77307, 77427 X 2, C61.

79) Answer B - The clinical history indicates that the specimen is from the soleus muscle of the right leg, which shows severe necrosis with patchy acute inflammation and neutrophilic infiltrates. The diagnosis given is "infective myositis," which is a type of muscle infection caused by microorganisms.

The CPT code for the examination of the tissue is 88304, which is used for the examination of a single tissue specimen by light microscopy. The code should be appended with modifier 26 since the interpretation of the specimen was done by a pathologist.

In addition to the CPT code, an ICD-10 code is also needed to indicate the diagnosis. The appropriate ICD-10 code for infective myositis is I96, which is used for infections of the musculoskeletal system and connective tissue.

Therefore, the correct answer is b) 88304-26, I96.

80) Answer D - The comprehensive metabolic panel (CMP), hemogram automated and manual differential WBC count (CBC), and thyroid-stimulating hormone (TSH) are all individual laboratory tests that can be reported using the CPT code 80050 - General health panel. This code covers a variety of tests that are commonly ordered as part of a routine annual physical exam or screening, including tests for glucose, electrolytes, liver function, and kidney function, among others.

Therefore, the correct CPT code for the lab tests ordered in this scenario is 80050.

81) Answer C - The patient has atrial fibrillation and is being monitored for digoxin levels. The CPT code for a quantitative digoxin level is 80162.

The ICD-10 codes to support medical necessity for this test are:

I48.91 - Atrial fibrillation, unspecified

Z51.81 - Encounter for therapeutic drug monitoring

Z79.899 - Other long-term (current) drug therapy

These codes indicate that the patient has atrial fibrillation, is receiving long-term digoxin therapy, and is undergoing therapeutic drug monitoring to ensure that the drug is being properly metabolized by the body and that the dose is appropriate.

Z44.2 is a code for fitting and adjustment of pacemaker, Z80.52 is a code for family history of stroke, and I50.3 is a code for congestive heart failure. These codes are not relevant to this scenario.

82) Answer D - The code 82540 refers to a creatinine test, which is a blood test that measures the levels of creatinine in the blood. The elevated creatinine levels may indicate kidney dysfunction or disease. The code R79.89 indicates an abnormal result of blood chemistry, specifically the creatinine level.

Therefore, the correct option for the repeat creatinine test with abnormal results is (d) 82540, R79.89.

83) Answer C - Urine pregnancy testing is coded with 81025. Often laboratories use the same test kit for urine and serum pregnancy testing. The code for qualitative serum pregnancy testing is 84703. The difference is not the methodology or analyte, but merely the specimen.

84) Answer B - The correct code for a transcutaneous bilirubin test is (b) 82247. This test measures the level of bilirubin in the skin using a non-invasive device. The code 82252 is used for a total bilirubin test in serum or plasma. Code 82248 is used for a direct bilirubin test in serum or plasma. Code 88720 is used for a flow cytometry test.

85) Answer C - The correct code is (c) 90960 for the dialysis procedure, N17.2 for acute kidney failure, and R19.5 for diarrhea. Code 90960 is used to report continuous ambulatory peritoneal dialysis (CAPD) and includes all necessary services provided during a 24-hour period. N17.2 is the code for acute kidney failure, which is the patient's primary diagnosis as he suffers from ESRD. R19.5 is used to report diarrhea, which the patient is experiencing. The other codes listed are not relevant to the documentation provided in the inpatient note.

86) Answer D - The correct answer is d) 93503, I21.9, I11.9.
The procedure described is the insertion of a Swan-Ganz catheter, which is used to measure pressures in the heart and lungs. The indication for the procedure is hypertension with newly diagnosed acute myocardial infarction. The diagnosis codes that best describe the patient's condition are I21.9 (Acute myocardial infarction, unspecified), which describes the patient's acute myocardial infarction, and I11.9 (Hypertensive heart disease without heart failure), which describes the patient's hypertension.
The procedure code for the insertion of a Swan-

Ganz catheter is 93503 (Insertion and placement of flow directed catheter (e.g., Swan-Ganz) for monitoring purposes), which should be reported as the primary procedure code. Additionally, an unspecified code for the patient's hypertension, I11.9, and an unspecified code for the patient's acute myocardial infarction, I21.9, should be reported as secondary diagnosis codes.

Therefore, the correct code assignment for this scenario is 93503, I21.9, I11.9.

87) Answer B - The correct answer is b) 92960, I48.92.

In this scenario, the patient was diagnosed with atrial flutter and underwent electrical cardioversion while under sedation with Versed and morphine. The procedure was successful in converting the atrial flutter to sinus tachycardia, and the patient was given Cardizem IV to lower her heart rate.

The CPT code for electrical cardioversion is 92960, and the ICD-10 code for atrial flutter is I48.92. Therefore, the correct answer is b) 92960, I48.92. There is no need to use any additional CPT or ICD-10 codes in this scenario, as the procedure and diagnosis are both adequately described by these codes.

88) Answer C - The correct answer is c) 96440, J9000.

The CPT code 96440 is used to report the therapeutic aspiration of a body cavity or organ, such as the pleural cavity. This procedure involves the insertion of a needle or catheter into the cavity to remove fluid or air.

The HCPCS code J9000 is used to report the chemotherapy drug doxorubicin hydrochloride. This drug is used to treat various types of cancer, including lung cancer, breast cancer, and lymphoma.

Since the patient is receiving doxorubicin hydrochloride via the pleural cavity, the appropriate codes to report this procedure are 96440 (thoracentesis) and J9000 (chemotherapy drug). Therefore, the correct answer is c)

96440, J9000.

The other options (a, b, and d) are incorrect because they include additional codes that are not necessary to report the procedure, such as 32554 (thoracoscopy) and/or 96446 (chemotherapy administration via indwelling catheter).

89) Answer B - The CPT code that would be used to report a home visit for a respiratory patient to care for mechanical ventilation is 99504. This code describes a comprehensive evaluation and management service provided in the patient's home, including the review of the patient's medical history, physical examination, and management of mechanical ventilation.

Here are brief descriptions of the other codes mentioned:

a) 99503 - This code is used for a home visit that involves a low complexity evaluation and management service.

b) 99504 - This code is used for a home visit that involves a moderate complexity evaluation and management service.

c) 99505 - This code is used for a home visit that involves a high complexity evaluation and management service.

d) 99509 - This code is used for a home visit that involves a team conference, such as a discussion between a patient, family member, and healthcare provider about the patient's care plan.

90) Answer B - The correct answer is (b) 92612.

CPT code 92612 describes a diagnostic procedure that involves the use of a flexible fiberoptic endoscope to evaluate swallowing function by recording a video. This code is used to report the technical component of the evaluation, which includes the use of equipment, supplies, and personnel necessary to perform the procedure.

CPT code 92611 describes a similar procedure, but without video recording. This code is used to report the technical component of a flexible fiberoptic endoscopic evaluation of swallowing (FEES) without recording.

CPT code 92610 describes a non-instrumental evaluation

of swallowing function.

CPT code 92613 describes a diagnostic procedure that involves the use of a flexible fiberoptic endoscope to evaluate swallowing function with interpretation and report.

Therefore, the appropriate CPT code for the technical component of an evaluation of swallowing by video recording using a flexible fiberoptic endoscope is 92612.

91) Answer B - The correct answer is b) Established patient.

According to the Centers for Medicare & Medicaid Services (CMS) definition, an established patient is one who has received professional services from a physician or another physician of the same specialty who belongs to the same group practice, within the past three years. Since the patient saw the Orthopedist 18 months ago, they would be considered an established patient if they return for another visit for the same or related problem.

Therefore, even though the patient did not return for a follow-up visit with the Orthopedist after being referred by their primary care physician, they are still considered an established patient if they return to the same Orthopedist for treatment of their lower back pain.

92) Answer B - The type of graft used in the procedure described is a split-thickness skin graft. This is indicated by the statement that "Split-thickness skin grafts measuring about a 10,000th inch thick were taken from both thighs, meshed with a 3:1 ratio mesher, and stapled to the wounds."

An allograft is a graft taken from a donor of the same species, while an autograft is a graft taken from the patient's own body. In this case, the graft was taken from the patient's own body, indicating that it is an autograft.

Therefore, the correct answer is b) Split thickness graft.

93) Answer A - The anesthesia procedure used for John's

operation was general anesthesia. This is because the patient needed to be completely unconscious and unaware of the surgical procedure due to the complexity and invasiveness of the surgery involved. General anesthesia allows the patient to be completely asleep and pain-free during the procedure, and it also provides muscle relaxation, which is necessary for certain types of surgeries. Regional anesthesia is typically used for surgeries that involve specific regions of the body, such as the arms, legs, or lower abdomen, while local anesthesia is used for minor surgical procedures that only require numbing of a small area of the body. Sedation, on the other hand, involves the use of medication to relax the patient during a surgical procedure, but the patient remains conscious and able to respond to commands.

In John's case, due to the severity of the injury and the need for extensive repair, general anesthesia was the most appropriate choice for his surgery.

94) Answer A - The correct answer is a) Proximal ileostomy.

In the given operative note, it is mentioned that the procedure performed was a "proximal ileostomy for diversion of colon" due to leakage from an intestinal anastomosis. An ileostomy is a surgical procedure that involves bringing the end or loop of the small intestine through an opening in the abdominal wall to create a stoma. This allows for the diversion of fecal matter and provides an alternative route for the elimination of waste products.

Therefore, the correct code for the colon diversion the doctor performed is a) Proximal ileostomy.

95) Answer B - In the given operative report, it is mentioned that the patient was placed in the lateral decubitus position with the left side up, and the lumbosacral area was sterilely prepped. This indicates that the area which was cleaned and prepared for the procedure was the lumbo sacral area.

The thoraco cavity refers to the chest cavity, which is not relevant to this procedure. The supine position refers to lying on the back, which is not the position described in the report. The lamellar region is not a medical term and is not relevant to this procedure.

Hence, option b) Lumbo sacral is the correct answer.

96) Answer C - The given scenario describes the presence of multiple eggs attached to eyelashes and a mobile foreign body, which is suggestive of an infestation with lice, a condition called pediculosis.

Blepharitis is a common condition that causes inflammation of the eyelid margins, but it does not involve the presence of lice or eggs on the eyelashes.

Preorbital cellulitis refers to an infection involving the tissues around the eye, which is not consistent with the given scenario.

A chalazion is a benign eyelid lesion that results from the blockage of a meibomian gland and does not involve the presence of lice or eggs on the eyelashes.

Therefore, the correct answer is c) Pediculosis.

97) Answer A - The medical sign described in the scenario is Keratosis nigricans, which is characterized by brown-to-black, poorly defined, velvety hyper-pigmentation of the skin. This condition is commonly associated with insulin resistance and is often seen in patients with type 2 diabetes. It can also be associated with obesity and certain medications.

Keratosis nigricans usually affects the folds and creases of the skin, such as the armpits, neck, groin, and under the breasts. It may also appear on the hands, elbows, and knees. The affected skin may feel thick and velvety, and there may be a strong odor in the affected areas.

The presence of Keratosis nigricans is an indicator of insulin resistance and an increased risk of developing type 2 diabetes, as well as other conditions such as metabolic syndrome, polycystic ovary syndrome, and certain types of cancer. Therefore, it is important for patients with this condition to undergo further evaluation and management of their underlying health conditions.

98) Answer B - The most appropriate laboratory test to order in this case is fasting blood glucose (option b).

The patient's presentation with hyper-pigmented tick plaque in both axillae, which has grown darker, thicker, and larger, could suggest acanthosis nigricans. Acanthosis nigricans is a skin condition characterized by hyperpigmentation and thickening of the skin, which is commonly associated with insulin resistance and type 2 diabetes mellitus.

Fasting blood glucose is a simple and cost-effective laboratory test that can help diagnose or rule out diabetes mellitus or impaired glucose tolerance as a cause of acanthosis nigricans. Other laboratory tests such as a fasting lipid panel or serum electrolytes may be useful in some clinical scenarios, but in this case, they are less likely to provide helpful information for diagnosing the cause of the patient's rash. Thyroid stimulating hormone (option a) is also less likely to be helpful in this case, as the patient does not have any other symptoms suggestive of thyroid disease.

99) Answer A - The birth defect described, in which the spine fails to close properly, resulting in a protrusion of nerves and skin, is known as spina bifida. Option (a) is the correct answer.

Spina bifida is a congenital defect that occurs during fetal development when the neural tube fails to close properly. This leads to an incomplete closure of the vertebrae, which allows the spinal cord and surrounding nerves to protrude through the opening. The severity of spina bifida can range from mild to severe, and it can cause a variety of physical and neurological symptoms depending on the location and extent of the defect.

Lordosis, kyphosis, and scoliosis are also spinal conditions, but they are not related to spina bifida. Lordosis refers to an excessive inward curvature of the spine, kyphosis refers to an excessive outward curvature of the spine, and scoliosis refers to a sideways curvature of the spine.

100)   Answer B - The neurologist orders a stat CT and MRI. Therefore, the correct answer is b) Computed tomography and Magnetic Resonance Imaging. These radiology tests are commonly ordered in cases of suspected closed head trauma to assess for the presence of bleeding or other injuries to the brain. The comprehensive testing, memory resonance imaging, continues testing, micro resonance imaging, compress testing, and mini resonance imaging are not standard radiology tests used for the evaluation of head trauma.

EXAM C

CODING GUIDELINES

1) Wound exploration codes include the following service(s):
   a) Exploration and repair
   b) Exploration, including enlargement, removal of foreign body(s), repair
   c)   Exploration, including enlargement, repair, and necessary grafting
   d)   Exploration, including enlargement, debridement, removal of foreign body(s), minor vessel ligation, and repair

2) The full description of CPT code 24925 is
   a) Secondary closure or scar revision
   b) Amputation, secondary closure or scar revision
   c) Amputation, arm through humerus; secondary closure or scar revision
   d)   Amputation, arm through humerus; with primary closure, secondary

3) Medical necessity means what?
   a)   Without treatment the patient will suffer permanent disability or death

b) The service requires medical treatment

c) The condition of the patient justifies the service provided

d) The care provided met quality standards

4) Which of the following place of service codes is reported for fracture care performed by an orthopedic physician in the ED?
   a) 11
   b) 20
   c) 22
   d) 23

5) Which of the following codes allows the use of modifier 51?
   a) 35600
   b) 44500
   c) 93600
   d) 45392

6) Category III codes are temporary codes for emerging technology, services, and procedures. If a Category III code exists it should be used instead of an "unlisted procedure" code in category I (example of an unlisted category I code: 60699).
   a) True
   b) False

7) CPT codes 22840-22848 are modifier 62 exempt?
   a) True
   b) False

REGULATORY AND COMPLIANCE

8) Which of the following is not one of the three components of HIPAA that is enforced by the office for civil rights?
   a)   Protecting the privacy of individually identifiable health information
   b)   Setting national standards for the security of electronic protected health information
   c)   Protecting identifiable information being used to analyze patient safety events and improve patient safety
   d)   Setting national standards regarding the transmission and use of protected health information

9) Which of the following statements is not true regarding Medicare Part A?
   a)   It helps cover home health care charges
   b)   It helps cover skilled nursing facility charges
   c)   It helps cover hospice charges
   d)   It helps cover outpatient charges

10) An ABN must be signed when?
   a)   Once the insurance company has denied payment
   b)   Before the service or procedure is provided to the patient
   c)   After services are rendered, but before the claim is filed
   d)   Once the denied claim has been appealed at the highest level

INTEGUMENTARY SYSTEM

11) John was in a fight at the local bar and presents to the ER with multiple lacerations. The physician evaluates John and determines that he has a 2.5 cm gash to his left forearm and a 4cm gash on his right shoulder, both which require

layered closure. He also has a simple 3cm laceration on his forehead that requires simple closure. What are the correct codes for the laceration repairs?

a) 12032-RT, 12031-LT, 12013-59
b) 12032, 12013-59
c) 13121, 12052-59
d) 12032-RT-LT, 12013-59

12) OPERATIVE REPORT

Preoperative Diagnosis: Basal Cell Carcinoma
Postoperative Diagnosis: Basal Cell Carcinoma
Location: Mid Parietal Scalp
Procedure: Prior to each surgical stage, the surgical site was tested for anesthesia and re-anesthetized as needed, after which it was prepped and draped in a sterile fashion. The clinically-apparent tumor was carefully defined and de-bulked prior to the first stage, determining the extent of the surgical excision. With each stage, a thin layer of tumor-laden tissue was excised with a narrow margin of normal appearing skin, using the Moh's fresh tissue technique. A map was prepared to correspond to the area of skin from which it was excised. The tissue was prepared for the cryostat and sectioned. Each section was coded, cut and stained for microscopic examination. The entire base and margins of the excised piece of tissue were examined by the surgeon. Areas noted to be positive on the previous stage (if applicable) were removed with the Moh's technique and processed for analysis. No tumor was identified after the final stage of microscopically controlled surgery. The patient tolerated the procedure well without any complication. After discussion with the patient regarding the various options, the best closure option for each defect was selected for optimal functional and cosmetic results.
Preoperative Size: 1.5 x 2.9 cm
Postoperative Size: 2.7 x 2.9 cm

Closure: Simple Linear Closure, 3.5cm, scalp
Total # of Moh's Stages: 2
Stage Sections Positive
6 blocks
2 blocks
a) 17311, 17315, 17312, 12002
b) 17311, 17312, 12002
c) 17311, 17315, 17312
d) 17311, 17312

13) A child is brought into the emergency department after having her fingers on her right hand closed in a car door. The physician evaluates the patient and diagnosis her with a 3cm laceration to her second finger and a subungual hematoma to her third finger. The physician then proceeds to cleanse the fingers with an iodine scrub and injects both digits with 2 mL of 1% lidocaine with epinephrine. The wound on the second finger was then irrigated with 500 cc of NS and explored for foreign bodies or structural damage. No foreign bodies were found, tendons and vessels were intact. The wound was then re-approximated. Three 5-0 absorbable mattress sutures were used to close the subcutaneous tissue and six 6-0 nylon interrupted sutures were used to close the epidermis. The finger was then wrapped in sterile gauze and placed in an aluminum finger splint. The physician then check that the digital block performed on the third finger was still effective. After ensuring the patient's finger was still numb he then proceeded to take an electronic cautery unit and created a small hole in the nail. Pressing slightly on the nail he evacuated the hematoma. The hole was then irrigated with 500cc of NS and the finger was wrapped in sterile gauze. The patient tolerated both procedures well without complaint.

a) 12042-F6, 11740-F7
b) 64400 (x2), 20103-51, 12042-51, 11740-51,59
c) 20103, 12042-F6, 11740-F7
d) 20103, 12042-51, F6, 11740-51, F7

14) The size of an excision of a benign lesion is determined by:
   a) Adding together the lesion diameter and the widest margins necessary to adequately excise the lesion.
   b) Adding together the lesion diameter and the narrowest margins necessary to adequately excise the lesion.
   c) The diameter of the lesion only, excluding any margins excised with it.
   d) The depth of the lesion plus the full diameter of the lesion.

15) A simple, single layered laceration requires extensive cleaning due to being heavily contaminated. The code selected would come from code range 12031-12057.
   a) True
   b) False

16) A patient is being treated for third degree burns to his left leg and left arm which cover a total of 18 sq cm. The burns are scrubbed clean, anesthetized, and three incisions are made with#11 scalpel, through the tough leathery tissue that is dead, in order to expose the fatty tissue below and avoid compartment syndrome. The burns are then re-dressed with sterile gauze.
   a) 97597
   b) 97602
   c) 16035, 16036 x2
   d) 16030, 16035, 16036 x2

MUSCULOSKELETAL SYSTEM

17) A patient comes into the emergency department complaining of sever wrist pain after falling onto her out stretched hands. The physician evaluates the patient taking a detailed history, a detailed exam, and medical decision making of moderate complexity. Upon examination the physician notes that there is a small portion of bone protruding through the skin. After ordering x-ray of the forearm and wrist the patient is diagnosed with an open distal radius fracture of the right arm. The physician provides an IV drip of morphine to the patient for pain and reduces the fracture. 5- 0 absorbable sutures were used to close the subcutaneous layer above the fracture and the surface was closed with 6-0 nylon interrupted sutures. Wound length was measured at 2.5 cm. It was then dressed with sterile gauze and the wrist was stabilized with a Spica fiberglass cast. The physician provided the patient with a prescription for Percocet for pain and instructions for her to follow up with her orthopedist in 7 days.
   a) 99284-25, 25574-RT
   b) 99284-57-25, 25605-54-RT, 12031
   c) 99284-57, 25574-54
   d) 99284-25, 25605-RT, 12031

18) A Scapulopexy is found under what heading
   a) Incision
   b) Excision
   c) introduction
   d) Repair, Revision, and/or Reconstruction

19) A patient with muscle spasms in her back was seen in her physician's office for treatment. The area over the myofascial spasm was prepped with alcohol utilizing

sterile technique. After isolating it between two palpating fingertips a 25-gauge 5" needle was placed in the center of the myofascial spasms and a negative aspiration was performed. Then 4 cc of Marcaine 0.5% was injected into three points in the muscle. The patient tolerated the procedure well without any apparent difficulties or complications. The patient reported feeling full relief by the time the block had set.

a) 64400
b) 20552
c) 64520
d) 20553

20) A general surgeon and a neurosurgeon are performing an osteotomy on the L4 vertebral segment. The general surgeon establishes the opening using an anterior approach. While the neurosurgeon performs the osteotomy the general surgeon performs a discectomy. After completion the general surgeon closes the patient up.

a) General: 22224-59, Neurosurgeon: 22224-54
b) General: 22224-62, Neurosurgeon: 22224-62
c) General: 22224-66, Neurosurgeon: 22224-66
d) General: 22224, Neurosurgeon: 22224-80

21) A patient comes into his physician's office with a prior diagnosis of a Colles type distal radius fracture. He complains that the cast he currently has on is too tight and is causing numbness in his fingers. The physician removes the cast and ensures the patient's circulation is intact. He then reapplies a short arm fiberglass cast and checks the patient's neurovascular status several times during the procedure. The patient is given instructions to follow-up with his orthopedist within seven days.

a) 25600-77
b) 25600-52
c) 29705, 29075
d) 29075

22) This 59-year-old female was brought to the operating room and placed on the surgical table in a supine position. Following anesthesia, the surgical site was prepped and draped in the normal sterile fashion. Attention was then directed to the right foot where, utilizing a # 15 blade, a 6 cm linear incision was made over the 1st metatarsal head, taking care to identify and retract all vita structures. The incision was medial to and parallel to the extensor hallucis longus tendon. The incision was deepened through subcutaneous underscored, retracted medially and laterally – thus exposing the capsular structures below, which were incised in a linear longitudinal manner, approximately the length of the skin incision. The capsular structures were sharply under scored off the underlying osseous attachments, retracted medially and laterally. Utilizing an osteotome and mallet the medial eminence of the metatarsal bone was removed and the head was remodeled with the Liston bone forceps and the bell rasp. The surgical site was then flushed with saline. The base and excised from the surgical site. There was no hemi implant used and Kirschner wire was used to hold the joint in place. Superficial closure was accomplished using Vicryl 5-0 in a running subcuticular fashion. Site was dressed with a light compressive dressing. The tourniquet was released. Excellent capillary refill to all the digits was observed without excessive bleeding noted.

a) 28296
b) 28292

c) 28899
d) 28298

RESPIRATORY AND CARDIOVASCULAR SYSTEM

23) A 50-year-old gentleman with severe respiratory failure is mechanically ventilated and is currently requiring multiple intravenous drips. With the patient in his Intensive Care Unit bed, mechanically ventilated in the Trendelenburg position, the right neck was prepped and draped with Betadine in a sterile fashion. A single needle stick aspiration of the right subclavian vein was accomplished without difficulty and the guide wire was advanced and a dilator was advanced over the wire. The triple lumen catheter was cannulated over the wire and the wire was then removed. No PVCs were encountered during the procedure. All three ports to the catheter were aspirated and flushed blood easily and they were all flushed with normal saline. The catheter was anchored to the chest wall with butterfly phalange using 3-0 silk suture, Betadine ointment and a sterile. Op-Site dressing were applied. Stat upright chest x-ray was obtained at the completion of the procedure to ensure proper placement of the tip in the subclavian vein.
   a) 36557
   b) 36555
   c) 36558
   d) 36556

24) A patient with chronic emphysema has surgery to remove both lobes of the left lung.
   a) 32440
   b) 32482

c) 32663x2
d) 32310

25) A thoracic surgeon makes an incision under the sternal notch at the base of the throat, introduces the scope into the mediastinal space and takes two biopsies of the tissue. He then retracts the scope and closes the small incision.
   a) 39401
   b) 32606
   c) 39000
   d) 32408

26) A patient has endoscopic surgery done to remove his anterior and posterior ethmoid sinuses. The surgeon dilated the maxillary sinus with a balloon using a trans-nasal approach, explored the frontal sinuses, removes two polyps from the maxillary sinus, and then performed the tissue removal.
   a) 31255, 31295, 31237
   b) 31201, 31295, 31237
   c) 31255, 31267
   d) 31255, 31295, 31267

27) A patient was taken into the operating room where after induction of appropriate anesthesia, her left chest, neck, axilla, and arm were prepped with Betadine solution and draped in a sterile fashion. An incision was made at the hairline and carried down by sharp dissection through the clavipectoral fascia. The lymph node was palpitated in the armpit and grasped with a figure-of eight 2-0 silk suture and by sharp dissection, was carried to hemoclip all attached structures. The lymph node was excised in its entirety. The wound was irrigated. The lymph node was

sent to pathology. The wound was then closed. Hemostasis was assured and the patient was taken to recovery room in stable condition.

a) 38308
b) 38500
c) 38510
d) 38525

28) Operative Note

Approach: Left cephalic vein.

Leads Implanted: Medtronic model 5076-45 in the right atrium, serial number PJN983322V. Medtronic 5076-52 in the right ventricle, serial number PJN961008V.

Device Implanted: Pacemaker, Dual Chamber, Medtronic EnRhythm, model P1501VR, serial number PNP422256H.

Lead Performance: Atrial threshold less than 1.3 volts at 0.5 milliseconds. P wave 3.3 millivolts. Impedance 572 ohms. Right ventricle threshold 0.9 volts at 0.5 milliseconds. R wave 10.3.

Impedance 855.

Procedure: The patient was brought to the electrophysiology laboratory in a fasting state and Intravenous sedation was provided as needed with Versed and fentanyl. The left neck and chest were prepped and draped in the usual manner and the skin and subcutaneous tissues below the left clavicle were infiltrated with 1% lidocaine for local anesthesia. A 2-1/2-inch incision was made below the left clavicle and electrocautery was used for hemostasis. Dissection was carried out to the level of the pectoralis fascia and extended caudally to create a pocket for the pulse generator. The deltopectoral groove was explored and a medium-sized cephalic vein was identified. The distal end of the vein was ligated and a venotomy was performed. Two guide wires were advanced to the superior vena cava and peel-away introducer sheaths were used to insert the two pacing leads. The venous pressures were elevated and there was a fair amount of back-bleeding from the vein, so a 30 Monocryl figure-of-eight stitch was placed around the tissue surrounding the vein for hemostasis.

The right ventricular lead was placed in the high RV septum and the right atrial lead was placed in the right atrial appendage. The leads were tested with a pacing systems analyzer and the results are noted above. The leads were then anchored in place with #0-silk around their suture sleeve and connected to the pulse generator. The pacemaker was noted to function appropriately. The pocket was then irrigated with antibiotic solution and the pacemaker system was placed in the pocket. The incision was closed with two layers of 3-0 Monocryl and a subcuticular closure of 4-0 Monocryl. The incision was dressed with Steri-Strips and a sterile bandage and the patient was returned to her room in good condition.

a) 33240, 33225, 33202
b) 33208, 33225, 33202
c) 33213, 33217
d) 33208

DIGESTIVE SYSTEM

29) The patient was scheduled for an esophagogastroduodenoscopy. Upon arrival they were placed under conscious sedation and instructed to swallow a small flexible camera. The camera was then manipulated into the esophagus, and through the entire length of the esophagus. The esophagus appeared to be slightly inflamed, but there was no sign of erosion or flame hemorrhage. A small 2cm tissue sample was taken to look for gastroesophageal reflux disease. There was no stricture or Barrett mucosa. The bony and the antrum of the stomach

were normal without any acute peptic lesions. Retroflexion of the tip of the endoscope in the body of the stomach revealed an abnormal cardia. There were no acute lesions and no evidence of ulcer, tumor, or polyp. The pylorus was easily entered, and the first, second, and third portions of the duodenum were normal.

a) 43202
b) 43206
c) 43235
d) 43239

30) After informed consent was obtained, the patient was placed in the left lateral decubitus position and sedated. The Olympus video colonoscope was inserted through the anus and was advanced in retrograde fashion through the sigmoid colon, descending colon, and to the splenic flexure. There was a large amount of stool at the flexure which appeared to be impacted. The physician decided not to advance to the cecum due to the impaction and the scope was pulled back into the descending colon and then slowly withdrawn. The mucosa was examined in detail along the way and was entirely normal. Upon reaching the rectum, retroflex examination of the rectum was normal. The scope was then straightened out, the air removed and the scope withdrawn. The patient tolerated the procedure well.

a) 45330-53
b) 45330
c) 45378-53
d) 45378

31) **Operative Note**
The 45-year-old male patient was taken to the operative suite, placed on the table in the supine position, and given a spinal anesthetic. The right inguinal region was

shaved, prepped, and draped in a routine sterile fashion. The patient received 1 gm of Ancef IV push. A transverse incision was made in the intraabdominal crease and carried through the skin and subcutaneous tissue. The external oblique fascia was exposed and incised down to, and through, the external inguinal ring. The spermatic cord and hernia sac were dissected bluntly off the undersurface of the external oblique fascia exposing the attenuated floor of the inguinal canal. The cord was surrounded with a Penrose drain. The sac was separated from the cord structures.

The floor of the inguinal canal, which consisted of attenuated transversalis fascia, was imbricated upon itself with a running locked suture of 2-0 Prolene. Marlex patch 1 x 4 in dimension was trimmed to an appropriate shape with a defect to accommodate the cord. It was placed around the cord and sutured to itself with 2-0 Prolene.

The patch was then sutured medially to the pubic tubercle, inferiorly to Cooper's ligament and inguinal ligaments, and superiorly to conjoined tendon using 2-0 Prolene. The area was irrigated with saline solution, and 0.5% Marcaine with epinephrine was injected to provide prolonged postoperative pain relief. The cord was returned to its position. External oblique fascia was closed with a running 2-0 PDS, subcu with 2-0 Vicryl, and skin with running subdermal 4-0 Vicryl and Steri-Strips. Sponge and needle counts were correct. Sterile dressing was applied.

a) 49505
b) 49505, 54520
c) 49505, 49568
d) 49505, 54520, 49568

32) **Preoperative Diagnosis**: Protein-calorie malnutrition
Postoperative Diagnosis: Protein-calorie malnutrition
Anesthesia: Conscious sedation per Anesthesia.
Complications: None

EGD: Dr. Brown

PEG Placement: Dr. Smith

History: The patient is a 73-year-old male who was admitted to the hospital with some mentation changes. He was unable to sustain enough caloric intakes and had markedly decreased albumin stores. After discussion with the patient and his son they agreed to place a PEG tube for nutritional supplementation.

Procedure: After informed consent was obtained the patient was brought to the endoscopy suite. He was placed in the supine position and was given IV sedation by the Anesthesia Department. An EGD was performed from above by Dr. Brown who has dictated his finding separately. The stomach was transilluminated and an optimal position for the PEG tube was identified using the single poke method. The skin was infiltrated with local and the needle and sheath were inserted through the abdomen into the stomach under direct visualization. The needle was removed and a guidewire was inserted through the sheath. The guidewire was grasped from above with a snare by Dr. Brown. It was removed completely and the Ponsky PEG tube was secured to the guidewire. The guidewire and PEG tube were then pulled through the mouth and esophagus and snug to the abdominal wall. There was no evidence of bleeding. Photos were taken. The Bolster was placed on the PEG site. A complete dictation for the EGD will be done separately by Dr. Brown. The patient tolerated the procedure well and was transferred to recovery room in stable condition. He will be started on tube feedings in 6 hours with aspiration and dietary precautions to determine his nutritional goal. What code(s) should Dr. Smith charge?

a) 43246-62

b) 49440

c) 43752

d) 43653

33) An 18-year-old female Rachel was found with a suicide note and an empty bottle of Tylenol. She was rushed into the emergency department where she had a large-bore gastric lavage tube inserted into her stomach and the contents were evacuated.
a) 43756
b) 43752
c) 43753
d) 43754

34) Which of the following organs is not part of the alimentary canal?
a) Gallbladder
b) Duodenum
c) Jejunum
d) Tongue

URINARY, MALE AND FEMALE REPRODUCTIVE SYSTEM

35) A patient was brought to the OR and sedated. She was then placed in the supine position on a water filled cushion. The C-Arm image intensifier was positioned in the correct anatomical location above the left renal and a total of 2500 high energy shock waves were applied from the outside of the body. Energy levels were slowly started and O2 increased up to 7. Gradually the 2.5cm stone was broken into smaller pieces as the number of shocks went up. The shocks were started at 60 per minute and slowly increased up to 90 per minute. The patient's heart rate and blood pressure were stable throughout the entire procedure. She was transported to recovery in good condition.
a) 50081, 74425

b) 50130, 76770
c) 50060
d) 50590

36) A patient recently underwent a total hysterectomy due to ovarian cancer, which has metastasized. She is now having cylinder rods placed for clinical brachytherapy treatment. Treatment will consist of high dose rate (HDR) brachytherapy once correct placements of the rods have been confirmed.
   a) 57155
   b) 57156
   c) 57155-58
   d) 57156-58

37) The patient was brought to the suite, where after oral sedation; the scrotum was prepped and draped. 1% lidocaine was used for local anesthesia. The vas was identified, skin was incised, and no scalpel instruments were used to dissect out the vas. A segment about 3 cm in length was dissected out. It was clipped proximally and distally, and then the ends were cauterized after excising the segment. Minimal bleeding was encountered and the scrotal skin was closed with 3-0 chromic. The identical procedure was performed on the contralateral side. The patient tolerated the procedure well. He was discharged from the surgical center in good condition with Tylenol with Codeine for pain.
   a) 55250-50
   b) 55400
   c) 55400-50
   d) 55250

38) A 74-year-old male with a weak urinary stream had his PSA tested. Results read 12.5and he was scheduled for a biopsy to determine whether he had a malignancy or BPH. He arrived for surgery and was placed in the left lateral decubitus position and he was sedated. The surgeon used ultrasonic guidance to percutaneously retrieve 3 biopsies, using the trans-perineal approach. The biopsies were examined and the patient was diagnosed with secondary prostate cancer with the primary site unknown. He was directed to schedule a PET scan and discharged in good condition.

a) 55875, 76965
b) 55706, 76942
c) 55700, 76942
d) 55705, 76942

39) **Procedure**: Hydrocelectomy

A scrotal incision was made and further extended with electrocautery. Once the hydrocele sac was reached, we then opened and delivered the testis which drained clear fluid. There was moderate amount of scarring on the testis itself from the tunica vaginalis. The hydrocele sac was completely removed. A drain was then placed in the base of the scrotum and then the testis was placed back into the scrotum in the proper orientation. The same procedure was performed on the left. The skin was then sutured with a running interlocking suture of 3-0 Vicryl and the drains were sutured to place with 3-0 Vicryl.

Bacitracin dressing, ABD dressing, and jock strap were placed. The patient was in stable condition upon transfer to recovery.

a) 55041
b) 54861

c) 55000-50

d) 55060

40) A urologist performs a cystometrogram with intra-abdominal voiding pressure studies in a hospital using calibrated electronic equipment that is provided for his use. He interprets the study and diagnosis the patient with neurogenic bladder.

a) 51726, 51797

b) 51729-26, 51797-26

c) 51726-26, 51797-26

d) 51729, 51797

NERVOUS SYSTEM, EYE AND EAR

41) **Operative Note**

Pre-operative Diagnosis: Increased intracranial pressure and cerebral edema due to severe brain injury.

Post-operative Diagnosis: Increased intracranial pressure and cerebral edema due to severe brain injury.

Procedure: Scalp was clipped. Patient was prepped with ChloraPrep and Betadine. Incisions are infiltrated with 1% Xylocaine with epinephrine 1:200000. Patient did receive antibiotics post procedure and was draped in a sterile manner. The incision made just to the right of the right mid-pupillary line 10 cm behind the nasion. A self-retaining retractor was placed. A hole was then drilled with the cranial twist drill and the dura was punctured. A brain needle was used to localize the ventricle and it took 3 passes to localize the ventricle. The pressure was initially high. The CSF was clear and colorless. The CSF drainage rapidly tapered off because of the brain swelling. With two tries, the ventricular catheter was then able to be placed into the ventricle and then brought out through a separate puncture

site; the depth of catheter was 7 cm from the outer table of the skull. There was intermittent drainage of CSF after that. The catheter was secured to the scalp with #2-0 silk sutures and the incision was closed with Ethilon suture. The patient tolerated the procedure well. No complications. Sponge and needle counts were correct. Blood loss is minimal.
a) 61107, 62160
b) 61210
c) 61107
d) 61210, 62160

42) A procedure in which corneal tissue from a donor is frozen, reshaped, and implanted into the anterior corneal stroma of the recipient to modify refractive error.
a) 65710
b) 65760
c) 65765
d) 65770

43) Which of the following organs is not part of the endocrine system?
a) Thyroid
b) Pancreas
c) Lymph nodes
d) Adrenal Glands

44) Using an operating microscope, the ophthalmologist places stay sutures into the rectus muscle. A cold probe is then placed over the sclera and is depressed sealing the choroid to the retina at the original tear site. He then performs a sclerotomy and places mattress sutures across the incision. Subretinal fluid is then drained. Next a silicone sponge, followed by a silicone band, are placed around the

eye and sutured into place to help support the healing scar. Rectus sutures are removed.

a) 67101
b) 67101, 69990
c) 67107
d) 67107, 69990

45) Following a motor vehicle collision, a 28-year-old male was given a CT scan of the brain which indicated an infratentorial hematoma in the cerebellum. The patient was taken to the OR where the neurosurgeon, using the CT coordinates, incised the scalp and drilled a burr hole into the cranium above the hematoma. Under direct visualization he then evacuated the hematoma using suction and irrigated with NS. Hemorrhaging was controlled and the dura was closed. The skull piece was then placed back into the drill hole and screwed into place. The scalp was closed and the patient was sent to recovery.

a) 61154
b) 61253, 61315
c) 61315
d) 61154, 61315

46) A postaurical incision is made on the right ear. With the use of an operating microscope the surgeon visualizes and reflects the skin flap and posterior eardrum forward. A small leak from the middle ear into the round window is noted. The surgeon then roughens up the surface of the window and packs it with fat. Upon retraction the eardrum and skin flap are replaced and the canal is packed. The surgeon then sutures the postaurical incision. He then repeats the procedure on the left ear.

a) 69666-50, 69990

b) 69667-50, 69990

c) 69666, 69990

d) 69667-50

EVALUATION AND MANAGEMENT

47) A patient comes into her doctor's office for her weekly blood sugar check. Her blood is drawn by the LPN on staff, the visit takes about 5 minutes total.
   a) 99214
   b) 99212
   c) 99211
   d) 99221

48) A 3-year-old child is brought into the ER after swallowing a penny. A detailed history and exam are taken on the child and medical decision making is of moderate complexity. The child is admitted to observation for three hours and is then discharged home.
   a) 99211
   b) 99214
   c) 99215
   d) 99235

49) A 20-month-old child is admitted to the hospital with pneumonia and acute respiratory distress. The physician spends 3 minutes intubating the child and spends 90 minutes of Critical Care time stabilizing the patient.
   a) 99291, 99292-25, 31500
   b) 99471-25, 31500
   c) 99291-25, 99292-25, 31500
   d) 99471

50) At the request of a physician who is delivering for a high-risk pregnancy, Dr. Smith, a pediatrician, is present in the delivery room to assist the infant if needed. After thirty minutes the infant is born, but is not breathing. The delivering physician hands the infant to Dr. Smith who provides chest compressions and resuscitates the infant. The pediatrician then performs the initial evaluation and management and admits the healthy newborn to the nursery. What codes should Dr. Smith submit on a claim?
a) 99360, 99465
b) 99465, 99460
c) 99360, 99460
d) 99360, 99465, 99460

51) Mr. Johnson is a 79-year-old established male patient that is seen by Dr. Anderson for his annual physical exam. During the examination Dr. Anderson notices a suspicious mole on Mr. Johnson's back. The Doctor completes the annual exam and documents a detailed history and exam and the time discussing the patient's need to quit smoking. Dr. Anderson then turns his attention to the mole and does a complete work up. He documents a comprehensive history and examination and medical decision making of moderate complexity. He also called a local dermatologist and made an appointment for Mr. Johnson to see him the next day for an evaluation and biopsy.
a) 99387, 99205
b) 99387, 99215
c) 99397, 99205
d) 99397, 99214

52) An infant is born six weeks premature in rural Arizona

and the pediatrician in attendance intubates the child and administers surfactant in the ET tube while waiting in the ER for the air ambulance. During the 45-minute wait, he continues to bag the critically ill patient on 100 percent oxygen while monitoring VS, ECG, pulse oximetry and temperature. The infant is in a warming unit and an umbilical vein line was placed for fluids and in case of emergent needs for medications. How is this coded?

a) 99291
b) 99471
c) 99291, 31500, 36510, 94610
d) 99434, 99464, 99465, 94610, 36510

ANESTHESIA

53) When does anesthesia time begin?
   a) After the induction of anesthesia is complete
   b) During the pre-operative exam prior to entering the OR
   c) When the anesthesiologist begins preparing the patient for the induction of anesthesia
   d) Once the supervising physician signs over the patient's care to the anesthesiologist

54) A 5-month-old is brought into the operating room for open heart surgery. The surgeon performs a repair of a small hole that was found in the lining surrounding the patient's heart. Anesthesia was provided as well as the assistance of an oxygenator pump.
   a) 00560, 99100
   b) 00561
   c) 00567, 99100
   d) 00561, 99100

55) A 72-year-old male with a history of severe asthma is placed under anesthesia to have a long tendon in his upper arm repaired. Code this Scenario.
a) 01712-P4, 99100
b) 01716-P3
c) 01714-P3, 99100
d) 01714-P4

56) Which of the following procedures can be coded separately when performed by the anesthesiologist?
a) Administration of blood
b) Monitoring of a central venous line
c) Capnography
d) Monitoring of an EKG

RADIOLOGY

57) Some radiology codes include two components. Often a radiologist will use the radiology equipment, which is known as the technical component, and the physician will provide the second half of the CPT code by supervising and interpreting the study. When this occurs what should the physician report?
a) The full CPT code
b) The CPT code with a modifier TC
c) The CPT with a modifier 26
d) The CPT with a modifier 52

58) A patient presents to the ER with intractable nausea and vomiting, and abdominal pain that radiates into her pelvis. The physician orders a CT scan of the abdomen, first without contrast and then followed by contrast, and a CT of

the pelvis, without contrast.
a) 74178
b) 74178, 74176-51
c) 74178 x2, 74177
d) 74176, 74178-51

59) If a prior study is available but it is documented in the medical records that there was inadequate visualization of the anatomy, then a diagnostic angiography may be reported in conjunction with an interventional procedure if modifier 59 is appended to the diagnostic S&I.
a) True
b) False

60) A physician performed a deep bone biopsy of the femur. The trocar was visualized and guided using a CAT scan and interpretation was provided.
a) 20245, 77012-26
b) 20225, 77012
c) 38221, 76998
d) 20225, 73700

61) A patient has a myocardial perfusion imaging study which included quantitative wall motion, ejection fraction by gated technique, and attenuation correction. The study was done during a cardiac stress test which was induced by using dipyridamole. The physician supervised, the interpretation and report were completed by the cardiologist.
a) 78451, 93016
b) 78453, 93016
c) 78451
d) 78453

62) A 35-year-old mother carrying twin gestations, who has a 3-year-old child with Down syndrome, comes in for a prenatal screening. She is in her 12th week of pregnancy and the physician requests that the amount of fluid behind the necks of the fetuses be measured. A transabdominal approach was used.
   a) 76801, 76802
   b) 76811, 76812
   c) 76813, 76814
   d) 76816, 76816-59

PATHOLOGY

63) A physician orders a patient's blood be tested for levels of urea nitrogen, sodium, potassium, transferase alanine and aspartate amnio, total protein, ionized calcium, carbon dioxide, chloride, creatinine, glucose, and TSH.
   a) 80053-52, 84443
   b) 80048, 84443, 84155, 84460, 84450
   c) 80047, 84460, 84450, 84155, 84443
   d) 80051, 84520, 84460, 84450, 84155, 82330, 82565, 82947, 84443

64) A specimen labeled "right ovarian cyst" is received for examination. It consists of a smooth-walled, clear fluid filled cyst measuring 13x12x7 cm and weighing 1351 grams with fluid. Both surfaces of the wall are pink-tan, smooth and grossly unremarkable. No firm or thick areas or papillary structures are noted on the cyst wall externally or internally. After removal the fluid, the cyst weight 68 grams. The fluid is transparent and slightly mucoid.
   a) 88300
   b) 88304

c) 88305

d) 88307

65) A patient presents to the ED with chest pain, shortness of breath, and a history of congestive heart failure. The physician performs a 12 lead EKG which indicates a myocardial infarction without ST elevations. The physician immediately orders myoglobin, quantitative troponin, and CK enzyme levels to be run once every hour for three consecutive hours.

a) 83874-99, 83874-76, 83874-91, 84484-99, 84484-76, 84484-91, 82250-99,

b) 82250-76, 82250-91

c) 83874, 83874-91 x2, 84484, 84484-91 x2, 82550, 82550-91 x2

d) 83874-91 x3, 84484-91 x3, 82250-91 x3

e) 83874 x3, 84484 x3, 82550 x3

66) A 17-year-old female presents in her family physician's office complaining of nausea, vomiting, and weight gain. She has been experiencing these symptoms on and off for two weeks. An analysis of the urine reveals a positive pregnancy test and hCG levels of 12500 mIU/ml confirm she is in her sixth week of pregnancy.

a) 81005, 84702

b) 81025, 84702

c) 81025, 84703

d) 81005, 84703

67) A couple that was unsuccessful at conceiving a child chooses to have in vitro fertilization done. The eggs and semen have been harvested and nine eggs were implanted with a sperm. The zygotes went through mitosis and

produced embryos. Three embryos were then implanted in the woman and the other six were kept for later use. What codes(s) would the lab technician charge for her services in preserving the remaining six embryos?

a) 89255 x6
b) 89258
c) 89268
d) 89342

68) A patient in her 30th week of pregnancy has a high oral glucose reading and her physician orders a glucose tolerance test. Upon arrival the laboratory technician draws the patient's blood and the patient then ingests a glucose drink. Her blood is then drawn one, two, and three hours after the ingestion. As the patient was leaving the laboratory the technician informs her that the samples were incorrectly labeled and that the test needed to be repeated. The patient has her blood drawn again, ingested the glucose drink again, and has her blood re-drawn at one-, two- and three-hour intervals.

a) 82951, 82951-91
b) 82946, 82946-91
c) 82947, 82950, 82950-91 x2
d) 82951

MEDICINE

69) A 52-year-old male is in the emergency department complaining of dizziness and states he passed out prior to arrival. The physician evaluates him, orders that a 12 lead EKG be performed, and has the nurse infuse 2 liters of NS over a 1 hour and 45-minute time period under his supervision. The EKG results were reviewed by the physician and were normal. A report was written and the

patient was diagnosed with syncope due to dehydration and released. In addition to the EM service what should the physician code for?

a) 93010, 96360, 96361
b) 93000, 96360
c) 93010
d) 93000, 96360, 96361

70) A 45-year-old patient with end stage renal disease has in home dialysis services initiated on the 15th of the month. The physician provides dialysis every day. On the 19th the patient was admitted to the hospital and discharged on the 24th. The physician and patient began in-home dialysis again on the 25th and continued every day until the 31st.

a) 90960
b) 90966
c) 90970
d) 90970 x11

71) A 73-year-old group home resident with end stage renal disease has a nurse come in on Mondays, Wednesdays, and Fridays to perform peritoneal dialysis. Each dialysis session lasts three hours. Once a week, (on Friday), the nurse also assists the patient with his meals, cleaning, and grocery shopping. What should the nurse charge for a month (30 days) of services if the 1st of the month landed on a Monday?

a) 99601, 99602 x25, 99509 x4
b) 99601 x13, 99602 x13, 99509 x4
c) 90966, 99509 x4
d) 99512 x 13, 99509 x4

72) The physician performs a non-imaging physiological

recording of pressure on the left leg with Doppler analysis of blood flow in both directions. ABIs were taken at the back and front lower aspect of the tibial and tibial/dorsalis pedis arteries. In addition, 2 levels of plethymography volume and oxygen tension were taken.

a) 93923-52
b) 93923
c) 93922
d) 93922-52

73) Due to a suspected gastric outlet obstruction a manometric study is performed. Using nuclear medicine, the physician monitors the time it takes for food to move through the patient's stomach, the time it take the patient's stomach to empty into the small intestine, and how fully it empties.

a) 91010
b) 91020
c) 91022
d) 91013

74) Which of the following drugs is not pending FDA approval?

a) 90664
b) 90666
c) 90667
d) 90668

MEDICAL TERMINOLOGY

75) The suffix "–ectomy" means

a) Cutting into
b) Surgical removal
c) A permanent opening

d) Surgical repair

76) The acronym "MMRV" stands for
   a) Measles, Mumps, and Rubella vaccine
   b) Measles, Mumps, and Rosella vaccine
   c) Measles, Mumps, Rubella, and Varicella
   d) Measles, Mumps, Rosella, and Varicella

77) "MRI" stands for
   a) Micro-wave Recording Instrument
   b) Medical Recording Instrument
   c) Magnetic Resolution Image
   d) Magnetic Resonance Imaging

78) The term "Salpingo-Oophorectomy" refers to
   a) The removal of the fallopian tubes and ovaries
   b) The surgical sampling or removal of fertilized egg
   c) Cutting into the fallopian tubes and ovaries for surgical purposes
   d) Cutting into a fertilized egg for surgical purposes

ANATOMY

79) The spleen belongs to what organ system?
   a) Endocrine
   b) Hemic and Lymphatic
   c) Digestive
   d) Nervous

80) The portion of the femur bone that helps makes up the knee cap is considered what?
   a) The posterior portion
   b) The proximal portion

c) The distal portion
d) The dorsal portion

81) How many regions are in the abdominopelvic cavity?
a) Four
b) Six
c) Eight
d) Nine

82) The Midsagittal plane refers to what portion of the body?
a) Top
b) Middle
c) Bottom
d) Back

ICD 10 CM

83)   Lucy was standing on a chair in her kitchen trying to change a light bulb when she slipped and fell. She struck the glass top stove, which shattered. She presents to the ER with a simple laceration to her forearm that has embedded glass particles.
a) S51.809A, W01.110A, Y92.099
b) S51.829A, W01.110A, W45.8XXA
c) S51.809A, W01.198A, Y92.099
d) S51.829A, W01.198A, W45.8XXA

84) A 60-year-old male is admitted for detoxification and rehabilitation. He has continuously abused amphetamines to the point that he cannot voluntarily stop on his own and has become dependent upon them. He also has a long-documented history of alcohol abuse and alcoholism. He experiences high levels of anxiety due to PTSD, which causes him to use and abuse substances.

a) F15.10, F15.20, F10.10, F10.20, F41.1, F43.10
b) F15.20, F10.20, F41.9, F43.10
c) F19.20, F10.10, F41.9, F43.10
d) F15.10, F15.20, F10.10, F10.20, F41.9, F43.10

85) A patient with uncontrolled type II diabetes is experiencing blurred vision and an increase in floaters appearing in her vision. She is diagnosed with diabetic retinopathy.
a) E11.9, E11.319
b) E11.311
c) E11.319
d) E11.39

86) Signs and symptoms that are associated routinely with a disease process should not be assigned as additional codes, unless otherwise instructed by classification.
a) True
b) False

87) A patient who is known to be HIV positive but who has no documented symptoms would be assigned code
a) B20, Z21
b) R75
c) Z21
d) Z11.4

HCPCS

88) A patient has a home health aide come to his home to clean and dress a burn on his lower leg. The aide uses a special absorptive, sterile dressing to cover a 20 sq. cm. area. She also covers a 15sq.cm. area with a self-adhesive sterile

gauze pad.
a) A6204, A6403
b) A6252, A6403
c) A6252, A6219
d) A6204, A6219

89) A 12-year-old arrives in his pediatrician's office after colliding with another player during a soccer game. He is complaining of pain in his right wrist. The physician orders an x-ray and diagnoses him with a hairline fracture of the distal radius. He has a short arm fiberglass cast applied and discharges him with follow up instructions.
a) Q4009
b) Q4012
c) Q4022
d) Q4010

90) A patient with Hodgkin's disease takes Neosar as part of his chemotherapy regiment. He receives 100 mg once a week through intravenous infusion.
a) J9100
b) J7502
c) J9070
d) J8999

CASE STUDY

91) CASE 1

Preoperative Diagnosis: Squamous cell carcinoma, left lower eyelid
Postoperative diagnosis: Squamous cell carcinoma, left lower eyelid Ill
Procedure Performed: Excision of squamous cell carcinoma of the left lower eyelid measuring10 cm with a 2.0 cm

squared rhomboid flap repair

Indications for Surgery: The patient is an 80-year-old female with biopsy-proven squamous cell carcinoma of her left lower eyelid. With her permission Dr. Violet marked this area for excision with gross normal margins of 2 mm, and drew her planned rhomboid flap for repair. The patient observed these markings in a mirror so she could understand the surgery, agreed on the location and we proceeded.

Description of Procedure: The patient was given 1 g of IV Ancef. The area was infiltrated with local anesthetic. The face was prepped and draped in a sterile fashion. Dr. Violet then excised the lesion as drawn into the subcutaneous fat. Suture was used to mark the specimen at its medial tip and this was labeled 12 0'clock. Meticulous hemostasis had been achieved using Bovie cautery. Dr. Violet put a stitch initially in this wound to see if she could close it primarily; however, it was pulling down on the patient's lower eyelid or creating ectropion, and because of that she felt she needed to proceed with the planned rhomboid flap reconstruction. She incised the rhomboid flap as she had drawn it, elevating the flap with the full thickness of skin and subcutaneous fat and rotated into the defect. The donor site was closed and the flap was inset in layers using 4-0 Monocryl, 5-0 Monocryl and 6-0 Prolene. Loupe magnification was used throughout the procedure, and the patient tolerated the procedure well. What are the correct CPT code and ICD codes?

92) CASE 2

Pre-procedure Diagnosis: Analysis of Vagal Nerve Stimulator (VNS), epilepsy with history of seizures

Post-procedure Diagnosis: Analysis of Vagal Nerve Stimulator (VNS), epilepsy with history of seizures (Post procedural diagnosis)

Procedure: Vagal Nerve Stimulator Analysis (VNS analysis)

Patient here for VNS implant analysis with possible adjustments.

The programming head was placed over the implanted neurostimulator located within the patient's neck-left side. Impedance was verified, ensuring parameters within normal limits. Parameters charted on flowchart within medical record. Operating status of the neurostimulator reflects on. Estimated time for analysis/interrogation was 20 minutes in duration.

Patient denies questions at this time. Will repeat analysis in three months. What is the correct CPT code reported?

93) CASE 3

Performed in the office

Pre-procedure Diagnosis: Gastro-esophageal reflux disease (GERD), Heartburn Post-procedure Diagnosis: GERD (Post procedure diagnosis used for coding.) Procedure: Esophageal pH monitoring with Bravo pH Capsule (Acid reflux testing)

Patient was placed in supine position on the examining bed, IV moderate sedation was administered. Visualization of esophagus with anatomic markers located during endoscopy. Endoscopy was removed and the Bravo pH Capsule delivery system was passed into the esophagus using the oral passage until the attachment site was obtained at approximately 5cm proximal to the upper margin of the LES. The external vacuum pump was activated pulling the adjacent esophageal mucosa into the fastening well. Vacuum gauge at 600 mm Hg and held for 10 seconds.

The plastic safety guard on the handle was then removed and the activation button was depressed and turned, attaching the pH capsule to the esophageal wall. (Placement of electrode placement.) The activation button on handle was then twisted 90 degrees and re-extended, releasing the pH capsule. Esophagoscopy was repeated to verify capsule attachment.

Prior to procedure, the Bravo pH capsule was activated and calibrated by submersion in pH buffer solutions.

The patient tolerated the procedure well and was transferred into the recovery room. The patient returned to the office two days later for download of the recording. The information was analyzed and interpreted. what is the correct CPT code reported?

94) CASE 4

Location: Imaging center; radiologist employed. (Radiologist is employed by the imaging center: the imaging center should report the global component.)

STUDY: MAMMOGRAM BILATERAL SCREENING, (Screening bilateral mammogram.) all VIEWS, PRODUCING DIRECT DIGITAL IMAGE

REASON: SCREEN BILATERAL DIGITAL MAMMOGRAPHY WITH COMPUTER-AIDED DETECTION (CAD) (Use of CAD.) No previous mammograms are available for comparison.

CLINICAL HISTORY: The patient has a positive family history of breast cancer. (Family history of breast CA.)

Mammogram was read with the assistance of GE iCAD (computerized diagnostic) system.

FINDINGS: Residual fibroglandular breast parenchymal tissue is identified bilaterally. No dominant spiculated mass or suspicious area of clustered pleomorphic microcalcifications are apparent. Skin and nipples are seen to be normal. The axilla is unremarkable.

IMPRESSION: BIRADS 1 – NEGATIVE (Negative screening.)

What are the CPT® and ICD-10-CM codes reported for this service?

95) CASE 5

Anesthesiologist personally permed case anesthesia time: 13:04 to 13:41

physical status 3

preoperative diagnosis: RLL lung cavity, possible CA of lung

postoperative diagnosis: Right lower lobe lung carcinoma

Procedure: bronchoscopy

Anesthesia: Monitored anesthesia care

Procedure description: With the patient under satisfactory anesthesia, a flexible fiberoptic bronchoscope was introduced via oral cavity and advanced passed the larynx for visualization of the bronchus. Cell washing obtained and sent to pathology. The bronchoscope was then removed. Patient tolerated the procedure well.

Cell washing obtained from the right lower lobe was confirmed by pathology as malignant carcinoma.

What CPT code reported for anesthesia?

96) CASE 6

Preoperative   Diagnosis/indication;   Traumatic pneumothorax/hemothorax/ pleural effusion

Postoperative Diagnosis: Decompressed pneumothorax/ drained hemothorax/drained pleural effusion

Procedure: Chest thoracostomy with indwelling tube

Procedure: After consent was obtained, the patient was then placed supine with the ipsilateral arm above his head. After donning cap, mask, sterile gown, and gloves, the patient's left chest wall from mid-clavicular line to posterior axillary line and from axilla to costophrenic line was scrubbed thoroughly with chlorhexidine solution and allowed to dry. Sterile drapes were applied covering the patient's upper torso including face, Landmarks were identified between the 4th and 5th intercostal space. 10 ccs of 2% Lidocaine with epinephrine were widely infiltrated subcutaneously for local analgesia. Using a 10-blade scalpel, the skin and subcutaneous tissues were incised parallel to the rib margins to a length of approx. 3 cm. Hemostats were then used to dissect bluntly to the intercostal musculature. The parietal pleura was then punctured with large Kelly clamps and the jaws were opened widely to allow an immediate escape of air. An 18 French chest tube with trocar was introduced into the pleural space to a level of 2 cm at the skin. The trocar was removed as the tube was advanced into position. The skin was approximated first, via 2-0 silk sutures in a horizontal mattress above and below the chest tube, then, the suture ends were tied around the indwelling tube. The tube was then placed to suction. Sterile petrolatum gauze was placed at the skin junction and covered with sterile 4x4's. The site was then taped with pressure tape and secured. The Pleuravac was checked and no air leak indicated. The patient tolerated the procedure well. There were no complications.

Follow-up CXR has been ordered for placement. What CPT and ICD 10 CM codes are reported?

97) CASE 7

Preoperative Diagnosis: Hypoxia Shortness of breath

Postoperative Diagnosis: Small cell carcinoma right lower lobe

Procedure: Surgical VATS, anatomic resection of the right lower lobe

Description of Procedure: After getting the appropriate consent for the operation and administering general anesthesia and intubation, the patient was placed in a full left lateral decubitus position with the table flexed at 30 degrees at the level between the nipples and the umbilicus to have better exposure of the right intercostal spaces. A 10-mm zero-degree thoracoscope was inserted in the right pleural cavity through a port site placed in the sixth intercostal space on the midaxillary line. Two additional port sites were placed in the fifth intercostal space on the posterior and anterior midaxillary line, respectively. lhe port sites were chosen with a possible thoracotomy in mind. The VATS exploration immediately revealed a mass in the base of the right lung. We wedge biopsied the mass and sent it to pathology for the frozen section. Results from pathology revealed small cell carcinoma so we proceeded with an anatomic resection of the mass. We were able to thoracoscopically remove the mass via anatomic resection of the right lower lobe 141 without having to open the thoracic cavity. Green load endoscopic stapling was used to retract the right lower wedge, which was bagged and sent to pathology. Inspection of the lung revealed normal pulmonary parenchyma. After closing the port sites and inserting a chest tube, the patient was extubated and was transferred to the surgical intensive care unit for observation. What CPT and ICD codes are reported?

98) CASE 8

Preoperative diagnosis:
phimosis
voiding dysfunction sexual disfunction
Postoperative Diagnosis: Phimosis Voiding dysfunction
Sexual dysfunction
Procedure: Circumcision
Anesthesia: General
Indications: Tie patient is a 17-year-old white male with severe phimosis since birth that does not allow him to retract his foreskin, He also notes bleeding and pain with sexual contact and some irritation from urine being trapped under the foreskin- He understood the risks and benefits of circumcision, and he and his grandparents (who are his guardians) elect to proceed.

Procedure Description: The patient was brought to the operating room and placed on the operating room table in the supine position. After adequate LMA anesthesia was accomplished, he was given a dorsal penile block and a modified ringblockwith 0.25% Marcaine plain

Two circumferential incisions were made around the patient's penis to allow for the maximal aesthetic result. Adequate hemostasis was then achieved with the Bovie, and the skin edges were approximated using 4-0 chromic simple interrupted sutures with a U-stitch at the frenulum. The patient was extubated and taken to the recovery room in good condition. Disposition: The patient was taken to the post anesthesia care unit and then discharged home in good condition. What are the CPT and ICD codes reported?

99) CASE 9

Preoperative Diagnosis: Shunt infection

Postoperative Diagnosis: Same

Operation: Replacement of externalized shunt with medium pressure ventriculoperitoneal shunt

Anesthesia: General

Estimated Blood Loss: less than 10 cc Complications: None

Specimen: CSF

Indications: Admitted for shunt tap documenting shunt infection resulting in externalized shunt. Culture of the staphylococcus aureus infection. Additional problems with chronic headaches and fibrous dysplasia.

Procedure:

After obtaining adequate general anesthesia, the patient was prepped and draped in the standard fashion. The right parietal scalp incision was reopened and the shunt catheter identified. The shunts reservoir was delivered from the wound and the distal catheter freed from it. The abdominal incision was reopened and the rectus sheath identified. A shunt passer was then passed from the abdominal wound to the head wound. The passer was then used to bring the wound distal catheter PI from the head wound to the abdominal.

The old ventricular catheter was then removed after freeing it from tethering material by twisting the catheter. A large piece of choroid plexus was entwined in the inlets of the catheter. A new ventricular-catheter was then inserted into the tract of the old catheter and fed into a distance equal to that of the old catheter (5 cm). Good flow was seen. It was attached to the shunt reservoir that was then seated after attaching a 0-25 shunt assistant valve to it. A small amount of CSF was then withdrawn from the distal end. An abdominal trocar was then used to pierce the rectus sheath and muscle and the abdominal cavity entered. The distal catheter was then fed into the peritoneal cavity.

The subcutaneous tissues were closed in a multi-layer fashion and the skin with staples. the monitor line was sewn to the scalp.

The patient tolerated the procedure well, had an estimated blood loss of cc and was taken to the PICU in stable condition. Sponge, needle, and cottonoid counts were correct. What is the correct CPT code reported?

100)   CASE 10

Indications: 24-year-old patient with feeding difficulties. Patient intubated and sedated due to respiratory distress and pneumonia. Placement of NG tube revealed coffee ground emesis.

Endoscopic   Procedure   Performed: Esophagogastroduodenoscopy performed with regular gastroscope to the second part of duodenum (depth of insertion 100 cm). 121 Diet: NPO >6 hours, Prep: None. Patient was in the supine position. Percutaneous endoscopic gastrostomy PI placement using a 20 Fr. Ponsky Gauderer pull.

Therapeutic Outcomes: Successful placement of feeding device

Specimens: No specimens obtained

Procedure Medications: 75 mg Meperidine administered by IV; 3 mg Midazolam administered by IV I'll

Recommendations: Can use tube in 4 hrs if bowel sounds are present Sedation performed by me.

Independent observation performed by Amy Smith, RN

Total time of Sedation: 30 minutes

Diagnoses:

Non-erosive duodenitis of duodenal bulb

Normal examination of whole stomach what are the surgery and ICD code reported?

EXAM C ANSWERS AND RATIONALES

1. Answer D – Wound exploration codes are 20100-20103. Directly above these codes is the wound exploration coding guidelines. In the guidelines it states that the following components are part of the codes description: surgical exploration and enlargement of the wound, extension of dissection, debridement, removal of foreign bodies, ligation or coagulation of minor subcutaneous and/or muscular blood vessel(s).

2. Answer C – In the CPT book there are two types of descriptions: common and unique. The common portion of a descriptor follows a code and end with a semi-colon (;). Any CPT that shares that description

is indented beneath the code. Any portion of the description following the semi-colon is the "Unique" portion of the descriptor and only belongs to a single code. In this case code 24900 contains the common descriptor "Amputation, arm through humerus". Codes 24920 through 24931 share that part of the description and so are indented beneath it with their unique portion of the descriptor beside them.

Amputation

24900	Amputation, arm through humerus; with primary closure
24920	open, circular (guillotine)
24925	secondary closure or scar revision

---

3. Answer C – Medical necessity is what adjudicates, or justifies, a claim for payment. If a physician wants to be paid for a laceration repair (CPT), then the ICD-10 code needs to describe a situation that says it is necessary (ICD-10 should be a laceration or open wound).

4. Answer D – Place of service codes are reported on the claim form to identify the site of the service provided. In this case, the services are rendered in the ED, which is reported with POS 23. The place of service codes can be found in the CPT manual.

5. Answer D – Appendix E lists all CPT codes that are modifier 51 exempt. Also, add-on codes should not be appended with modifier 51. Beside each code in the tabular there is a convention that looks like a circle with a backslash through it. This convention means that the code next to it is modifier 51 exempt. Code 45392 is the only code not listed in appendix E and that does not have this convention beside it. Also, this is not

an add-on code.

6. Answer A – Category III codes are located between the Category II codes and Appendix A in the back of the CPT manual. Category III coding guidelines state that these codes are to be used before assigning an unlisted procedure code from category I codes.

7. Answer A – Just prior to code 22840 there are some code specific coding guidelines. In the third paragraph it states, "do not append modifier 62 to spinal instrumentation codes 22840- 22848 and 22850-20938".

Spinal Instrumentation

Segmental instrumentation is defined as fixation at each end of the construct and at least one additional interposed bony attachment.

Non-segmental instrumentation is defined as fixation at each end of the construct and may span several vertebral segments without attachment to the intervening segments.

Insertion of spinal instrumentation is reported separately and in addition to arthrodesis. Instrumentation procedure codes 22840-22848, 22853, 22854, 22859 are reported in addition to the definitive procedure(s). Do not append modifier 62 to spinal instrumentation codes 22840-22848, 22850, 22852, 22853, 22854, 22859.

---

8. Answer D – HIPAA has three rules; Privacy, Security, and Patient Safety. Standards for transmitting PHI are not regulated by HIPAA but the security of this information while it is being transmitted is. Once transmission rules are set HIPAA then set the standards on how this information should be protected.

9. Answer D – Medicare parts A is hospital insurance and

helps cover inpatient care in hospitals, skilled nursing facility, hospice, and home health care. Medicare part B helps cover medically-necessary services like doctors' services, outpatient care, home health services, and other medical services. It also covers some preventive services.

10. Answer B – ABN stands for advanced beneficiary notice, and is a document that a patient sign stating that they will pay for the procedure they are having done if insurance does not cover it. This is something taught in a medical billing and/or coding class, or something read in preparation of the exam. This answer is not located in one of the coding books.

11. Answer B – According to the laceration coding guidelines (above code 12001, titled "Repair (closure)"), lacerations of the same depth and same anatomical grouping should have their lengths added together and a single code should be selected. Since the arm lacerations share the same anatomical location (arm), and both are of the same depth (layered lacerations), their length is added together (2.5 + 4 = 6.5 cm). Code 12032 is the correct code because it meets all three specifications: 1) Length = 6.5cm, 2) Depth = layered laceration 3) Anatomical Location = the arm. The facial laceration would have a separate CPT code because it has a different depth (simple laceration) as well as a different anatomical location (face). Code 12013 is correct because it also meets all three specifications: 1) Length = 3cm 2) Depth = Simple 3) Anatomical Location = Face. According to the laceration repair guidelines "When

more than one classification of wound is repaired, list the more complicated as the primary procedure and the less complicated as the secondary procedure, using modifier 59." Option B correctly sequences the most complicated code first (12032), followed by the least severe code (12013) with an appended 59 modifier.

12. Answer A – The easiest way to determine exactly what was done during this procedure is to look at the information at the very end of the operative note. Here we have the information that is most important to us: simple linear closure was performed; two stages (described as Mohs), were performed, and the number of sections in each stage are reported. According to the Mohs microsurgery guidelines, repairs are not bundled into the procedure and can be billed additionally. This means that the repair code 12002 (simple repair, 6.5cm, scalp), is correct and we can eliminate options C and D. Options A and B share three of the same codes, with one additional code in option A. So at this point the question is do you need code 17315 or not? Going through the Stages and sections: Stage I Section 1-5 is coded with 17311; Stage I Section 6 is coded with 17315; Stage II Section 1-5 (only 2 sections were performed in our scenario) is coded with; And code 12002 describes the simple, 3.5cm closure of the scalp.

13. Answer A

14. Answer B

15. Answer A – True. According to the laceration "Repair (closure)" coding guidelines (above code 12001), under the heading "Definitions, intermediate repair". "Single-layer closure of heavily contaminated wounds that have required extensive cleaning or removal of particulate matter also constitutes intermediate repair"

> *Intermediate repair* includes the repair of wounds that, in addition to the above, require layered closure of one or more of the deeper layers of subcutaneous tissue and superficial (non-muscle) fascia, in addition to the skin (epidermal and dermal)
>
> closure. It includes limited undermining (defined as a distance less than the maximum width of the defect, measured perpendicular to the closure line, along at least one entire edge of the defect). Single-layer closure of heavily contaminated wounds that have required extensive cleaning or removal of particulate matter also constitutes intermediate repair.

16. Answer C – Code 97597 and 97602 are found in the medicine chapter and describe active open wound care (Ex. Decubitus ulcers). Beneath the Active Wound Care Management coding guidelines there is a notation that states "For debridement of burn wounds, see 16020- 16030). This eliminates options A and B. Code 16030 is used to describe the removal of dead tissue on second degree (partial thickness) burns. Not only is the degree of burn different, but in our scenario, there was no mention of tissue removal, only cleansing and incisions. This eliminates option D. Code 16035 describes an Escharotomy (note the suffix "– otomy" means to "cut into"). An Escharotomy is a procedure performed on healing third degree burns. Incisions are made into the thick dead tissue to keep underlying nerves and vessels from being

injured or constricted. Code 16036 is an add on code which is used in conjunction with code 16035. This add on code should be used for each additional incision. So, code 16035 describes the first incision and code 16036 x2 describes the second and third incision.

17. Answer B – Open fractures do not always utilize "open fracture treatment" codes. In the ICD- 10 an open fracture means that the skin has been broken. In the CPT book "open" and "closed" are term used to refer to the type of treatment. If the patient is taken to the operating room and an incision is made in order to visualize the fracture, this would be considered "open" treatment. If the physician manipulates the fracture without creating an opening it is considered "closed treatment". In this scenario the patient has an open fracture but "closed fracture treatment" is utilized. Codes 25574 describe an "open treatment" and so options A and C are incorrect. Option B and D both have the same CPT codes, but different modifiers. Any procedure with a 90 global period can be broken down into three portions: pre-operative assessment and/or decision for surgery; Surgical (the actual procedure); post-operative follow-up care. In this scenario the fracture care has a 90 global period and can be broken down into these three portions. The E/M service is considered the pre-operative evaluation and the decision for surgery since the patient has to give consent to proceed, because of this the E/M should have the 57-modifier appended. The 57 modifier describes "decision for surgery" (see appendix A). The 25 modifier is also appended to

the E/M because of the additional procedure (12031, laceration repair). The fracture care is considered the "surgical" portion of the package and so modifier 54 is appended to the fracture care code. Modifier 54 is used to describe "Surgical care only" (see appendix A). The HCPCS modifier RT is used to describe which arm was receiving care. (See appendix A for RT modifier's full description).

18. Answer D – Knowing medical terminology will help you choose the answer for this question. Specific medical prefixes usually fall under a specific heading, such as: The prefix "–otomy" which means to "cut into", is usually under the heading "incisions". The prefix "–ectomy" which means "to remove", is usually found under the "excision" heading. The prefixes "–plasty" and "–pexy" mean to repair, and so terms with these prefixes usually fall under the heading "repair", such as Scapulopexy. If you don't know medical terminology you can also try looking up the term scapulopexy in the index, which will lead you to code 23400. Code 23400 is under the heading "Repair, Revision, and/or Reconstruction".

19. Answer B – The procedure being performed in this question is a trigger point injection. Codes 64400 and 64520 are used to describe nerve blocks. These are injections involving the nervous system, instead of injecting muscles, as was done in our scenario. This eliminates options A and C. Codes 20552 and 20553 both describe trigger point injections and both codes include multiple injections. Code 20552 describes 1 or more injections into 1 – 2 muscles, and code 20553

describes 1 or more injections into 3 or more muscles. Since only one muscle was being injected multiple times, code 20552 is correct.

20. Answer B – In this scenario each answer has the identical codes, only with different modifiers. Modifiers can be referenced quickly on the CPT book's front cover, and can be found with a full description and guidelines in Appendix A. Guidance for this question really comes from looking at the guidelines above the two codes that were provided. According to osteotomy guidelines (above code 22206) when two surgeons work together as primary surgeons performing distinct parts of an anterior spine osteotomy each surgeon should report their distinct operative work by appending modifier 62 to the procedure code.

   62 Two Surgeons: When 2 surgeons work together as primary surgeons performing distinct part(s) of a procedure, each surgeon should report his/her distinct operative work by adding modifier 62 to the procedure code and any associated add-on code(s) for that procedure as long as both surgeons continue to work together as primary surgeons. Each surgeon should report the co-surgery once using the same procedure code. If additional procedure(s) (including add-on procedure[s]) are performed during the same surgical session, separate code(s) may also be reported with modifier 62 added. **Note:** If a co-surgeon acts as an assistant in the performance of additional procedure(s), other than those reported with the modifier 62, during the same surgical session, those

   services may be reported using separate procedure code(s) with modifier 80 or modifier 82 added, as appropriate.

21. Answer D – "Fracture care", as described by code 25600, includes pain management, fracture reduction (if necessary), and initial stabilization. Since the patient came into the physician's office with a cast already in place, we can deduct that the patient already received initial fracture care. Coding 25600

would be inappropriate then, because the patient was already charged for fracture care once. The physician performed only a cast application, as described by code 29075. Option C is also incorrect. Although the physician did remove the prior cast, it was never specified to be a full arm cast. I was most likely a short arm cast, but you cannot draw assumptions while coding.

Application of Casts and Strapping

▶ All services that appear in the Musculoskeletal System section include the application and removal of the first cast, splint, or traction device, when performed. Supplies are reported separately. If a cast is removed by someone other than the physician or other qualified health care professional who applied the cast, report the cast removal code (29700, 29705, 29710).

Subsequent replacement of cast, splint, or strapping (29000-29750) and/or traction device (eg, 20690, 20692) during or after the global period may be reported separately.

A cast, splint, or strapping is not considered part of the preoperative care; therefore, the use of modifier 56 for preoperative management only is not applicable. ◀

22. Answer B – Most CPT books (like the one published by the AMA and required by the AAPC for the CPC Exam), have diagrams with detailed descriptions accompanying these codes. If your CPT book has their diagrams, reading the detailed captions will direct you to the correct code selection. In this scenario the diagram provided for code 28290 describes the correct "medial eminence of the metatarsal bone" being removed, but since there is no mention of the Kirschner wire used to stabilize the joint, this code is incorrect. The diagram for code 28294 describes

a bunionectomy but describes a tendon transplant being an integral component of this procedure, and this was not performed in our question. The diagram for code 28298 describes the removal of the "medial eminence" and the Kirschener wire stabilization, but also includes the additional removal of several bone wedges from the base of the phalanx. Our scenario describes the surgeon cutting into the foot, moving tendons and other structures out of the way, removing the medial eminence, stabilizing the joint with Kirschner wire, and closing the patient up. This is procedure is best described by code 28292, and is accurately depicted in the accompanying diagram.

Hallux Valgus Correction
28292

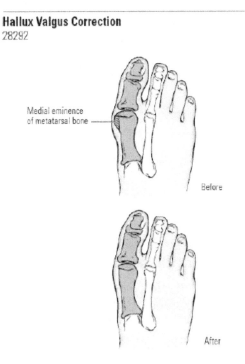

Medial eminence
of metatarsal bone

Before

After

23. Answer D – Option A and C share the same description and provide different age brackets and options B and

D share the same description and provide different age brackets. Option A and C are both for kids five years and under. Since our patient is 50 years old so we can eliminate options A and C. The difference between the remaining options B and D is the description "tunneled" catheter verses a "non-tunneled" catheter. A tunneled catheter is one that enters the body, tunnels under the skin, and exits the body in a different place. A non- tunneled catheter is one that enters the body and resides in the point of entry. Our scenario describes the catheter entering and residing in/near the point of entry (subclavian). Most CPT books (like the AMA's professional edition) provide diagrams of these procedures above or below the corresponding codes and include a short description of the process. The diagram for code 36556 specifically states "the catheter tip must reside in the subclavian, innominate, or other iliac veins".

24. Answer A – The right lung has three lobes so when two lobes are removed it is called a bilobectomy and when the whole lung is removed it is called a total pneumonectomy. The left lung only has two lobes (so the heart has room to expand). When one lobe of the left lung is removed it is called a lobectomy and when two lobes are removed it is called a total pneumonectomy (because the whole lung is being removed). Because our question describes the left lung, code 32482 is incorrect. Code 32482 describes a bi-lobectomy, but in the case of the left lung, that would be the entire lung (total pneumonectomy). A pleaurectomy is the removal if the pleura, not the lung or its lobes (32310). In our scenario a total

pneumonectomy was performed, and it was in an open fashion (not laparoscopically- 32663).

25. Answer A – In our scenario the surgeon took a biopsy of tissue from the mediastinal space using a scope. Noting that a scope was used we can eliminate options C and D because these are codes describing open procedures. The difference between option A and B is the approach used. A thoracoscopy of the mediastinal space (32606) approaches through the chest wall and then manipulate the scope from the thorax into the mediastinal space. Mediastinoscopies (39400) approach by making an incision under the sternal notch at the base of the throat and enter directly into the mediastinum.

26. Answer C – Reading the notations below several of these codes is how you will choose the best option here. Code 31237 states beside it "separate procedure", which means if it was performed at the same time as another procedure then it cannot be coded and is bundled into the primary procedure. This means option A and B can be eliminated because this code is listed. In addition, option B can also be eliminated because code 31201 describes. Also, 31295 and 31267 can't be coded together.

27. Answer D – Code 38308 describes surgery done on a lymphatic channel instead of a lymph node, so this code is incorrect. What the surgeon performed was a biopsy of a lymph node in the armpit (axillia). Code 38500 describes a biopsy, but is for a superficial one. The procedure describes dissection through the

fascia (this covers the muscle), and the full excision of the entire lymph node (which was then sent to pathology). Code 38510 has the correct common descriptor, which begins at code 38500 and reads "Biopsy or excision of lymph node(s);". The unique descriptor of this code describes the location being on the neck instead of the axillia though, so this code is also incorrect. Code 38525 accurately describes the biopsy/excision of the deep axillary nodes.

28. Answer D – In this question the surgeon placed a permanent dual chamber pace maker. Code 33240 in option A describes a cardioverter-defibrillator instead of a pacemaker, this rules out option A. Option B has the correct code 33208 to describe the pacemaker placement with leads in both the atrial and ventricular chambers. Codes 33225 and 33202 are incorrect though, because according to the pacemaker coding guidelines (found above code 33202) and the notations below code 33208, transvenous placement of electrodes is included in code 33208. Codes 33225 and 33202 should only be used when additional electrodes are placed. Code 33213 in option C describes only the battery portion of the unit being placed. The notation below this codes states that if electrodes are coded to use 33202 or 33203 (not code 33217, as given in option C). Option D accurately describes the placement of both the pacemaker generator and the two transvenous electrode.

29. Answer D – The term esophagogastroduodenoscopy (abbreviated EGD) describes the viewing of the

esophagus (esophago), the stomach (gastro), and the duodenum (duodeno), with a camera/scope (oscopy). Option A, 43202, describes an esophagoscopy with a biopsy, but does not move farther than the esophagus. Option B, 43206, describes use of a special type of optical endo-microscope (not mentioned in the description), and further, this code does not describe a full EGD. Option C correctly describes an EGD, but a tissue sample is not the same as obtaining cells through brushing or washing, since the physician actually took a sample, this code is also incorrect. Option D, code 43239, uses the same common descriptor in code 43235, but the unique descriptor (beside code 43239) correctly describes the tissue biopsy. There may also be a diagram of code 43235 which describes a scope going through the esophagus, stomach, and to the duodenum. This diagram may also help narrow down the options to C and D.

30. Answer C – By reading the Endoscopy coding guidelines (above code 45300) and the Colonoscopy "coding tip" (above code 45355) we can learn that a sigmoidoscopy is an endoscopy that advances to the descending colon but no further, and a colonoscopy is an endoscopy that advances past the splenic flexure, into the cecum, and may go as far as the terminal ileum. The physician had planned to advance into the cecum, which means he was going to perform a colonoscopy. He chose not to perform the entire colonoscopy though, due to unforeseen circumstances (fecal impaction). According to "coding tip" coding guidelines (above code 45355 in the AMA Professional Edition), we should still code

for the colonoscopy and then add modifier 53 to indicate that the entire procedure was not completed. This means that code 45378 with a 53 modifier is correct.

—— *Coding Tip* ———————————————————

Definition of Colonoscopy

Colonoscopy is the examination of the entire colon, from the rectum to the cecum, and may include the examination of the terminal ileum or small intestine proximal to an anastomosis.

When performing a diagnostic or screening endoscopic procedure on a patient who is scheduled and prepared for a total colonoscopy, if the physician is unable to advance the colonoscope to the cecum or colon-small intestine anastomosis due to unforeseen circumstances, report 45378 (colonoscopy) or 44388 (colonoscopy through stoma) with modifier 53 and provide appropriate documentation.

CPT Coding Guidelines, Endoscopy

31. Answer A – The operative note describes the open repair of a unilateral inguinal hernia with mesh placement (Marlex patch). Code 49505 accurately describes the repair of a unilateral inguinal hernia (open) and includes the mesh placement (see hernia coding guidelines above code 49491 which state in the fourth paragraph "With the exception of the incisional hernia repairs (49560-49566) the use of mesh or other prostheses is not separately reported"). Beneath code 49507 there is a notation stating that if a simple orchiectomy (removal of a testicle) is also performed during the hernia repair, that codes 49505 and/or 49507 should be used in conjunction with code 54520. In our scenario an orchiectomy was not performed though, so using codes 49505 or 49507

with code 54520 would be incorrect. This eliminates options B and D. Code 49568 describes the use of mesh during the repair of an incisional or ventral hernia only (our hernia was inguinal), and beneath this code is a list of the CPT codes it should be used in conjunction with. Code 49505 is not included in that list. Also, remember the hernia coding guidelines (above code 49491) states that "with the exception of the incisional hernia repairs (codes 49560-49566) the use of mesh or other prostheses in not separately reported".

32. Answer A – The operative note describes an endoscopic percutaneous gastrostomy tube placement. Code 43246 describes this correctly (see code 43235 for the common descriptor). Modifier 62 is needed because Dr. Smith only performed the tube placement. If he were to charge code 43246 with no modifier, he would be reimbursed for the EDG as well. Since Dr. Brown performed the EDG potion of this code he would also charge code 43246-62. This way each physician is reimbursed half. Code 49440 describes a non-endoscopic gastostomy tube placement. Code 43752 is also a non- endoscopic procedure. Code 43653 is a laparoscopic procedure, which means they created a small incision through which the camera entered the body; instead of an endoscopic procedure, which enters the body through an existing opening (ex. mouth).

33. Answer C – Code 43756 is not used for evacuation of stomach contents, but for things like bile studies. The duodenum is also where the stomach and small

intestine connect, which was not mentioned in our scenario. Code 43752 describes the placement of a permanent tube that is meant not for evacuation, but for introducing nutrients or medication into the body. Code 43753 is the correct code. Gastric intubation is the introduction of a tube into the stomach and aspiration is synonymous with evacuation. Some CPT books (like the AMA's professional edition) have an added diagram of this code and a detailed description that includes key terms like: "large-bore gastric lavage tube" and "evacuation of stomach contents". It also includes examples of why this code would be used, including poisonings. Option D describes a gastric intubation as well (which was performed here), but this code it is only performed for diagnostic purposes, not to correct an already known problem (which would be therapeutic).

34. Answer A – The digestive system is made up of two portions: the alimentary canal, and the accessory organs. The alimentary canal starts at the mouth and ends at the anus. The alimentary canal is also what food passes through during the digestive process. Parts of the alimentary canal include the mouth, esophagus, stomach, and intestines. Accessory organs are organs that aid in digestion but do not come in direct contact with the food. Accessory organs include the gallbladder, liver, and pancreas. This information is not listed in the CPT book. Since the AAPC allows notations to be made in your books, it is a good idea to make a notation regarding this beside your digestive system diagram (prior to code

40490 and following code 39599).

35. Answer D – This question describes a patient with renal calculi (kidney stone) and the procedure that breaks the stone into smaller pieces, which is called lithotripsy. The term "lith" means stone and the term "trip" means to break. Code 50590 describes the use of the lithotripsy wave machine (C-Arm image intensifier) to send shock waves from the outside of the body in (extracorpeal). This code may also have a diagram describing lithotripsy in more detail. Radiology codes, such as 74425 and 76770 were not utilized here. Code 50081 describes a percutaneous procedure that enters the kidney from the outside (likely using a needle), and then retrieves the stone, without destroying it. Codes 50060 & 50130 both describe open procedures. The suffix "–otomy" means to cut into. The terms nephrolithotomy and pyelolithotomy both mean to cut into the kidney (nephro and pyelo both mean kidney) and remove a stone (lith). Since neither an open procedure nor incisions were made in our scenario, these codes are also incorrect.

36. Answer B – Code 57155 describes the placement of small radioactive elements, which are left in the patient for the course of treatment prescribed and then later removed. Code 57156 describes the insertion of a vaginal radiation afterloading apparatus for clinical brachytherapy. This code should be used for the placement of vaginal cylinder rods, or similar afterloading devices. This procedure is also typically performed in a posthysterectomy

patient. An "afterloading apparatus" is described as a technique where the radioactivity is loaded after proper placement of the apparatus has been confirmed. The rods (or afterloading device) should have an access port on the outside of the body which can then be hooked up to an external machine which can deliver either high dose or low dose rate brachytherapy. Although the patient recently had a hysterectomy it does not state exactly how long ago or by whom, and since we cannot assume anything so modifier 58 is not applied.

37. Answer D – Our scenario in this question is describing a vasectomy. Option A describes the "ligation" of the vas deferens, which is one form of a vasectomy that ties off, or strangulates, the vas deferens in order to block the exit of semen. This procedure does not require any dissection or removal of the tube though, as is described in our scenario. Option B and C are used to describe a vasectomy reversal. As the two suffixes imply; -ostomy means to create a permanent opening (as in opening a ligated vas deferns) and –orraphy means to repair. Depending on the version of the CPT book you own, you may be able to locate common terms like these in the front of the manual (ex. AMA professional edition on page xiv). Code 55250 in option D accurately describes the performance of a vasectomy, unilateral or bilateral.

38. Answer C – PSA is an antigen tested in males to detect prostate cancer. Any reading over 10 is considered high. In this scenario the patient is having a prostate biopsy performed to determine is he

has prostate cancer or benign prostate hypertrophy. Option A describes a needle or catheter being place by the transperineal approach, for the purpose of entering small radioactive elements into the body to kill cancerous cells. Option B also describes a transperineal approach with the use of a needle for a prostate biopsy, however, it also describes a sterotactic template guided saturation sampling. A saturation biopsy is an alternative technique utilized by urologists to detect cancer in high risk patients by taking multiple samples (usually 30 or more). This code also includes the imaging guidance so a 70000 code (like 76942) should not be coded in addition to it. Code 55705 in option D is used to describe a biopsy taken by an open procedure. This would include an incision and repair. Code 55700 accurately describes a prostate biopsy, by needle or punch, by any approach (including retroperineal). Notations beneath this code also direct you to code 76942 for ultrasonic guidance if performed.

39. Answer A - A hydrocele is a pathological fluid filled sack within the scrotum. This question describes a bilateral hydrocelectomy of the tunic vaginalis. What makes this question more difficult is that medicinally a hydrocelectomy and a hydrocele repair are sometimes used synonymously. Code 54861in option B describes a procedure removing both of the Epididymis tubes and has no mention of a hydrocele, so this easily rules out option B. Code 55000-50 in option C describes a procedure performed on both tunic vaginalis, but it is a puncture aspiration (a hole punched with a needle to drain the fluid), so this can be ruled out as well since our physician performed an

incision and dissection. Code 55060 in option D and code 55041 in option A comes down to the type of procedure and its details. Code 55060 is a "bottle type procedure, also known as "Andrews Procedure". This procedure requires a 2-3cm incision in the hydrocele sack near the superior portion (or top) and requires tacking the cut edges around the cord structures, leaving the everted sac open. Also, when choosing between these two codes note the heading each one is under. Code 55041 is under the "Excision" heading and code 55060 is under the "Repair" heading. In a hydrocele excision (code 55041) the majority of the sac is removed. In a hydrocele repair (code 55060) the sac is cut open and the edges are tacked back. The procedure is also stated as being a "hydrocelectomy" and the suffix "–ectomy" means to remove (similar to the excision).

40. Answer B – Code 51797 should not be used without its primary code. Beneath code 51797 it states that this code should be used in addition to either code 51728 or 51729. Since options A and C utilized code 51797 without its primary code these two options are incorrect. Code 51729 utilizes the common descriptor next to code 51726 but also include its own unique descriptor "with voiding pressure studies", making its full description "Complex cystometrogram (i.e. Calibrated electronic equipment); with voiding pressure studies". Code 51797 is an add-on code describing the "intraabdominal" portion and notes that it should be used in addition to code 51729. This would make the codes in options B and C both correct. According to the Urodynamics coding

guidelines (above code 51725), if the physician did not provide the equipment and is simply operating it and interpreting the report then modifier 26 should be added to these codes. Since they physician in our scenario is utilizing hospital equipment and not his own adding modifier 26 would be correct.

41. Answer C – Code 62160 in options A and D describe the use of a neuroendoscope, which was not mentioned in our scenario, so these options are in correct. Options B and C are very similar, but code 61210 describes a burr hole and code 61107 describes a twist drill hole. The difference is that a burr hole is created with an electronic drill and a special bit, and the twist drill is a manually operated hand tool that is twisted to make a hole. Code 61107 also describes a puncture method (performed with a needle) instead of an incision made with a scalpel.

42. Answer A – Keratoplasty is the term for cornea transplant where the cornea of a donor is taken, frozen, reshaped and transplanted to the recipient

43. Answer C – The endocrine system codes start with code 6000 and end with code 60699. The first heading in the endocrine chapter is "thyroid gland". Following the codes through the chapter you come to code 60500 and the next (and final) heading (directly above this code), which reads "Parathyroid, Thymus, Adrenal Glands, Pancreas, and Carotid Body". The only organ not listed in the endocrine chapter is the Lymph nodes, which are part of the hemic-lymphatic system located at the end of the 30000 codes.

44. Answer C – The coding guidelines above code 69990 (operating microscope) state that it should not be coded in addition to multiple codes. Among the codes listed is code range 65091-68850. Since both code 67107 and 67101 are within that code range the operating microscope should not be coded with them. This eliminates options B and D. Code 67101 and code 67107 differ little, but code 67107 does include the terms "sclera buckling" and "with or without implant". The band placed around the eye causes sclera buckling and in scenario there was not an implant. This code is also further explained in some CPT books that contain diagrams.

45. Answer C – The neurosurgeon performed a crainiotomy (he cut into the skull; Craini means headand "–otomy" means to cut into), and drained an intracerebellar hematoma (which is a collection of blood). Code 61154 describes the burr hole accurately, but no craniotomy, it also describes the evacuation of the hematoma correctly, but it is missing the location (intracerebellum). This means you can eliminate options A and D. Code 61315 correctly describes the scenario, "Craniectomy or crainiotomy for evacuation of hematoma, infratentorial; intracerebellar. Although the neurosurgeon did create a burr hole during the procedure, notations beneath code 61253 state that "if burr holes or trephine are followed by a crainiotomy at the same operative session, use 61304-61321; do not use 61250 or 61253"

46. Answer B – The procedure performed is a repair to a fistula in the round window. Code 69666 and code 69667 both accurately describes this procedure, but code 69666 is performed on the oval window and code 69667 is performed on the round window. Options A and C can be ruled out, because they describe they utilize the oval window code instead of the round window code. There are no notations beneath code 69667 excluding modifier 50, and coding guidelines state that if a procedure is not stated it as a bilateral operation (or is not specified in the guidelines), then it is assumed to be uni-lateral. Since code 69667 is not noted as being bilateral we must assume it is unilateral. Since the surgeon performed this procedure on both ears modifier 50 would be correct. Code 69990 has a list of CPT codes it cannot be coded in conjunction with (see Operating Microscope Coding Guidelines above code 69990), however, code 69667 is not one of them, therefore, coding 69990 in addition to code 69667 is correct.

47. Answer C - This code states that the visit may not (necessarily) require the presence of a physician or other qualified health care professional (such as LPN, MA). However, physicians or other qualified health care professionals may use this code when they provide this type of E/M. Code 99211 would apply in this circumstance since the patient was seen by an LPN. The description of this code also gives a hint, as it states these codes are for visits that are "typically 5 minutes".

48. Answer D – Option A, B and C are incorrect because it is for Office or other outpatient codes. Hence D is the answer.

▶ Hospital Inpatient or Observation Care Services (Including Admission and Discharge Services) ◀

▶ The following codes are used to report hospital inpatient or observation care services provided to patients admitted and discharged on the same date of service.

For patients admitted to hospital inpatient or observation care and discharged on a different date, see 99221, 99222, 99223, 99231, 99232, 99233, 99238, 99239.

Codes 99234, 99235, 99236 require two or more encounters on the same date of which one of these encounters is an initial admission encounter and another encounter being a discharge encounter. For a patient admitted and discharged at the same encounter (ie, one encounter), see 99221, 99222, 99223. Do not report 99238, 99239 in conjunction with 99221, 99222, 99223 for admission and discharge services performed on the same date. ◀

▶ (For discharge services provided to newborns admitted and discharged on the same date, use 99463) ◀

⚠ 99234   **Hospital inpatient or observation care,** for the evaluation and management of a patient including admission and discharge on the same date, which requires a medically appropriate history and/or examination and straightforward or low level of medical decision making.

When using total time on the date of the encounter for code selection, 45 minutes must be met or exceeded.

⚠ 99235   **Hospital inpatient or observation care,** for the evaluation and management of a patient including admission and discharge on the same date, which requires a medically appropriate history and/or examination and moderate level of medical decision making.

When using total time on the date of the encounter for code selection, 70 minutes must be met or exceeded.

49. Answer D – If you were to compare the 99291 codes in A and C to the 99471 codes in B and D you would discover that the critical care code 99291, although good, is incorrect. The 99471 is for initial critical care for an inpatient pediatric (29 day old to 24 months). This code is more specific since the patient was admitted (inpatient) and is only 20 months old (pediatric). This then narrows down your options between B and D. B is incorrect because it includes a charge for the intubation, which according to the pediatric critical care coding guidelines, is a bundled service.

50. Answer D – The physician performed three services: Stand by, resuscitation, and an E/M. By reading the descriptions of these codes and the guidelines provided for each code, you can determine which of them can or cannot be code in conjunction with one another. The coding guidelines for code 99360 state that the code "should not be used if the period of standby ends with the performance of a procedure". Initially you would think that this would then rule out the use of this code since Dr. Smith did end up rendering a procedure (resuscitation). However, there is a special notation in parentheses beneath code 99360 that states "99360 may be reported in addition to 99460, 99465 as appropriate". The next CPT code 99465 describes new born resuscitation in the delivery room. This was the procedure that Dr. Smith provided, and is correct. The last code is 99460. This code describes the new born E/M that the physician provided. This code has no special notations or exclusions and is also correct. There is also a notation beneath code 99465 that states "99465 may be reported in conjunction with 99460". This means that all three codes can be used together.

51. Answer D – Comparing code 99387 to 99397: Both are for an annual wellness exam, and according to their descriptions, include age/gender appropriate history, exam, counseling (ex. smoking cessation), guidance, risk factors, etc. Code 99387 is for a new patient though and 99397 is for an established patient (both state the correct age). Since Mr. Johnson is stated as being an established patient, options A and B can be eliminated because of code 99387 (new patient). For options C and D you will then compare codes

99205 and 99215. Both of these codes describe an in-office E/M with a primary care physician. Code 99205 is for a new patient. This code is incorrect because the patient is established (not new), and the MDM provided was only of moderate complexity (this code requires high complexity MDM). Code 99214 is for an established patient and the MDM for this code states moderate, which the physician provided. This means option D, which includes both 99397 and 99214, is correct.

52. Answer C – Rationale: When neonatal services are provided in the outpatient setting, Inpatient Neonatal Critical Care guidelines direct the coder to use critical care codes 99291 Critical care, evaluation and management of the critically ill or critically injured patient; first 30-74 minutes and 99292 … each additional 30 minutes (List separately in addition to code for primary service). Care is documented as lasting 45 minutes with the physician in constant attendance. The physician also administered intrapulmonary surfactant (94610), placed an umbilical vein line (36510) and intubated the patient (31500). These services can be separately billed as they are not included in 99291.

53. Answer C – The answer to this question is located in the Anesthesia coding guidelines under the title "Time Reporting"

54. Answer B – The lining surrounding the heart is called the pericardium, knowing this term helps to narrow down the options. Code 00560 accurately describes

the surgery that was performed; however, this code is meant to be used for patients over the age of 1, and does not include the oxygenator pump. Code 00561, in answer B, states that this code is for children under 1 year of age and includes an oxygenator pump. When the age is specified in the code's description it is not necessary to add a qualifying circumstance code (99100), re-stating the extreme age. Also stated directly beneath code 00561, there is a notation stating "Do not report 00561 in conjunction with 99100, 99116, and 99135". This eliminates option D. Option C is incorrect because it does not describe surgery on the pericardium, but on the great vessels of the heart instead.

55. Answer C - By recognizing the patient's age you can narrow down your options to A or C (because of the qualifying circumstance code 99100 depicts extreme age, which is patients under the age of 1 and over the age of 70). Qualifying circumstance codes can also be located in either the Anesthesia coding guidelines and/or in the medicine chapter. Knowing your medical terminology will also help you eliminate options here. Option A describes a ten-otomy, the term "-otomy" means to cut into, or to make an incision. Option B describes a teno-desis, the suffix "–esis" means to remove fluid. In our question a repair was being done though. Code 01714 uses the term tenoplasty, and the suffix "– plasty" means to repair. Option C and D provide the same code, but D does not list the qualifying circumstance code 99100. Also, the P modifier for severe asthma would be P3.

56. Answer B – The answer to this question is found in the bottom half of paragraph two in the Anesthesia coding guidelines.

57. Answer C – The full CPT code has both components, technical and professional, and if the physician did not perform both components, he cannot be reimbursed for them both. The TC modifier is used to depict the technical component, which is what the radiologist often utilizes. Modifier 26 is the professional component, which is what the physician should append to his CPT code. Modifier 52 is used when a physician must terminate a procedure or attempts an entire procedure but has unsuccessful results. A full description of modifiers 26 and 52 can be found in appendix A. Modifier TC in a HCPCS modifier and should be referenced in the HCPCS book.

58. Answer A – According to the chart provided above code 74176, the guidelines above that, and the notation beneath code 74178, code 74178 is a standalone code. Guidelines state "do not report more than one CT of the abdomen or CT of the pelvis for any single session". Using the chart, the last box across the top should be selected (in bold) "74170 CT of the Abdomen without contrast followed by with contrast (abbreviated WO//W Contrast)", and the top box on the side should be selected, "72192, CT of the Pelvis without contrast (abbreviated WO Contrast)". Following both selections to the point where they meet you end up in the last box in the first (non-bold) column, which contains code "74178". Notations

beneath this code state, "Do not report 74176 – 74178 in conjunction with 72192 – 72194, 74150 – 74170.

59. Answer A – The "Aorta and Arteries" coding guidelines (above code 75600) state that a diagnostic angiography may be reported with an interventional procedure when performed together under specific circumstances. One such circumstance is when a prior report is recorded in the medical record but states there is inadequate visualization of the anatomy. These guidelines also state modifier 59 would need to be appended to the diagnostic radiological supervision and interpretation. To find this information you would use the alphabetic index and look up the term "angiography". The index would direct you to "see aortography". Looking up the term "Aorta, aortography" would lead you to code 75600, and the guidelines above it.

60. Answer B – For the bone biopsy, code 20225 accurately describes a percutaneous, deep bone, biopsy. Code 20245 describes the same thing; only open instead of percutaneous (requiring an incision instead of a needle). Code 38221 is a biopsy of the bone marrow (not the actual bone). Beneath code 20225 the notations state to use either code 77002, 77012, or 77021 for radiological supervision and interpretation. Code 77012 accurately depicts the CAT scan (computed tomography). Code 76998 describes the use of an ultrasound instead of a CAT scan, and code 73700 is used when a diagnostic CAT scan is being taken, not a procedural one.

61. Answer A – There is little difference between codes

78451 and 78453. Code 78451 is done by SPECT and includes attenuation correction and code 78453 is a planar type image. In our scenario code 78451 is correct. This rules-out options B and D. According to the Radiology Cardiovascular System coding guidelines, (above code 78414), when a myocardial perfusion study using codes 78451-78454 or 78472-78492 is performed in conjunction with a stress test, then the stress test should be coded in addition to the study using codes 93015 – 93018. In our scenario code 93016 is correct because the physician did not provide the interpretation and report (the cardiologist did).

62. Answer C – The fluid at the back of the fetuses' neck is also known as the nuchal fold or the nuchal translucency. When this is too thick it is an indication, the fetus may have Down syndrome. Option A describes an ultrasound for both the fetuses and the mother. In our scenario only the fetuses are being evaluated though, so this eliminates option A. Option B also includes a maternal evaluation, so this too is incorrect. Option C correctly describes the first trimester, fetus evaluation only, is specific to the nuchal translucency, and includes a transabdominal approach. Add-on code 76814 is also correct when reporting multiple gestations, (per. notations beneath code 76814, it should be used in conjunction with code 76813 when reporting multiple gestations). Option D describes a re-evaluation to confirm a prior finding. In our scenario there is no mention of a prior screening.

63. Answer C – When coding a panel every test in that panel must be performed or that panel cannot be coded. Every code listed in our scenario is listed beneath code 80053 except the TSH (which is coded using code 84443). Code 80053 also has an additional test for Albumin listed. Since an Albumin level was not ordered we cannot use code 80053, even with a 52 modifier. This eliminates option A. Option B lists total calcium levels being ordered instead of ionized calcium levels, so this is incorrect. Option C is correct because every test listed beneath code 80047 was ordered. In addition to 80047, the lab tests not listed are accurately coded individually. Option D seems like a good option because it does accurately capture each test listed in our scenario, however, code 80047 captures a larger number of tests while still being correct and utilizes fewer codes overall which makes this the better option. When give the option between choosing a panel or listing each test individually, you should select the panel.

64. Answer A – Only a gross examination was performed here. There is no mention of a microscopic examination, so even though an ovary is not specifically listed beneath code 88300, it is the only code that does not include the microscopic examination.

65. Answer B – Appendix "A" has a full description of each modifier and how it should or should not be used. Modifier 99 should be used when a single CPT code has two or more modifiers appended to it. Modifier 99

could be used in place of the multiple modifiers and the specific modifiers could then be listed elsewhere on a claim form. Modifier 76 is meant to be used on a service and/or procedure code, not laboratory codes. The use of modifier 76 eliminates option A. Modifier 91 is meant to be used on laboratory codes, and is used to when a test is purposely ran more than once on the same day. Modifier 91 should only be appended to the second test and beyond though, and not to the first test performed (like in option C). Option B is correct because it lists each test once without a modifier and then the second and third time each of those tests were ran modifier 91 was appended, indicating that it was actually performed multiple times in one day. If option D was billed, the insurance company would pay each test only once and then deny the second and third time the test was run as a "duplicate charge", this is because the 91 modifier was not appended to indicate they were not duplicates.

66. Answer B – Code 81005 is used for an analysis of the urine for things like protein, glucose, and bacteria. This is often performed by way of a dip stick and may be accompanied by a microscopic examination. This is not what is described in our scenario, and eliminates options A and D. Code 81025 accurately describes a urine test that provides a positive or negative result, in this case, pregnancy. Code 84702 and 84703 are both used when testing for the growth hormone hCG. Code 84703 is a qualitative test and tests if hCG is present or not. Code 84702 is a quantitative test, usually run to confirm a pregnancy, and provides a specific level of the hormone, such as

12500 mIU/ml.

67. Answer B – Code 89255 is used to describe a fertilized egg being prepared for implantation into a woman's uterus. Code 89258 is the code used when taking an embryo and preserving it by freezing, (the medical prefix cryo- means cold). This is what the technician did in our scenario. Code 89268 describes the egg (oocyte) being fertilized with the sperm to form a zygote. And code 89342 is a code that is used when an embryo is already frozen and is simply being stored.

68. Answer D – A glucose tolerance test (GTT) requires the patient to have a blood draw prior to the glucose, they then receive glucose in some form, and then have their blood drawn at intervals to determine how their body metabolizes the glucose. Code 82951 is the correct code for this test and includes the pre-glucose blood draw, the glucose dose, and the three blood draws following the ingestion. Code 82946 is also a tolerance test, but it is for glucagon and not glucose. Code 82950 is a glucose test that is very similar to the GTT, but does not require a blood draw prior to the glucose and is usually only checked once, 2 hours after the glucose dose is received. According to appendix "A" modifier 91 should not be used when a test is re-run due to a testing problem. Because the issue was caused by the laboratory the patient's insurance should not be charged for two tests.

69. Answer A – The physician did not perform the actual EKG but ordered another individual to run it, so the physician cannot charge code 93000 which

includes reimbursement for performing the test. In this scenario code 93010 would accurately describe the report and interpretation. This eliminates options B and D. Normal saline (NS) was also infused for 1 hour and 45 minutes. According to the hydration coding guidelines (above code 96360), normal saline is included in the 96360 and 96361 codes and can be charged by a physician who is supervising, but not actually performing, the hydration. Code 96360 may only be reported once for the initial hour and each increment of time beyond that must utilize the add-on code 96361. Although the 96361-code description says it is for each additional hour, a notation beneath the code states that code 96361 may be used for time increments of 30 minutes or greater if the total infusion time is at least 1 hour and 30 minutes (or longer).

70. Answer D – Reading the "End-Stage Renal Disease Services" coding guidelines (above code 90951) is the key to selecting this code. According to these guidelines code 90960 is used when providing these services in an out-patient setting (like a physician's office), not for home dialysis. This eliminates option A. Code 90966 is for home dialysis and correctly describes our patient's age bracket (20 and older), however, according to the coding guidelines these codes cannot be used for patients receiving services for less than a full month (30 days). This eliminates option B. Code 90970 is the correct code, but per. the description of this code, and per. the coding guidelines, this code should be reported for each day of service outside any inpatient setting. This

eliminates option C and makes option D correct. The physician performed dialysis on the 15th – 18th (4 days), and then resumed dialysis on the 25th – 31st (7 days). For the month the physician should charge 11 days

71. Answer B – The simplest way to code this would be to code for one day and then just multiple that for the number of visits in the month. When coding for a single day you would use code 99601 as the initial peritoneal infusion code and code 99602 for the additional hour. These codes would be used on all three days the nurse visits and code 99509 would be added on once each week for the additional services performed on Fridays. Code 90966 would not be correct because this code is only for physician use (not nurses). Code 99512 is also incorrect because this code is for hemodialysis and not peritoneal dialysis. Beneath this code there is even a notation stating that if coding for home infusion of peritoneal dialysis to use codes 99601 and 99602. The number of Mondays, Wednesdays, and Fridays in the month add up to 13, It would be incorrect to code one initial infusion code (99601) and the rest of the visits as code (99602 x25), because code 99601 states that it should be used "per visit". This means that code 99601 should be used for each individual date of service with the add-on code 99602 for each date of service. (99601 x13 and 99602 x13). In a month there were also 4 Fridays and so code 99509 would be coded as 99509 x4.

72. Answer D –Code 93923 includes what is described in our scenario, but also has additional studies as well

(ex. 3 levels instead of 2 levels of plethymograohy volume were taken, 3 or more oxygen tension measurements are taken instead of 2. Etc.) This eliminates options A and B. Code 93922 accurately describes what is performed in our scenario. Requirements for using this code are also given in the coding guidelines (above code 93880), under the heading "Noninvasive Vascular Diagnostic Studies", in the 5th paragraph titled, "Limited studies for lower extremity". These guidelines stipulations include items stated in our questions, such as " ABI's (ankle/ brachial indices) being taken at the posterior (back) and anterior (front) lower aspects of the tibial and tibial/dorsalis pedis arteries; Plethymography levels; Oxygen tension reading, etc. The notation beneath code 93922 also states that if a single extremity, (instead of both), are being studied to append modifier 52 to the procedure code.

73. Answer B – Code 91010 is a manometric study, but it is of the esophagus (throat) and/or where the stomach and esophagus meet (gastroesophageal junction; gastro meaning stomach and esophageal meaning the esophagus). Code 91020, (Gastric motility), is also a manometric study, and accurately describes our scenario. The term "gastric" (or gastro), means the stomach and the word "motility" is a biological term referring to the ability to move. In this case it is referring to the ability of food to move through the stomach. Code 91022 is similar to code 91020, except the anatomical location is different, it is studying the duodenum. The duodenum is the first portion of the small intestine, and code 91022 is the

study of movement through this. Code 0240T is a category III code located between category II codes and Appendix A in the back of the CPT book. Code 0240T is also a motility study but this particular code is for study of just the esophagus and/or gastroesophageal junction, and does not include the stomach and gastric outlet into the small intestine.

74. Answer A – To the left of each code are listed any coding conventions. Conventions each have their own meaning which can be found with a short description at the bottom of each page or in their full description at the front of the CPT book. The coding convention that looks like a lightning bolt means "FDA approval pending". Codes 90666, 90667, and 90668 each have this convention listed beside them. Code 90664 does not have this coding convention listed beside it; hence we know it has FDA approval.

75. Answer B – Cutting into is the term "otomy"; surgical removal is the "ectomy"; a permanent opening is the term "ostomy"; surgical repair is the term "plasty". Some CPT books have common medical terms like these listed in the first few pages of the book.

76. Answer C – In your CPT book turn to the index and look up the word vaccination. Indented beneath vaccination look for the abbreviation MMRV or the word Measles. You will see the full description "Measles, Mumps, Rubella, and Varicella" and beneath it you will see the abbreviation MMRV.

77. Answer D – Each term listed can be looked up in the

CPT book's index (if they do not exist in the index move to the next one). Beside the term magnetic resonance imaging you will see the abbreviation MRI.

78. Answer A – Knowing some medical terminology is useful here. The term "salp" means tube, the term "ooph" refers to the ovary, and the suffix "ectomy" means to surgically remove. Some CPT books have common medical terms like these listed in the first few pages of the book.

79. Answer B – The answer to this question can be found the same two ways as the explanation above describes

80. Answer C – Some CPT books will have a few diagrams located in the front of the CPT book. These diagrams describe body planes, regions, quadrant, and directional terms (Ex. Posterior). If your book does not contain these diagrams try looking up the term "femur, fracture, and then each term (distal, etc.)" in the index. The terms that do not exist in the index should indicate they are not the correct answer. Flip to the code provided for the terms that are in the index and look at any anatomical diagrams. Ex. Femur, fracture, distal gives codes 27508, 27510, and 27514. If a diagram is not provided remember that CPT codes are sequenced from the top of the body down, so code 27508 is closer to the hip (top of the body) and code 27514 is closer to the knee.

81. Answer D – Again, look for an anatomical diagram first. Either in the front of the CPT or in the guidelines of the digestive system. If no diagrams are provided in

your book, then try looking up the term "abdominal" in your CPT or ICD-10 book and search for diagrams or wording to help you.

82. Answer B – This is another occasion that either you will find the answer in the diagrams in the front of your CPT book, or your book does not provide them. If you do not have these diagrams then this question would need to be an educated guess. Knowing medical terminology could also assist here. In this case the term "mid" means middle.

83. Answer D – The correct open wound code is S51.829A because the wound has a foreign body. In the alphabetic index under the term "open, wound" there is a box that describe when to use the "complicated" option (this includes foreign bodies and infections). By selecting code S51.829A, your choices are narrowed down to option B or D. Option B has a second code describing a fall resulting in striking a sharp object. This is incorrect because she struck the stove top (which was not sharp until it was broken by her fall). Option D's second code describes falling and striking an object and W45.8XXA describes being cut by broken glass.

84. Answer B

85. Answer C – The patient does not have macular edema.

86. Answer A – This is true according the ICD-10-CM coding guidelines, Signs and symptoms that are associated routinely with a disease process should

not be assigned as additional codes, unless otherwise instructed by the classification.

87. Answer C – The coding guidelines, (found at the beginning of the ICD-10-CM manual), specify the HIV coding rules, these guidelines state that Z21 should be coded for asymptomatic HIV that has no documented symptoms, and may include the terms "HIV positive", "known HIV", and "HIV test positive".

88. Answer C – Options A and D can be eliminated when comparing codes A6204 and A6252. Code A6204 states composite dressing is used and code A6252 states special absorptive sterile dressing is used (which is correct). When choosing between options B and C code A6219 meets the correct size requirements and also has an adhesive border.

89. Answer D – Option A is a plaster cast so it is incorrect. Option B is for a pediatric cast and it states beneath the code that a pediatric cast is considered 0-10 years old, since the patient is 12 this code would be incorrect. Option C meets most of the description but it is for a splint and not a cast.

90. Answer C – The correct answer is C for J9070. Neosar directs you to Cyclophosphamide 100 mg, which is a Chemotherapy drug used intravenously. Answer A for J9100 is for Cytarabine 100 mg, which is not the correct medication. Answer B for J7502 is for Cyclosporine oral medication, which is an immunosuppressive drug. Answer D is J8999 and is a prescription oral chemotherapeutic drug and our

patient is getting IV infusion.

91. Answer 14060, C44.129, The correct CPT code for this procedure is 14060, which is defined as "Excision, tumor, soft tissue of face or scalp, subcutaneous; less than 2.0 cm." This code covers the excision of the squamous cell carcinoma on the left lower eyelid. The correct ICD-10 code is C44.129, which is defined as "Squamous cell carcinoma of skin of unspecified eyelid, including canthus." This code accurately describes the diagnosis of the patient's squamous cell carcinoma of the left lower eyelid.

It's important to note that ICD-10 codes describe the patient's diagnosis, while CPT codes describe the procedures performed during the patient's visit. Accurate coding ensures proper documentation, billing, and reimbursement for medical services.

92. Answer 95970, he correct CPT code for the described procedure is 95970, which is defined as "Electronic analysis of implanted neurostimulator pulse generator system (e.g., rate, pulse amplitude, pulse duration, configuration of wave form, battery status, electrode selectability, output modulation, cycling, impedance and patient compliance measurements); simple or complex brain, spinal cord, or peripheral (i.e., cranial nerve, peripheral nerve, sacral nerve, neuromuscular) neurostimulator pulse generator/ transmitter, without reprogramming."

The procedure described in the scenario involves the analysis of a vagal nerve stimulator (VNS) implant, which is a type of neurostimulator. The programming head was placed over the implanted neurostimulator to verify impedance and ensure that the parameters were within normal limits. The estimated time for the analysis was 20 minutes. The procedure did not involve any reprogramming of the device.

Therefore, based on the description provided, CPT code 95970 is the most appropriate code to report for this procedure.

93. Answer 91035, The correct CPT code for this procedure is 91035, which is used for esophageal pH monitoring with Bravo pH Capsule. This code covers the placement and recording of the pH capsule and the subsequent data analysis and interpretation. It is important to note that the post-procedure diagnosis of GERD should be used for coding, as specified in the provided information.

94. Answer 77067, Z12.31, Z80.3, The CPT® code reported for this service is 77067 - Screening mammography, bilateral (two view study of each breast), including computer-aided detection (CAD) when performed.

The ICD-10-CM codes reported for this service are:

Z12.31 - Encounter for screening mammogram for malignant neoplasm of breast

Z80.3 - Family history of malignant neoplasm of breast

The reason for reporting Z12.31 is that the patient underwent a screening mammogram for breast cancer, and Z80.3 is reported because the patient has a positive family history of breast cancer.

It is also worth noting that the imaging center should report the global component for the professional component of the mammogram interpretation, which is not reported in the CPT® code.

95. Answer 00520-AA-QS-P3, the correct CPT code reported for anesthesia is 00520-AA-QS-P3.

The CPT code 00520 is used to report anesthesia for procedures performed on the lower abdomen, including the peritoneum, and pelvic organs. The AA modifier indicates that the anesthesia is performed by an anesthesiologist, and the QS modifier indicates that the service is a monitored anesthesia care.

The P3 modifier is used to indicate that the patient has a severe systemic disease, which is reflected in the physical status of 3 mentioned in the clinical information.

Therefore, the correct CPT code reported for anesthesia in this case is 00520-AA-QS-P3

96. Answer 32551, S27.2XXA, J20, The correct CPT code for the procedure described is 32551 - Tube thoracostomy, includes connection to drainage system.

The ICD-10-CM diagnosis code for traumatic pneumothorax/hemothorax/pleural effusion is S27.2XXA - Traumatic pneumothorax with open wound into thorax, initial encounter.

Additionally, J20 - Acute bronchitis is included as a secondary diagnosis since it was mentioned in the procedure note that a follow-up CXR has been ordered for placement.

Therefore, the reported codes are:

CPT code: 32551

ICD-10-CM codes: S27.2XXA, J20

97. Answer 32663-RT, C34.31, CPT Code: 32663-RT (Anatomic pulmonary lobectomy, lower lobe, open or thoracoscopic approach)

This is the Current Procedural Terminology (CPT) code for anatomic pulmonary lobectomy, which is the surgical removal of a lobe of the lung. In this case, the code is modified with RT to indicate that the procedure was performed on the right side of the body. The code also specifies that the procedure can be performed using an open approach or a thoracoscopic approach, which is the minimally invasive technique used in this case.

ICD Code C34.31: This is the International Classification of Diseases (ICD) code for malignant neoplasm (cancer) of the lower lobe of the right lung. This code is used to indicate the reason for the procedure, which was the presence of a small cell carcinoma in the right lower lobe of the lung.

Note: RT is used to indicate that the procedure was performed on the right side of the body.

98. Answer 54161, N47.1, CPT code: 54161 (Circumcision, surgical excision of foreskin (including local anesthesia and follow-up care))

ICD-10 code: N47.1 (Phimosis)

The voiding dysfunction and sexual dysfunction are not specific enough to assign a separate diagnosis code, so they would not be reported separately. It's possible that they would be considered symptoms of the phimosis and not warrant separate coding.

99. Answer 62230, 62225, the correct CPT code to report for this procedure is actually a combination of codes 62230 and 62225.

Code 62230 is for the insertion of a ventricular catheter for drainage of cerebrospinal fluid without the use of image guidance. This code is appropriate for the insertion of the new ventricular catheter.

Code 62225 is for the revision or replacement of a ventricular catheter using image guidance. In this case, the documentation mentions that the right parietal scalp incision was reopened and the shunt catheter was identified. It is possible that image guidance was used during this part of the procedure, although it is not explicitly stated in the documentation. Therefore, it would be appropriate to report code 62225 in addition to code 62230.

So, the correct CPT code to report for this procedure would be 62230 for the insertion of the new ventricular catheter and 62225 for the revision of the existing ventricular catheter. Both codes would be reported together to accurately describe the procedure that was performed.

100. Answer 43246, R63.3, K29.80, The surgery code reported is 43246, which represents the placement of a percutaneous endoscopic gastrostomy (PEG) tube.

The ICD-10 diagnosis codes reported are:

R63.3 - Feeding difficulties

K29.80 - Duodenitis, unspecified, without bleeding

Therefore, the full diagnosis code is: R63.3 + K29.80.

EXAM D

1) The Medicare program is made up of several parts. Which part is affected by the Centers for Medicare and Medicaid Services - hierarchal condition categories (CMS-HCC)?
   a) Part A
   b) Part B
   c) Part C
   d) Part D

2) Healthcare providers are responsible for developing _____ and policies and procedures regarding privacy in their practices.
   a) Patient hotlines
   b) Work around procedures
   c) Fees
   d) Notices of Privacy Practices

3) How many components should be included in an effective compliance plan?
   a) 3
   b) 4

c) 7

d) 9

4) According to the AAPC Code of Ethics, Member shall use only ___ and ___ means in all professional dealings.
   a) private and professional
   b) efficient and inexpensive
   c) legal and profitable
   d) legal and ethical

5) Which option below is NOT a covered entity under HIPAA?
   a) Medicare
   b) Medicaid
   c) BCBS
   d) Worker's' Compensation

6) Muscle is attached to bone by what method?
   a) Tendons, ligaments, and directly to bone
   b) Tendons and aponeurosis
   c) Tendons, aponeurosis and directly to bone
   d) Tendons, ligaments, aponeurosis, and directly to bone

7) Which respiratory structure is comprised of cartilage and ligaments?
   a) Alveoli
   b) Lung
   c) Bronchiole
   d) Trachea

8) Upon leaving the last portion of the small intestine, nutrients move through the large intestine in what order?
   a) Cecum, transverse colon, ascending colon, descending colon, sigmoid colon, rectum, anus
   b) Cecum, ascending colon, transverse colon, descending

colon, sigmoid colon, rectum, anus
- c)   Cecum, ascending colon, transverse colon, sigmoid colon, descending colon, rectum, anus
- d)   Cecum, descending colon, transverse colon, ascending colon, sigmoid colon, rectum, anus

9)   What are chemicals which relay amplify and modulate signals between a neuron and another cell?
- a) Neurotransmitters
- b) Hormones
- c) Interneurons
- d) Myelin

10) A surgeon performs an "escharotomy." This procedure is best described as:
- a)   Removal of scar tissue resulting from burns or other injuries
- b) Removal of a basal cell carcinoma
- c) Debridement of a pressure ulcer
- d) Removal of a fingernail

11) A vesiculotomy is defined as:
- a) Removal of an obstruction from the vas deferens
- b) Surgical cutting into the seminal vesicles
- c) Removal of one of the seminal vesicles
- d) Incision into the prostate

12) A form of milk produced the first few days after giving birth is:
- a) Chorion
- b) Lactose
- c) Colostrum
- d) Prolactin

13) The root for pertaining to uterus is:
   a) Cyt/o
   b) Hyster/o
   c) Pancreat/o
   d) Endocrin/o

14) What is the meaning of "provider" in the ICD-10-CM guidelines refers to?
   a) the hospital
   b) the physician
   c) insurance Company
   d) the patient

15) When can you use the code for HIV (B20)?
   a) The test result is inconclusive
   b)   The test result is confirmed by the physician's diagnostic statement
   c) Known HIV without symptoms
   d) Suspected HIV

16) The instructions and conventions of the classification take precedence over?
   a) Physicians
   b) Official Coding Guidelines
   c) CPT
   d)   Nothing, they are only used in the event of no other instruction.

17) What diagnosis code(s) should be reported for spastic cerebral palsy due to meningitis?
   a) G03.9, G80.1
   b) G80.1, G09
   c) G80.1, G03.9

d) G09, G80.1

18) 32-year-old sees her obstetrician about a lump in the right breast. Her mother and aunt both have a history of breast cancer. What diagnosis code(s) should be reported?
a) N63, Z85.3
b) N63.10
c) C50.919, Z80.3
d) N63.10, Z80.3

19) A 50-year-old female visits her physician with symptoms of insomnia and upset stomach. The physician suspects she is pre-menopausal. His diagnosis is impending menopause. What diagnosis code(s) should be reported?
a) G47.00, K30
b) N92.0
c) Z78.0, G47.09, K30
d) Z78.0

20) When the type of diabetes mellitus is not documented in the medical note, what is used as the default type?
a) Type II
b) Type I
c) Can be Type I or II
d) Secondary

21) A patient is coming in for follow-up of his essential hypertension and cardiomegaly. Both conditions are stable and he is told to continue with his medications. What ICD-10-CM code(s) should be reported?
a) I11.9, I51.7
b) I51.7, I10

c) I11.9
d) I51.7

22) A 2-month-old is seeing his pediatrician for a routine health check examination. The physician notices a diaper rash and prescribes an ointment to treat it. What ICD-10-CM code(s) should be reported?
   a) L22
   b) Z00.121, L22
   c) L22, Z00.121
   d) Z00.129, L22

23) A patient is coming in for follow-up of a second-degree burn on the arm. The physician notes the burn is healing well. He is to come back in two weeks for another check-up. What ICD-10-CM code(s) should be reported?
   a) Z51.89, T22.20XA
   b) T22.20XD
   c) Z09, T22.20XD
   d) Z09

24) 40-year-old woman, 25-weeks-pregnant with her second child, is seeing her obstetrician. She is worried about decreased fetal movement. During the examination the obstetrician detects bradycardia in the fetus. What ICD-10-CM code(s) should be reported?
   a) O09.12, O09.41
   b) P29.12, O09.41
   c) O09.41, O09.522
   d) O09.522, O76

25) HCPCS Level II includes code ranges which consist of what type of codes?
   a)   Category II codes, temporary national codes, miscellaneous codes, permanent national codes.
   b)   Dental codes, morphology codes, miscellaneous codes,

temporary national codes, permanent national codes.

c) Permanent national codes, dental codes, category II codes.

d) Permanent national codes, miscellaneous codes, dental codes, and temporary national codes.

26) A patient is seen in the OR for an arthroscopy of the medial compartment of his left knee. What is the correct coding to report for the Anesthesia services?
   a) 01400
   b) 01402
   c) 29870-LT
   d) 29880-LT

27) What is the correct CPT code for the wedge excision of skin of nail fold for an ingrown toenail?
   a) 11720
   b) 11750
   c) 11765
   d) 11760

28) What is the code for partial laparoscopic colectomy with anastamosis and coloproctostomy?
   a) 44208
   b) 44210
   c) 44145
   d) 44207

29) What is the correct CPT code for strabismus reparative surgery performed on 2 horizontal muscles?
   a) 67311
   b) 67312
   c) 67314
   d) 67316

30) What is commonly known as a boil of the skin?
   a) Abscess
   b) Furuncle
   c) Lesion
   d) Impetigo

31) A patient presents with a recurrent seborrheic keratosis of the left cheek. The area was marked for a shave removal. The area was infiltrated with local anesthetic, prepped and draped in a sterile fashion. The lesion measuring 1.8 cm was shaved using an 11-blade. Meticulous hemostasis was achieved using light pressure. The specimen was sent for permanent pathology. The patient tolerated the procedure well. What CPT® code(s) is reported?
   a) 11200
   b) 11312
   c) 11442
   d) 11642

32) A 45-year-old male with a previous biopsy positive for malignant melanoma, presents for definitive excision of the lesion. After induction of general anesthesia, the patient is placed supine on the OR table, the left thigh prepped and draped in the usual sterile fashion. IV antibiotics are given, patient had previous MRSA infection. The previous excisional biopsy site on the left knee measured approximately 4 cm and was widely elipsed with a 1.5 cm margin. The excision was taken down to the underlying patellar fascia. Hemostasis was achieved via electrocautery. The resulting defect was 11cm x 5cm. Wide advancement flaps were created inferiorly and superiorly using electrocautery. This allowed skin edges to come together without tension. The wound was closed using

interrupted 2-0 monocryl and 2 retention sutures were placed using #1 Prolene. Skin was closed with a stapler. What CPT® code(s) is/are reported?

a) 27328
b) 14301
c) 14301, 27328-51
d) 15738, 11606-51

33) Operative Report

PREOPERATIVE DIAGNOSIS: Diabetic foot ulceration.

POSTOPERATIVE DIAGNOSIS: Diabetic foot ulceration.

OPERATION PERFORMED: Debridement and split thickness autografting of left foot

ANESTHESIA: General endotracheal.

INDICATIONS FOR PROCEDURE: This patient with multiple complications from Type II diabetes has developed ulcerations which were debrided and homografted last week. The homograft is taking quite nicely; the wounds appear to be fairly clean; he is ready for autografting.

DESCRIPTION OF PROCEDURE: After informed consent the patient is brought to the operating room and placed in the supine position on the operating table. Anesthetic monitoring was instituted, internal anesthesia was induced. The left lower extremity is prepped and draped in a sterile fashion. Staples were removed and the homograft was debrided from the surface of the wounds. One wound appeared to have healed; the remaining two appeared to be relatively clean. We debrided this sharply with good bleeding in all areas. Hemostasis was achieved with pressure, Bovie cautery, and warm saline-soaked sponges. With good hemostasis a donor site was then obtained on the left anterior thigh, measuring less than 100 cm2. The wounds were then grafted with a split-thickness autograft that was harvested with a patch of Brown dermatome set at 12,000 of an inch thick. This was meshed 1.5:1. The donor site was infiltrated with bupivacaine and dressed. The skin graft was then applied over the wound, measured approximately 60 cm2 in dimension on the left foot. This was secured into place with skin staples and was then dressed with Acticoat 18's, Kerlix incorporating a catheter, and gel pad. The patient tolerated the procedure well. The right foot was redressed with skin lubricant sterile gauze and Ace wrap.

Anesthesia was reversed. The patient was brought back to the ICU in satisfactory condition. What CPT® and ICD-9-CM codes are reported?

a) 15220-58, 15004-58, E10.621, L97.508
b) 15120-58, 15004-58, E11.621, L97.529
c) 15950-78, 15004-78, E11.622, L97.526
d) 11044-78, 15120-78, E11.622, L97.809

34) A patient is seen in the same day surgery unit for an arthroscopy to remove some loose bodies in the shoulder area. What CPT® code(s) should be reported?

a) 29805
b) 29806
c) 29807
d) 29819

35) A patient presented with a closed, displaced supracondylar fracture of the left elbow. After conscious sedation, the left upper extremity was draped and closed reduction was performed, achieving anatomical reduction of the fracture. The elbow was then prepped and with the use of fluoroscopic guidance, two K-wires were directed crossing the fracture site and pierced the medial cortex of the left distal humerus. Stable reduction was obtained, with full flexion and extension. K-wires were bent and cut at a 90-degree angle. Telfa padding and splint were applied. What

CPT code(s) should be reported?
a) 24535
b) 24538
c) 24582
d) 24566

36) A 27-year-old tri-athlete is thrown from his bike on a steep downhill ride. He suffered a severely fractured vertebra at C5. An anterior approach is used to dissect out the bony fragments and strengthen the spine with titanium cages and arthrodesis. The surgeon places the patient supine on the OR table and proceeds with an anterior corpectomy at C5 with discectomy above and below. Titanium cages are placed in the resulting defect and morselized allograft bone is placed in and around the cages. Anterior Synthes plates are placed across C2-C3 and C3-C5, and C5-C6. What CPT® code(s) should be reported?
a) 22326, 22554-51, 22845, 22851, 20930
b) 63081, 22554-51, 22846, 22851, 20930
c) 63001, 22554-51, 22845, 20931
d) 22326, 22548-51, 22846, 20931

37) This 45-year-old male presents to the operating room with a painful mass of the right upper arm. General anesthesia was induced. Soft tissue dissection was carried through the proximal aspect of the teres minor muscle. Upon further dissection a large mass was noted just distal of the IGHL (inferior glenohumeral ligament), which appeared to be benign in nature. With blunt dissection and electrocautery, the 4-cm mass was removed en bloc and sent to pathology. The wound was irrigated, and repair of the teres minor with subcutaneous tissue was closed with triple-0 Vicryl. Skin was closed with double-0 Prolene in a subcuticular

fashion. What CPT® code(s) should be reported?

a) 23076-RT

b) 23066-RT

c) 23075-RT

d) 11406-RT

38) A 50-year-old male had surgery on his upper leg one day ago and presents with serous drainage from the wound. He was taken back to the operating room for evaluation of the hematoma. His wound was explored, and there was a hematoma at the base of the wound, which was very carefully evacuated. The wound was irrigated with antibacterial solution. What CPT® and ICD-10-CM codes should be reported?

a) 10140-79, M96.840

b) 27603-78, M96.840

c) 10140-76, L76.01

d) 27301-78, M96.840

39) A patient presents with a healed fracture of the left ankle. The patient was placed on the OR table in the supine position. After satisfactory induction of general anesthesia, the patient's left ankle was prepped and draped. A small incision about 1 cm long was made in the previous incision. The lower screws were removed. Another small incision was made just lateral about 1 cm long. The upper screws were removed from the plate. Both wounds were thoroughly irrigated with copious amounts of antibiotic ontaining saline. Skin was closed in a layered fashion and sterile dressing applied. What CPT® code(s) should be reported?

a) 20680

b) 20680, 20680-59

c) 20670

d) 20680, 20670-59

40) A 31-year-old secretary returns to the office with continued complaints of numbness involving three radial digits of the upper right extremity. Upon examination, she has a positive Tinel's test of the median nerve in the left wrist. Anti-inflammatory medication has not relieved her pain. Previous electrodiagnostic studies show sensory mononeuropathy. She has clinical findings consistent with carpal tunnel syndrome. She has failed physical therapy and presents for injection of the left carpal canal. The left carpal area is prepped sterilely. A 1.5 inch 25- or 22- gauge needle is inserted radial to the palmaris longus or ulnar to the carpi radialis tendon at an oblique angle of approximately 30 degrees. The needle is advanced a short distance about 1 or 2 cm observing for any complaints of paresthesias or pain in a median nerve distribution. The mixture of 1 cc of 1% lidocaine and 10 mg of Kenalog is injected slowly along the median nerve. The injection area is cleansed and a bandage is applied to the site. What CPT® code(s) should be reported?

a) 20526, J3301

b) 20551, J3302

c) 20526, J3303

d) 20550, J3302

41) What CPT® code should be reported for a frontal sinusotomy, non-obliterative, with osteoplastic flap, brow incision?

a) 31080

b) 31087

c) 31084

d) 31086

42) A 14-year-old boy presents at the Emergency Department experiencing an uncontrolled epistaxis. Through the nares, the ED physician packs his entire nose via anterior approach with medicated gauze. In approximately 15 minutes the nosebleed stops. What CPT® and ICD-10-CM codes should be reported?
   a) 30903-50, R04.0
   b) 30901-50, R04.0
   c) 30901, R04.0
   d) 30905, R04.0

43) A surgeon performs a high thoracotomy with resection of a single left lung segment on a 57-year-old heavy smoker who had presented with a six-month history of right shoulder pain. An apical lung biopsy had confirmed lung cancer. What CPT® and ICD-10-CM code(s) should be reported?
   a) 32100, C34.11, F17.219
   b) 32484, C34.12, F17.218
   c) 32503, C34.12, F17.210
   d) 19271, 32551-51, C34.10, M25.511, F17.218

44) Code the procedure for removal of two lobes of lungs, one from the right lung and other from the left lung with bronchoscopy.
   a) 32482
   b) 32484-50
   c) 32480-50
   d) 32482-50

45) Physician changes the old battery to a new battery on a patient's dual chamber permanent pacemaker.

a) 33212
b) 33229
c) 33213, 33233-51
d) 33228

46) A 35-year-old patient presented to the ASC for PTA of an obstructed hemodialysis AV graft in the venous anastomosis and the immediate venous outflow. The procedure was performed under moderate sedation administered by the physician performing the PTA. The physician performed all aspects of the procedure, including radiological supervision and interpretation & intraservice time is about 1 hour. Code for all services performed.
a) 36903, 99151, 99153×3, 75989-26
b) 36901, 99152, 99153×1, 75978-26
c) 36902, 99152, 99153×3
d) 35476, 99155, 99157×3, 75978-26

47) What is included in all vascular injection procedures?
a) Catheters, drugs, and contrast material
b) Selective catheterization
c) Just the procedure itself
d) Necessary local anesthesia, introduction of needles or catheters, injection of contrast media with or without automatic power injection, and/or necessary pre and post injection care specifically related to the injection procedure.

48) Preoperative Diagnosis: Coronary artery disease associated with congestive heart failure; in addition, the patient has diabetes and massive obesity.
Postoperative Diagnosis: Same Anesthesia: General endotracheal Incision: Median sternotomy
Indications: The patient had presented with severe

congestive heart failure associated with her severe diabetes. She had significant coronary artery disease, consisting of a chronically occluded right coronary artery but a very important large obtuse marginal artery coming off as the main circumflex system. She also has a left anterior descending artery, which has moderate disease and this supplies quite a bit of collateral to her right system. The decision was therefore made to perform a coronary artery bypass grafting procedure, particularly because she is so symptomatic. The patient was brought to the operating room.

Description of Procedure: The patient was brought to the operating room and placed in supine position. Myself, the operating surgeon was scrubbed throughout the entire operation. After the patient was prepared, median sternotomy incision was carried out and conduits were taken from the left arm as well as the right thigh. The patient weighs almost three hundred pounds and with her obesity there was some concern as to taking down the left internal mammary artery. Because the radial artery appeared to be a good conduit, she should have an arterial graft to the left anterior descending artery territory. She was cannulated after the aorta and atrium were exposed and after full heparinization. Attention was turned to the coronary arteries. The first obtuse marginal artery was a very large target and the vein graft to this target indeed produced an excellent amount of flow. Proximal anastomosis was then carried out to the foot of the aorta. The left anterior descending artery does not have severe disease but is also a very good target, and the radial artery was anastomosed to this target, and the proximal anastomosis was then carried out to the root of the aorta. Sternal closure was then done using wires. The subcutaneous layers were closed using Vicryl suture. The skin was approximated using staples.

a) 33533, 33510
b) 33511
c) 33533, 33517
d) 33533, 33517, 35600

49) CLINICAL SUMMARY: The patient is a 55-year-old female with known coronary disease and previous left anterior descending and diagonal artery intervention, with recent recurrent chest pain. Cardiac catheterization demonstrated continued patency of the stented segment, but diffuses borderline changes in the ostial/proximal portion of the right coronary artery.

PROCEDURE: With informed consent obtained, the patient was prepped and draped in the usual sterile fashion. With the right groin area infiltrated with 2% Xylocaine and the patient given 2 mg of Versed and 50 mcg of fentanyl intravenously for conscious sedation and pain control, the 6-French catheter sheath from the diagnostic study was exchanged for a 6French sheath and a 6-French JR4 catheter with side holes utilized. The patient initially received 3000 units of IV heparin, and then IVUS interrogation was carried out using an Atlantis Boston Scientific probe. After it had been determined that there was significant stenosis in the ostial/proximal segment of the right coronary artery, the patient received an additional 3000 units of IV heparin, as well as Integrilin per double-bolus injection. A 3.0, 16-mm-long Taxus stent was then deployed in the ostium and proximal segment of the right coronary artery in a primary stenting procedure with inflation pressure up to 12 atmospheres applied. Final angiographic documentation was carried out, and then the guiding catheter pulled, the sheath upgraded to a 7-French system, because of some diffuse oozing around the 6-French-sized sheath, and the patient is now being transferred to telemetry for post-coronary intervention observation and care. RESULTS: The initial guiding picture of the right coronary artery demonstrates the right coronary artery to be dominant in distribution, with luminal irregularities in its proximal and mid third with up to 50% stenosis in the ostial/proximal segment per angiographic criteria, although some additional increased radiolucency observed in that segment.

IVUS interrogation confirms severe, concentric plaque formation in this ostial/proximal portion of the right coronary artery with over 80% area stenosis demonstrated. The mid, distal lesions are not significant, with less than 40% stenosis per IVUS evaluation.

Following the coronary intervention with stent placement, there is marked increase in the ostial/proximal right coronary artery size, with no evidence for intimal disruption, no intraluminal filling defect, and TIMI III flow preserved.

CONCLUSION: Successful coronary intervention with drug-eluting Taxus stent placement to the ostial/proximal right coronary artery.

a) 92928-RC, 92978-RC
b) 92928-RC, 92924-RC, 92978-59-RC
c) 92920-RC, 92978-51-RC
d) 92920-RC, 92924-59 RC, 92978-51-RC

50) What CPT® code(s) is/are reported for a percutaneous endoscopic direct placement of a tube gastrostomy for a patient who previously underwent a partial esophagectomy?
a) 49440, 43116
b) 43246, 43116
c) 49440
d) 43246

51) A patient suffering from cirrhosis of the liver presents with

a history of coffee ground emesis. The surgeon diagnoses the patient with esophageal varices. Two days later, in the hospital GI lab, the surgeon ligates the varices with bands via an UGI endoscopy. What CPT® and ICD-10-CM codes are reported?

a) 43205, I85.10
b) 43244, K74.60, I85.10
c) 43227, K74.60, I85.11
d) 43235, I85.11

52) A 45-year-old patient with liver cancer is scheduled for a liver transplant. The patient's brother is a perfect match and will be donating a portion of his liver for a graft. Segments II and III will be taken from the brother and then the backbench reconstruction of the graft will be performed, both a venous and arterial anastomosis. The orthotopic allotransplantation will then be performed on the patient. What CPT® code(s) is/are reported?

a) 47140, 47146, 47147, 47135
b) 47141, 47146, 47135
c) 47140, 47147, 47146, 47136
d) 47141, 47146, 47136

53) Circumcision with adjacent tissue transfer was performed. What CPT® code(s) is/are reported for this service?

a) 14040
b) 54161-22
c) 54163
d) 54161, 14040

54) The patient presents to the office for CMG (cystometrogram) procedure(s). Complex CMG cystometrogram with voiding pressure studies is done,

intrabdominal voiding pressure studies, and complex uroflow are performed. What CPT® code(s) is/are reported for this service?

a) 51726

b) 51726, 51728, 51797

c) 51728, 51797, 51741

d) 51728-26, 51797-26, 51741-26

55) Preoperative diagnosis: Cytologic atypia and gross hematuria

Postoperative diagnosis: Cytologic atypia and gross hematuria

Procedure performed: Cystoscopy and random bladder biopsies and GreenLight laser ablation of the prostate. Description: Bladder biopsies were taken of the dome, posterior bladder wall and lateral side walls. Bugbee was used to fulgurate the biopsy sites to diminish bleeding. Cystoscope was replaced with the cystoscope designed for the GreenLight laser. We introduced this into the patient's urethra and performed GreenLight laser ablation of the prostate down to the level of verumontanum (a crest near the wall of the urethra).

There were some calcifications at the left apex of the prostate, causing damage to the laser but adequate vaporization was achieved. What CPT® code(s) is/are reported for this service?

a) 52648, 52204

b) 52647

c) 52649, 52224-59

d) 52648, 52224-59

56) What is a root word for vagina?

a) Uter/o

b) Colp/o

c) Hyster/o
d) Metri/o

57) The patient presents with a recurrent infection of the Bartholin's gland which has previously been treated with antibiotics and I&D. At this visit her gynecologist incises the cyst, draining the material in it and tacks the edges of the cyst open creating an open pouch to prevent recurrence. How is this procedure coded?
a) 56405
b) 56420
c) 56440
d) 56740

58) What CPT® code is used to report a complete unilateral removal of the vulva and deep subcutaneous tissues?
a) 56630
b) 56633
c) 56625
d) 56620

59) Vulvar cancer in situ can also be documented as:
a) VIN I
b) VIN II
c) Adenocarcinoma of the vulva
d) VIN III

60) Patient wishes permanent sterilization and elects laparoscopic tubal ligation with falope ring. What is/are the CPT® code(s) reported for this service?
a) 58671
b) 58600
c) 58615
d) 58670

61) A patient presents with cervical cancer, it has spread and metastasized throughout the pelvic area. She receives a total abdominal hysterectomy with bilateral salpingo oophorectomy, cystectomy and creation of an ileal conduit and partial colectomy. What is/are the CPT® code(s) reported for this service?
a) 58150, 51590, 44140
b) 58152, 44141
c) 58150, 51590, 44140, 58720
d) 58240

62) A pregnant patient presents with the baby in a breech presentation. During the delivery the doctor attempts to turn the baby while it is still in the uterus. The baby turns but then immediately resumes his previous position. Can this service be billed? If so, what is the code?
a) No, since the doctor was unable to successfully turn the baby.
b) No, this procedure is included in the obstetrical global package
c) Yes, since the doctor did the work, even though the outcome was unsuccessful. Report this procedure with code 59412
d) Yes, only billing it with postpartum care 59515

63) What are the four lobes of the brain?
a) Frontal, Parietal, Temporal, Occipital
b) Sulci, Cerebellum, Pons, Medulla
c) Frontal, Cerebral, Cerebellum, Pons
d) Frontal, Cerebrum, Temporal, Occipital

64) A neurosurgeon excised a berry aneurism outside the duramatter which was in the branches of anterior cerebral

artery. The procedure was performed through orbitocranial approach into anterior cranial fossa
a) 61584
b) 61584, 61600
c) 61584, 61600-51
d) 61592

65) The physician removes the thymus gland in a 27-year-old female with myasthenia gravis. Using a transcervical approach, the blood supply to the thymus is divided and the thymus is dissected free from the pericardium and the thymus is removed. What CPT® code(s) is reported for this procedure?
a) 60520
b) 60521
c) 60522
d) 60540

66) A patient is having a decompression of the nerve root involving two segments of the lumbar spine via transpedicular approach. What CPT® code(s) is/are reported?
a) 63056
b) 63056, 63057
c) 63030, 63035
d) 63030

67) A patient with a herniated cervical disc undergoes a cervical laminotomy with a partial facetectomy and excision of the herniated disc for cervical interspace C3-C4. What CPT® and ICD-10-CM codes are reported?
a) 63050, M50.20
b) 63020, M50.20

c) 63020, 63035, M50.20

d) 63050, M50.20

68) A 37-year-old has multilevel lumbar degenerative disc disease and is coming in for an epidural injection. Localizing the skin over the area of L5-S1, the physician uses the transforaminal approach. The spinal needle is inserted, and the patient experienced paresthesias into her left lower extremities. The anesthetic drug is injected into the epidural space. What CPT® code(s) is/are reported for this procedure?

a) 64483, 64484

b) 64493

c) 64493, 64494

d) 64483

69) A patient receives a paravertebral facet joint injection at three levels on both sides of the lumbar spine using fluoroscopic guidance for lumbar pain. What CPT® and ICD-10- CM codes are reported?

a) 64493, 64494 x 2, M54.89

b) 64493-50, 64494-50, 64495-50, M54.5

c) 64493, 64495 x 2, M54.5

d) 64495-50, M54.5

70) 70. A 47-year-old female presents to the OR for a partial corpectomy to three thoracic vertebrae. One surgeon performs the transthoracic approach while another surgeon performs the three vertebral nerve root decompressions necessary. How both providers do involved code for their portions of the surgery?

a) 63087-52, 63088-52 x 2

b) 63085-62, 63086-62 x 2

c) 63087-80, 63088-80 x 2
d) 63085, 63086-82 x 2

71) A patient had recently experienced muscle atrophy and noticed she did not have pain when she cut herself on a piece of glass. The provider decides to obtain a biopsy of the spinal cord under fluoroscopic guidance. The biopsy results come back as syringomyelia. What CPT® and ICD-10-CM codes are reported?
a) 62270, G95.0, R20.9
b) 62270, G95.0
c) 62269, G95.0, R20.9
d) 62269, G95.0

72) A 26-year-old patient presents with headache, neck pain, and fever and is concerned he may have meningitis. The patient was placed in the sitting position and given 0.5 mg Ativan IV. His back was prepped and a 20-gauge needle punctured the spine between L4 and L5 with the return of clear fluid. The cerebral spinal fluid was reviewed and showed no sign of meningitis. What CPT® code(s) is reported?
a) 62270
b) 62272
c) 62282
d) 62268

73) Patient had an abscess in the external auditory canal, which was drained in the office. What CPT® code(s) should be reported?
a) 69540
b) 69105
c) 69020

d) 69000

74) What CPT® code(s) should be reported for removal of foreign body from the external auditory canal w/o general anesthesia?
   a) 69205
   b) 69220
   c) 69200
   d) 69210

75) A patient with a cyst-like mass on his left external auditory canal was visualized under the microscope and a microcup forceps was used to obtain a biopsy of tissue along the posterior superior canal wall. What CPT® code(s) should be reported?
   a) 69100-RT
   b) 69105-LT
   c) 69140-RT
   d) 69145-LT

76) Following labor and delivery, the mother developed acute kidney failure. What ICD-10- CM code(s) is reported?
   a) O26.90
   b) PO1.9
   c) O90.4
   d) N19

77) A 42-year-old patient was undergoing anesthesia in an ASC and began having complications prior to the administration of anesthesia. The surgeon immediately discontinued the planned surgery. If the insurance company requires a reported modifier, what modifier is reported best describing the extenuating circumstances?
   a) 53

b) 23

c) 73

d) 74

78) Code 00350, Anesthesia for procedures on the major vessels of the neck, has a base   value of ten (10) units. The patient is a P3 status, which allows one (1) extra base unit. Anesthesia start time is reported as 11:02, and the surgery began at 11:14. The surgery finished at 12:34 and the patient was turned over to PACU at 12:47, which was reported as the ending anesthesia time. Using fifteen-minute time increments and a conversion factor of $100, what is the correct anesthesia charge?
   a) $1,500.00
   b) $1,600.00
   c) $1,700.00
   d) $1,800.00

79) A CRNA is personally performing a case, with medical direction from an anesthesiologist. What modifier is appropriately reported for the CRNA services?
   a) QY
   b) QZ
   c) QK
   d) QS

80) A 40-year-old female in good physical health is having a laparoscopic tubal ligation. The anesthesiologist begins to prepare the patient for surgery at 0830. Surgery begins at 0900 and ends at 1000. The anesthesiologist releases the patient to recovery nurse at 1015. What is the total anesthesia time and anesthesia code?
   a) 1 hour 30 minutes, 00840

b) 1 hour 45 minutes, 00851
c) 1 hour, 00840
d) 1 hour 15 minutes, 00851

81) Procedure: Body PET-CT Skull Base to Mid-Thigh
History: A 65-year-old male Medicare patient with a history of rectal carcinoma presenting for restaging examination. Description: Following the IV administration of 15.51 mCi of F-18 deoxyglucose (FDG), multiplanar image acquisitions of the neck, chest, abdomen and pelvis to the level of mid-thigh were obtained at one-hour post-radiopharmaceutical administration. (Nuclear Medicine Tumor imaging). What CPT code(s) is/are reported?
a) 78815
b) 78815, 96365
c) 78816, 96365
d) 78815, 96374

82) 25-year-old female in her last trimester of her pregnancy comes into her obstetrician's office for a fetal biophysical profile (BPP). An ultrasound is used to first monitor the fetus movements showing three movements of the legs and arms (normal). There are two breathing movements lasting 30 seconds (normal). Non-stress test (NST) of 30 minutes showed the heartbeat at 120 beats per minute and increased with movement (normal or reactive). Arms and legs were flexed with fetus head on its chest, opening and closing of a hand. Two pockets of amniotic fluid at 3cm were seen in the uterine cavity (normal). Biophysical profile scored 9 out of 10 points (normal or reassuring). What CPT® code(s) is/are reported by the obstetrician?
a) 76818
b) 76819
c) 76815

d) 59025, 76818

83) 65-year-old female has a 2.5 cm by 2.0 cm non-small cell lung cancer in her right upper lobe of her lung. The tumor is inoperable due to severe respiratory conditions. She will be receiving stereotactic body radiation therapy under image guidance. Beams arranged in 8 fields will deliver 25 Gy per fraction for 4 fractions. What CPT® and ICD- 10-CM codes are reported?
   a) 77435-26, C34.11, Z51.0
   b) 77371-26, C34.11
   c) 77373-26, Z51.0, C34.11
   d) 77431-26, Z51.0, C34.12

84) A patient with thickening of the synovial membrane undergoes a fluoroscopic guided radiopharmaceutical therapy joint injection on his right knee. What CPT® code(s) is/are reported by the physician if performed in an ASC setting?
   a) 79440
   b) 79440, 20610
   c) 79999, 77002
   d) 79440-26, 77002-26, 20610

85) A patient with bilateral lower extremity deep venous thromboses has a history of a recent pulmonary embolus. Under ultrasound guidance an inferior vena cavagram was performed demonstrating the right and left renal arteries at the level of L1. A tulip filter device was passed down the sheath, positioned, and deployed with excellent symmetry. It showed the filter between the renal veins and the confluence of the iliac veins but well above the bifurcation of the inferior vena cava. What CPT® code(s) is reported?

a) 75825
b) 75827
c) 75820
d) 75860

86) An oncology patient is having weekly radiation treatments with a total of seven conventional fractionated treatments broken up five on one day and two on the next. What radiology code is appropriate for this series of clinical management fractions?
a) 77427
b) 77427x7
c) 77427x2
d) 77427-22

87) A patient in her 2nd trimester with a triplet pregnancy is seen for an obstetrical ultrasound only including fetal heartbeats and position of the fetuses. What CPT® code(s) is/are reported for the ultrasound?
a) 76805, 76810, 76810
b) 76811, 76812, 76812
c) 76815 x 3
d) 76815

88) In what section of the Pathology chapter of CPT® would a coder find codes for a FISH test?
a) Cytopathology
b) Immunology
c) Chemistry
d) Other Procedures

89) A patient has a severe traumatic fracture of the humerus. During the open reduction procedure, the surgeon removes several small pieces of bone embedded in the nearby

tissue. They are sent to Pathology for examination without microscopic sections. The pathologist finds no evidence of disease. How should the pathologist code for his services?
a) This service cannot be billed
b) 88304
c) 88300
d) 88309, 88311

90) A patient presents with right upper quadrant pain, nausea, and other symptoms of liver disease as well as complaints of decreased urination. Her physician orders an albumin; bilirubin, both total and direct; alkaline phosphatase; total protein; alanine amino transferase; aspartate amino transferase, and creatinine. What CPT® code(s) is/are reported?
a) 82040, 82247, 82248, 84075, 84155, 84460, 84450, 82565
b) 80076, 82565
c) 80076
d) 80076-22

91) A urine pregnancy test is performed by the office staff using the Hybritech ICON (qualitative visual color comparison test). What CPT® code(s) is reported?
a) 84703
b) 84702
c) 81025
d) 81025, 36415

92) A pediatrician is asked to be in the room during the delivery of a baby at risk for complications. The pediatrician is in the room for 45 minutes. The baby is born and is completely healthy, not requiring the services of

the pediatrician. What CPT® code(s) does the pediatrician report?

a) 99219
b) 99252
c) 99360
d) 99360 x 2

93) An infant is born six weeks premature in rural Arizona and the pediatrician in attendance intubates the child and administers surfactant in the ET tube while waiting in the ER for the air ambulance. During the 45-minute wait, he continues to bag the critically ill patient on 100 percent oxygen while monitoring VS, ECG, pulse oximetry and temperature. The infant is in a warming unit and an umbilical vein line was placed for fluids and in case of emergent needs for medications. How is this coded?

a) 99291
b) 99471
c) 99291, 31500, 36510, 94610
d) 99434, 99464, 99465, 94610, 36510

94) Patient comes in today at four months of age for a checkup. She is growing and developing well. Her mother is concerned because she seems to cry a lot when lying down but when she is picked up she is fine. She is on breast milk but her mother has returned to work and is using a breast pump, but hasn't seemed to produce enough milk.
PHYSICAL EXAM: Weight 12 lbs 11 oz, Height 25in., OFC 41.5 cm. HEENT: Eye: Red reflex normal. Right eardrum is minimally pink, left eardrum is normal. Nose: slight mucous Throat with slight thrush on the inside of the cheeks and on the tongue. LUNGS: clear. HEART: w/o murmur. ABDOMEN: soft. Hip exam normal. GENITALIA normal although her mother says there was a diaper rash

earlier in the week.

ASSESSMENT

Four-month-old well check Cold

Mild thrush Diaper rash

PLAN: Okay to advance to baby foods Okay to supplement with Similac

Nystatin suspension for the thrush and creams for the diaper rash if it recurs. Mother will bring child back after the cold symptoms resolve for her DPT, HIB and polio What E/M code(s) are reported?

a) 99212

b) 99391

c) 99391, 99212-25

d) 99213

95) A new patient wants to quit smoking. The patient has constant cough due to smoking and some shortness of breath. No night sweats, weight loss, night fever, CP, headache, or dizziness. He has tried patches and nicotine gum, which has not helped. Patient has been smoking for 40 years and smokes 2 packs per day. He has a family history of emphysema. A limited three system exam was performed. Physician discussed the pros and cons of medications used to quit smoking in detail. Counseling and education done for 46-minute visit and moderate level of medical decision making. Prescription for Chantrix and Tetracylcine were given. Patient to follow up in 1 month. We will consider chest X-ray and cardiac work up. Select the appropriate CPT code(s) for this visit:

a) 99203

b) 99204

c) 99204, 99354

d) 99214, 99354

96) A patient with coronary atherosclerosis underwent a PTCA in the left anterior descending and in the first diagonal of the LD. What CPT® code(s) is/are reported?
a) 92920, 92921 - LD
b) 92920×2
c) 92924
d) 92925, 92996

97) Margaret has food allergies, comes to her physician for her weekly allergen immunotherapy that consists of two injections prepared and provided by the physician. What is the correct CPT code?
a) 95125
b) 95117
c) 95131
d) 95146

98) A baby was born with a ventricular septal defect (VSD). The physician performed a right heart catheterization and transcatheter closure with implant by percutaneous approach. What codes are reported?
a) 93530, 93581-59, Q21.9
b) 93581, Q21.0
c) 93530, Q24.0
d) 93530, 93591-59, Q21.0

99) 30-year-old male cut his left hand on a piece of aluminum repairing the gutter on his house. 6 days later, it became infected. He went to the intermediate care center in his neighborhood, his first visit there. The wound was very red and warm with purulent material present. The wound was irrigated extensively with sterile water and covered with a clean sterile dressing. An injection of Bicillin CR, 1,200,000

units was given. The patient was instructed to return in 3-4 days. The physician diagnosed open wound of the hand with cellulitis. A problem focused history and examination with a low MDM were performed. What are the CPT and ICD-10-CM codes?

a) 96372, L02.113
b) 99202, J0558 x 4, L03.119
c) 99203, 96372, J0558 x 12, L03.114
d) 99284, L03.114

100)   Mrs. Salas had 30 minutes of angin a decubitus and was admitted to the Coronary Care Unit with a diagnosis of R/O MI. The cardiologist (private practice based) takes her to the cardiac catheterization suite at the local hospital for a left heart catheterization. Injection procedures for selective coronary angiography and left ventriculography were performed and imaging supervision and interpretation for the selective coronary angiography and left ventriculography was provided. What CPT® code(s) are reported for the services?

a) 93452-26
b) 93458-26
c) 93453-26
d) 93453-26, 9346

EXAM D ANSWERS AND RATIONALES

1) Answer C – Part C.

   The Centers for Medicare and Medicaid Services - Hierarchical Condition Categories (CMS-HCC) is used to determine payment rates for Medicare Advantage plans, which are offered under Part C of the Medicare program. CMS-HCC is a risk adjustment model that uses demographic and health status information to predict healthcare costs for beneficiaries enrolled in Medicare Advantage plans. This information is used to calculate the payment rates that Medicare Advantage plans receive from the federal government.

2) Answer D – The answer is d) Notices of Privacy Practices.

Notices of Privacy Practices (NPP) are documents that healthcare providers are required to develop and distribute to their patients under the Health Insurance Portability and Accountability Act (HIPAA) Privacy Rule. The NPP informs patients about how their medical information may be used and disclosed, as well as their rights to access and control their protected health information (PHI).

Developing NPPs and policies and procedures regarding privacy are important for healthcare providers to ensure that they comply with HIPAA regulations and protect the privacy and security of patients' PHI. These policies and procedures may include things like training staff on HIPAA requirements, implementing physical and electronic safeguards to protect PHI, and responding to breaches of PHI.

Patient hotlines, work around procedures, and fees are not directly related to the development of privacy policies and procedures for healthcare providers.

3) Answer C – The answer is c) 7.

An effective compliance plan for a healthcare organization should include seven key components. These components are:

Written policies and procedures: This component includes the development of policies and procedures that outline the organization's commitment to compliance and provide guidance for employees on how to comply with regulations.

Compliance officer and compliance committee: This component involves designating a compliance officer and establishing a compliance committee to oversee the organization's compliance program.

Training and education: This component includes providing training and education to employees on compliance policies, procedures, and regulations.

Communication: This component involves establishing

effective lines of communication for reporting compliance issues and providing feedback to employees.

Auditing and monitoring: This component includes implementing auditing and monitoring processes to assess the effectiveness of the compliance program and identify areas for improvement.

Enforcement and discipline: This component involves establishing a system for enforcing compliance policies and procedures and disciplining employees who violate them.

Response and corrective action: This component involves establishing a system for responding to compliance issues and taking corrective action to prevent similar issues from occurring in the future.

By including these seven components in a compliance plan, healthcare organizations can effectively manage compliance risks and promote a culture of compliance within the organization.

4) Answer D – The correct answer is D) legal and ethical.

The American Academy of Professional Coders (AAPC) is a professional organization that provides certification and training for medical coders. The AAPC has established a Code of Ethics that outlines the standards of conduct that its members should adhere to.

One of the key principles of the AAPC Code of Ethics is that members should use only legal and ethical means in all professional dealings. This means that members should comply with all applicable laws and regulations and act in a manner that is consistent with accepted ethical standards.

By using legal and ethical means in their professional dealings, members can promote trust and confidence in the medical coding profession and uphold the integrity of the healthcare system. This helps to ensure that patients receive high-quality care and that healthcare providers are fairly compensated for their services.

5) Answer D - The option that is NOT a covered entity under

HIPAA is d) Worker's Compensation.

Under HIPAA (Health Insurance Portability and Accountability Act), covered entities are healthcare providers, health plans, and healthcare clearinghouses. Worker's Compensation is not considered a covered entity under HIPAA because it is not a healthcare provider, health plan, or healthcare clearinghouse.

However, it is important to note that while Worker's Compensation is not considered a covered entity under HIPAA, it is still subject to other privacy and security laws and regulations that protect the confidentiality of personal health information.

6) Answer C – The answer is actually c) Tendons, aponeurosis and directly to bone.

Muscles attach to bone through a combination of tendons, aponeurosis, and direct attachment. Tendons are tough bands of connective tissue that attach muscles to bones, while aponeurosis is a flat, sheet-like structure that connects muscle to bone. Direct attachment occurs when muscle fibers attach directly to the bone surface.

Therefore, while tendons and aponeurosis play an important role in attaching muscles to bones, direct attachment also occurs. Hence, option c) is the correct answer.

7) Answer D - The answer is d) Trachea.

The trachea, also known as the windpipe, is a respiratory structure that connects the larynx (voice box) to the bronchi in the lungs. It is a tube-like structure that is made up of rings of cartilage that help keep it open and prevent it from collapsing. The trachea also contains ligaments that connect the cartilage rings together and help provide flexibility.

The alveoli are small air sacs located in the lungs where gas exchange occurs between the air and the blood. The lungs are the main respiratory organs responsible for gas exchange. The bronchioles are small airways in the lungs that branch off from the bronchi and lead to the alveoli.

Therefore, among the given options, only the trachea is composed of cartilage and ligaments. Hence, the answer is d) Trachea.

8) Answer B - The correct answer is b) Cecum, ascending colon, transverse colon, descending colon, sigmoid colon, rectum, anus.

After leaving the last portion of the small intestine (ileum), the nutrients, water, and electrolytes pass through the ileocecal valve and enter the cecum, which is the first part of the large intestine. From there, the food moves up the ascending colon, across the transverse colon, down the descending colon, and into the sigmoid colon. Finally, the fecal matter moves into the rectum and is eliminated through the anus.

Option b) is the correct answer because it lists the order of movement of fecal matter through the large intestine in the correct order, starting with the cecum and ending with the anus. The other options either have an incorrect order or are missing one or more parts of the large intestine.

It is important to note that the large intestine is responsible for absorbing water and electrolytes from the remaining indigestible food matter and producing and storing fecal matter until it is eliminated from the body.

9) Answer A - The chemicals that relay, amplify, and modulate signals between a neuron and another cell are called neurotransmitters.

Neurotransmitters are chemicals that are released by neurons and allow for communication between neurons and other cells, such as muscle cells or other neurons. When a nerve impulse reaches the end of a neuron, neurotransmitters are released into the synapse, which is the small gap between the neurons or between a neuron and its target cell. The neurotransmitters then bind to receptors on the target cell and either excite or inhibit the activity of that cell.

Hormones are chemical messengers that are produced by glands and released into the bloodstream to travel to other parts of the body where they regulate various bodily functions. Interneurons are neurons that relay signals between other neurons, whereas myelin is a fatty substance that covers and insulates nerve fibers, allowing for faster transmission of nerve impulses.

Therefore, among the given options, the correct answer is a) Neurotransmitters, as they are specifically involved in the communication between neurons and other cells.

10) Answer A - The correct answer is a) Removal of scar tissue resulting from burns or other injuries.

An escharotomy is a surgical procedure that involves making incisions through the burned or injured tissue to relieve pressure and restore circulation. This is typically done in cases of severe burns or other injuries that result in the formation of eschar, which is a hard, leathery scab or tissue that can cause constriction and compression of underlying tissues and blood vessels.

The procedure involves cutting through the eschar to relieve the pressure and restore blood flow to the affected area. This can be a life-saving procedure, as the constriction caused by eschar can lead to tissue death and other complications.

Option b) Removal of a basal cell carcinoma refers to a type of skin cancer and is not related to an escharotomy. Debridement of a pressure ulcer involves the removal of dead or infected tissue from a wound, and removal of a fingernail is a different type of surgical procedure altogether.

Therefore, among the given options, the correct answer is a) Removal of scar tissue resulting from burns or other injuries.

11) Answer B - The correct answer is b) Surgical cutting into the seminal vesicles.

A vesiculotomy is a surgical procedure that involves cutting into the seminal vesicles. The seminal vesicles are a pair of glandular structures located near the prostate gland that secrete seminal fluid, which is an important component of semen.

Vesiculotomy is a rare procedure and is typically only done in cases of severe inflammation or infection of the seminal vesicles, known as seminal vesiculitis. The procedure involves making an incision into the seminal vesicles to drain any fluid or pus that has accumulated and to allow for better drainage and healing.

Option a) Removal of an obstruction from the vas deferens refers to a different type of surgical procedure that involves removing a blockage from the duct that carries sperm from the testicles to the urethra. Option c) Removal of one of the seminal vesicles is a more drastic procedure that may be done in cases of cancer or other serious conditions affecting the seminal vesicles. Option d) Incision into the prostate is a different surgical procedure that may be done to treat conditions such as prostate cancer or benign prostatic hyperplasia (BPH).

Therefore, among the given options, the correct answer is b) Surgical cutting into the seminal vesicles.

12) Answer C - The correct answer is c) Colostrum.

Colostrum is a form of milk that is produced by the mammary glands of female mammals, including humans, during the first few days after giving birth. It is a thick, yellowish fluid that contains high levels of protein, immunoglobulins, and other important nutrients that are important for the health and development of newborns.

Colostrum is sometimes referred to as "first milk" or "premilk" and is produced before the production of mature breast milk begins. It provides important nutrients and antibodies that help to protect the newborn against infections and other health problems.

Option a) Chorion is a membrane that surrounds the developing embryo and helps to form the placenta. Option b) Lactose is a sugar that is found in milk and other dairy products. Option d) Prolactin is a hormone that is produced by the pituitary gland and stimulates the production of milk in the mammary glands.

Therefore, among the given options, the correct answer is c) Colostrum.

13) Answer B - The correct answer is b) Hyster/o.

Hyster/o is a root that pertains to the uterus, which is a female reproductive organ that plays an important role in pregnancy and childbirth. For example, the term "hysterectomy" refers to the surgical removal of the uterus.

Option a) Cyt/o pertains to cells. Option c) Pancreat/o pertains to the pancreas, which is a glandular organ located in the abdomen that produces digestive enzymes and hormones. Option d) Endocrin/o pertains to the endocrine system, which is a collection of glands that produce hormones that regulate various bodily functions.

Therefore, among the given options, the correct answer is b) Hyster/o.

14) Answer B - In the ICD-10-CM guidelines, the term "provider" typically refers to the healthcare professional who is providing medical care or treatment to the patient. This can include physicians, nurse practitioners, physician assistants, and other healthcare professionals who are licensed or otherwise authorized to provide medical care.

Option a) the hospital refers to a healthcare facility where medical care is provided, including inpatient and outpatient care. Option c) insurance company refers to an organization that provides health insurance coverage to individuals or groups. Option d) the patient refers to the individual who is receiving medical care or treatment.

Therefore, among the given options, the correct answer is b) the physician.

15) Answer B - The appropriate use of the ICD-10-CM code B20 (Human Immunodeficiency Virus [HIV] disease) depends on the accuracy and specificity of the diagnosis. In general, the code should only be used when the diagnosis of HIV has been confirmed by the physician's diagnostic statement or by laboratory testing.

Option a) The test result is inconclusive: If the HIV test result is inconclusive, it is not appropriate to use the code B20. Additional testing may be necessary to determine whether the patient has HIV.

Option b) The test result is confirmed by the physician's diagnostic statement: When the physician confirms the diagnosis of HIV through clinical evaluation or laboratory testing, the code B20 can be used to indicate the diagnosis.

Option c) Known HIV without symptoms: If the patient has a confirmed diagnosis of HIV, but is asymptomatic, the code B20 can be used to indicate the presence of the disease.

Option d) Suspected HIV: If the physician suspects that the patient may have HIV, but has not yet confirmed the diagnosis, it is not appropriate to use the code B20. Additional testing and evaluation may be necessary before the diagnosis can be confirmed.

Therefore, among the given options, the correct answer is b) The test result is confirmed by the physician's diagnostic statement.

16) Answer B - The ICD-10-CM classification system has specific instructions and conventions that must be followed in order to assign accurate and appropriate codes. These instructions and conventions take precedence over other sources of information when assigning codes.

Option a) Physicians: While physicians provide important information for coding, the instructions and conventions of the classification system take precedence over their input.

Option b) Official Coding Guidelines: The Official Coding Guidelines provide specific instructions for coding and take precedence over other sources of information when assigning codes. The guidelines provide instructions on how to assign codes for various types of situations, including when the documentation is unclear or conflicting.

Option c) CPT: The Current Procedural Terminology (CPT) is a separate classification system used to code medical procedures. While CPT codes are important for medical billing and documentation, they do not take precedence over the instructions and conventions of the ICD-10-CM classification system.

Option d) Nothing, they are only used in the event of no other instruction: This option is incorrect. The instructions and conventions of the classification system should always be followed, regardless of whether other sources of information are available.

Therefore, among the given options, the correct answer is b) Official Coding Guidelines.

17) Answer C - The correct answer is c) G80.1, G03.9.

Cerebral palsy (CP) is a group of disorders that affect movement and posture. Spastic cerebral palsy is the most common type of CP, characterized by increased muscle tone and stiffness, which can affect mobility and coordination.

In this case, the underlying cause of spastic cerebral palsy is meningitis, which is an inflammation of the meninges (the membranes that cover the brain and spinal cord) usually caused by a bacterial or viral infection.

The ICD-10 diagnosis code for spastic cerebral palsy is G80.1. The diagnosis code for meningitis is G03.9, which is the code for unspecified meningitis.

Therefore, the correct diagnosis codes for spastic cerebral palsy due to meningitis are G80.1 (spastic cerebral palsy) and G03.9 (unspecified meningitis). So, the correct answer is c) G80.1, G03.9.

18) Answer D - The correct answer is d) N63.10, Z80.3.

In this case, the patient presents with a breast lump, and she has a family history of breast cancer, which is a significant risk factor for developing breast cancer.

The ICD-10 diagnosis code for a breast lump is N63.10, which is used for unspecified lump in the breast, and the diagnosis code for family history of breast cancer is Z80.3.

Therefore, the correct diagnosis codes for this case are N63.10 (unspecified lump in the breast) and Z80.3 (family history of breast cancer). So, the correct answer is d) N63.10, Z80.3.

19) Answer D - The correct answer is d) Z78.0.

In this case, the patient presents with symptoms of insomnia and upset stomach, and the physician suspects that she is pre-menopausal. The diagnosis given is impending menopause.

The ICD-10 diagnosis code for impending menopause is Z78.0, which is used for the observation of suspected menopausal and climacteric conditions. The diagnosis codes for insomnia and upset stomach are not necessary since they are symptoms, not the primary diagnosis.

Therefore, the correct diagnosis code for this case is Z78.0 (observation of suspected menopausal and climacteric conditions). So, the correct answer is d) Z78.0.

20) Answer A - When the type of diabetes mellitus is not documented in the medical note, the default type that is typically used is a) Type II.

Type II diabetes is the most common type of diabetes and is often associated with obesity, inactivity, and advanced age. It is also more likely to be asymptomatic or have mild symptoms, which can make it easier to miss or overlook in medical documentation.

21) Answer B - The correct answer is b) I51.7, I10.

In this case, the patient is coming in for a follow-up visit for two existing conditions: essential hypertension and cardiomegaly. Both conditions are stable, and the patient is told to continue with his medications.

The ICD-10 diagnosis code for essential hypertension is I10, and the diagnosis code for cardiomegaly is I51.7.

Therefore, the correct diagnosis codes for this case are I51.7 (cardiomegaly) and I10 (essential hypertension). So, the correct answer is b) I51.7, I10.

Answer a) (I11.9, I51.7) is not the correct answer because I11.9 is the code for hypertensive heart disease without heart failure, which is not the same as essential hypertension. While essential hypertension is a type of high blood pressure that is not caused by any underlying medical condition, hypertensive heart disease is a condition where long-term high blood pressure has caused damage to the heart.

22) Answer B - The answer is b) Z00.121, L22.

The reason for this is that in ICD-10-CM coding, the first-listed or primary diagnosis should be the reason for the encounter. In this case, the reason for the encounter is a routine health check examination, which should be reported first with the code Z00.121. The diaper rash is a secondary diagnosis and should be reported with the additional code L22.

23) Answer B - The correct answer is b) T22.20XD.

T22.20XD is the ICD-10-CM code for a second-degree burn of the left upper arm, subsequent encounter. The "D" at the end of the code indicates that this is a subsequent encounter for the injury, which is appropriate in this case as the patient is coming in for follow-up.

Z51.89 is a code for other specified aftercare, while Z09 is a code for follow-up examination after completed treatment for conditions other than malignant neoplasm. These codes are not appropriate for reporting a second-degree burn.

Therefore, the appropriate ICD-10-CM code to report for this encounter is T22.20XD.

24) Answer D - The correct answer is d) O09.522, O76.

O09.522 is the ICD-10-CM code for a patient with a pregnancy-related problem with abnormal fetal heart rate or rhythm. O76 is the ICD-10-CM code for a complication of labor and delivery, which may be relevant if the patient requires delivery due to the abnormal fetal heart rate.

While O09.41 is the ICD-10-CM code for a patient with a pregnancy-related problem with decreased fetal movements, it is not necessary to report this code in addition to O09.522 in this scenario.

P29.12 is the ICD-10-CM code for neonatal bradycardia, which is not appropriate for reporting a condition in the fetus during pregnancy. O09.12 is the ICD-10-CM code for a patient with a pregnancy-related problem with excessive weight gain, which is not relevant to this patient's condition.

Therefore, the appropriate ICD-10-CM codes to report for this encounter are O09.522 and O76.

25) Answer D - Permanent national codes, miscellaneous codes, dental codes, and temporary national codes are included in the code ranges of HCPCS Level II.

26) Answer A - the correct anesthesia code to report for an arthroscopy of the medial compartment of the left knee would be 01400

The anesthesia code for arthroscopic procedures of the knee joint is 01400, which includes procedures such as diagnostic arthroscopy, surgical arthroscopy, and removal of loose or foreign bodies. Thank you for bringing this to my attention and I apologize for any confusion my previous response may have caused.

27)   Answer   C   -

11765   Wedge excision of skin of nail fold (eg. for ingrown toenail)
   ⊃ *CPT Assistant* Dec 02:4

28) Answer D - The correct answer for the code of partial laparoscopic colectomy with anastomosis and coloproctostomy is d) 44207.
Code 44208 refers to a laparoscopic-assisted partial colectomy, which is not the same as a laparoscopic partial colectomy with anastomosis and coloproctostomy.
Code 44210 is used for a laparoscopic total colectomy.
Code 44145 refers to a laparoscopic-assisted proctocolectomy with ileoanal anastomosis, which is a different procedure than the one described in the question.
Therefore, the correct code for the procedure described in the question is 44207.

29) Answer B - The correct CPT code for strabismus reparative surgery performed on 2 horizontal muscles is indeed option (b) 67312.
CPT code 67312 is used for Strabismus surgery involving two horizontal muscles, with or without vertical muscle(s). The code describes the surgical correction of misaligned eyes by repositioning two of the muscles that control eye movement, usually the horizontal muscles. The code includes all related pre-operative and post-operative care.

30) Answer B - Furuncle is commonly known as a boil of the skin. It is a painful, pus-filled bump that develops under the skin, usually caused by a bacterial infection. Furuncles typically occur on the neck, face, armpits, buttocks, and thighs. Treatment may include antibiotics, warm compresses, and in some cases, surgical drainage.

31)   Answer   B   -

11310 Shaving of epidermal or dermal lesion, single lesion, face, ears, eyelids, nose, lips, mucous membrane; lesion diameter 0.5 cm or less

⟲ *CPT Assistant* Feb 00:11, Feb 08:1, Feb 13:16, Mar 13:6, Dec 17:14, Feb 18:10, Jan 19:9

11311 lesion diameter 0.6 to 1.0 cm

⟲ *CPT Assistant* Feb 00:11, Feb 08:1, Feb 13:16, Mar 13:6, Feb 18:10, Jan 19:9

11312 lesion diameter 1.1 to 2.0 cm ⟵

⟲ *CPT Assistant* Feb 00:11, Feb 08:1, Feb 13:16, Mar

32) Answer B - The correct answer is b) 14301.

CPT® code 14301 describes a complex repair of a wound that requires more than layered closure, such as the creation of multiple flaps. In this case, wide advancement flaps were created using electrocautery to allow the skin edges to come together without tension, which meets the requirements for code 14301.

CPT® code 27328 describes a repair of a patellar tendon, which is not performed in this case.

The -51 modifier is not appropriate in this case because only one procedure was performed.

CPT® code 15738 describes a split-thickness skin graft, which is not performed in this case.

CPT® code 11606 describes the excision of a malignant lesion that has already been performed on this patient and is not applicable to this procedure.

33) Answer B - The correct answer is b) 15120-58, 15004-58, E11.621, L97.529.

CPT® code 15120 describes the split-thickness autografting of the patient's left foot. The -58 modifier is used to indicate that this is a staged or related procedure performed during the global period of the previous surgery.

CPT® code 15004 describes the debridement of the wound

from the surface of the wounds. The -58 modifier is used to indicate that this is a staged or related procedure performed during the global period of the previous surgery.

ICD-10-CM code E11.621 represents type 2 diabetes mellitus with foot ulcer. This code is used to describe the patient's underlying condition.

ICD-10-CM code L97.529 represents non-pressure chronic ulcer of other part of left foot with unspecified severity. This code is used to describe the patient's foot ulcer.

Therefore, the correct CPT® and ICD-10-CM codes to report for this operative report are 15120-58, 15004-58, E11.621, L97.529.

34) Answer D - The correct CPT® code for arthroscopy to remove loose bodies in the shoulder area is 29819. This code is used for arthroscopy, shoulder, surgical; with extensive debridement, bursectomy, or arthroplasty (e.g., total shoulder replacement).

Codes 29805 and 29806 are also used for arthroscopy of the shoulder, but they are not appropriate for this specific procedure because they describe different procedures. Code 29805 is used for arthroscopy, shoulder, surgical; debridement, limited and code 29806 is used for arthroscopy, shoulder, surgical; decompression of subacromial space with partial acromioplasty, with coracoacromial ligament (C-C ligament) release, when performed.

Code 29807 is used for arthroscopy, shoulder, surgical; with rotator cuff repair, when performed, and code 29819 is not used for rotator cuff repair.

Therefore, the correct CPT® code for the given scenario is 29819.

35) Answer B - The correct CPT code for the described procedure is 24538.

24535 is used for open treatment of supracondylar humerus fracture with or without internal fixation.

24538 is used for closed treatment of supracondylar humerus fracture with manipulation and percutaneous K-wire fixation.

24582 is used for closed treatment of supracondylar humerus fracture without manipulation.

24566 is used for open treatment of supracondylar humerus fracture with internal fixation and/or cast application.

Since the patient presented with a closed fracture and the procedure involved closed reduction and percutaneous K-wire fixation, the appropriate code is 24538.

36) Answer B - The correct CPT codes for the procedure described are:

63081 Anterior vertebral segmental decompression, discectomy, with decompression of spinal cord and/or nerve root(s), including osteophytectomy; cervical, single interspace (List separately in addition to code for primary procedure)

22554-51 Arthrodesis, anterior interbody technique, including minimal discectomy to prepare interspace (other than for decompression); cervical below C2

22846 Posterior non-segmental instrumentation (eg, Harrington rod technique, pedicle fixation across one interspace, atlantoaxial transarticular screw fixation, sublaminar wiring at C1, facet screw fixation) (List separately in addition to code for primary procedure)

22851 Application of intervertebral biomechanical device(s) (eg, synthetic cage(s), methylmethacrylate) to vertebral defect or interspace (List separately in addition to code for primary procedure)

20930 Allograft, includes packing and dressing

Option b is correct because it includes all the correct codes for the procedure.

Code 63081 describes the anterior corpectomy and discectomy procedure performed at C5.

Codes 22554-51, 22846, and 22851 describe the placement of the titanium cages and Synthes plates across C2-C3, C3-C5, and C5-C6.

Code 20930 is reported for the use of morselized allograft bone.

Option a is incorrect because it includes code 22326, which is for the placement of interbody biomechanical device(s) using a posterior approach. This is not the approach used in this case.

Option c is incorrect because it includes code 63001, which is for the excision of an intervertebral disc in conjunction with a cervical fusion performed via a posterior approach. This is not the approach used in this case.

Option d is incorrect because it includes code 22548, which is not a valid code. The correct code for arthrodesis, anterior interbody technique, including minimal discectomy to prepare interspace (other than for decompression); cervical above C2 is 22551. However, the patient had the arthrodesis procedure performed below C2, so code 22551 is not applicable in this case.

37) Answer A - The appropriate CPT code for the procedure described is 23076-RT.

CPT code 23076 describes the excision of a soft tissue tumor or cyst of the upper arm or elbow area that is 3 cm or greater in diameter. In this case, a 4 cm mass was removed en bloc from the right upper arm, which meets the criteria for code 23076.

Codes 23066 and 23075 describe excision of soft tissue tumors or cysts of the upper arm or elbow that are smaller in size, so they do not apply to this case.

Code 11406 describes the excision of benign lesions, such as skin tags or moles, by any method other than shaving. This code does not apply to the removal of a soft tissue mass from the upper arm.

38) Answer D - The correct answer is d) 27301-78, M96.840.

CPT® code 27301 describes the evacuation of a hematoma, which was done in this case. The modifier 78 indicates that the procedure was performed due to complications or unexpected circumstances that required the patient to return to the operating room.

ICD-10-CM code M96.840 is used to report postprocedural hematoma, seroma, and lymphocele following a procedure. This code accurately reflects the patient's condition of developing a hematoma following surgery.

Therefore, the correct coding for this scenario is 27301-78 for the hematoma evacuation with the modifier 78 indicating that it was a repeat procedure, and the ICD-10-CM code M96.840 to report the postprocedural hematoma.

39) Answer A - The appropriate CPT® code for the procedure described is 20680, "Removal of implant; deep (e.g., buried wire, pin, screw, metal band, nail, rod or plate)". This code is used for the removal of deep implants, such as screws or plates, from bone. In this case, the patient had previously undergone surgery to have a plate and screws placed in their left ankle to help heal a fracture. The plate and screws were removed during this procedure, which qualifies as a deep implant removal.

Codes 20680-59 and 20670 are not appropriate in this case. Code 20670, "Removal of implant; superficial (e.g., buried wire, pin or rod) (separate procedure)", is used for the removal of superficial implants, such as wires or pins, that are located close to the skin surface. Since the implant in this case was a plate and screws that were inserted deep into the bone, code 20670 is not appropriate.

Code 20680-59 is an add-on code used to report a second or subsequent removal of a deep implant during the same surgical session as the first removal. Since only one implant was removed during this procedure, code 20680-59 is not appropriate.

Therefore, the correct answer is a) 20680.

40) Answer A - The correct answer is (a) 20526, J3301.

Carpal tunnel injection is a therapeutic injection used to treat carpal tunnel syndrome. In this scenario, the injection is administered into the left carpal canal. The injection consists of a mixture of 1 cc of 1% lidocaine and 10 mg of Kenalog.

CPT® code 20526 (Injection, therapeutic [e.g., local anesthetic, corticosteroid], carpal tunnel) is used to report the carpal tunnel injection procedure. It is a unilateral code, which means it is reported once for each hand.

J3301 (Injection, triamcinolone acetonide, per 10 mg) is a HCPCS Level II code that represents the Kenalog medication administered during the procedure.

Therefore, the correct codes to report for this scenario are:

20526 (Injection, therapeutic [e.g., local anesthetic, corticosteroid], carpal tunnel), once for the left hand

J3301 (Injection, triamcinolone acetonide, per 10 mg), reported once for the 10 mg of Kenalog injected.

So, the correct answer is (a) 20526, J3301.

41) Answer D - The correct answer is d) 31086. A frontal sinusotomy with osteoplastic flap and brow incision is a surgical procedure that involves the removal of the frontal sinus walls and reconstruction of the sinus with a flap of bone taken from the skull. CPT® code 31086 describes this procedure specifically.

42) Answer A- The correct answer is a) 30903-50, R04.0. The ED physician packed the entire nose via an anterior approach to control the epistaxis. CPT® code 30903 describes the packing of the nasal cavity using anterior, posterior or nasal approach. The -50 modifier is used to indicate that the procedure was performed bilaterally. The ICD-10-CM code R04.0 is used to report the diagnosis of epistaxis.

43) Answer B - The correct answer is b) 32484, C34.12,

F17.218. A high thoracotomy with resection of a single left lung segment is described by CPT® code 32484. The ICD-10-CM code C34.12 is used to report the diagnosis of malignant neoplasm of the upper lobe, left lung. The additional diagnosis code F17.218 is used to report the patient's history of tobacco use.

44) Answer A - The correct answer is a) 32482.

Code 32482 is used to report the removal of one lobe of the lung, and it is used twice in this case to report the removal of two lobes, one from each lung. Additionally, bronchoscopy is not separately reported as it is included in the primary procedure code.

Option b) 32484-50 is incorrect as it is used to report bilateral procedures performed on the same anatomical site, which is not the case here.

Option c) 32480-50 is incorrect as it is used to report unilateral procedures performed on the opposite side of a previous unilateral procedure, which is not the case here.

Option d) 32482-50 is incorrect as the modifier -50 is used to report bilateral procedures performed on the same anatomical site, which is not the case here.

45) Answer D - The correct answer is d) 33228.

Code 33228 is used to report replacement of the battery in a dual chamber permanent pacemaker.

Option a) 33212 is incorrect as it is used to report removal of a single lead from a pacemaker system.

Option b) 33229 is incorrect as it is used to report removal of a dual lead from a pacemaker system.

Option c) 33213, 33233-51 is incorrect as 33213 is used to report insertion of a single lead into a pacemaker system and 33233-51 is used to report imaging supervision and interpretation, which are not relevant to this procedure.

46) Answer C - The correct answer is c) 36902, 99152, 99153×3.

Code 36902 is used to report percutaneous transluminal angioplasty (PTA) of an arteriovenous graft in hemodialysis access. Code 99152 is used to report moderate sedation services provided by the physician performing the procedure. Code 99153 is used to report additional time spent beyond the first 30 minutes of moderate sedation. As the intraservice time is approximately 1 hour, 3 units of 99153 are reported. No other codes are necessary as the physician performed all aspects of the procedure and radiological supervision and interpretation is included in the PTA code.

Option a) 36903, 99151, 99153×3, 75989-26 is incorrect as 36903 is used to report PTA of an autogenous dialysis fistula or graft, which is not the case here. Code 75989 is used to report imaging of vascular access performed during a dialysis procedure, which is not relevant to this case.

Option b) 36901, 99152, 99153×1, 75978-26 is incorrect as 36901 is used to report transluminal balloon angioplasty of a noncoronary vessel, which is not the case here. Code 75978 is used to report imaging of vascular access performed during a non-dialysis procedure, which is not relevant to this case.

Option d) 35476, 99155, 99157×3, 75978-26 is incorrect as 35476 is used to report PTA of the renal artery or branch, which is not the case here. Code 99155 is used to report additional time spent beyond the first 30 minutes of anesthesia administered by a physician, which is not relevant to this case. Code 99157 is used to report additional time spent beyond the first 30 minutes of anesthesia administered by a qualified non-physician, which is not relevant to this case. Code 75978 is used to report imaging of vascular access performed during a non-dialysis procedure, which is not relevant to this case

47) Answer D - The answer is d) Necessary local anesthesia, introduction of needles or catheters, injection of contrast

media with or without automatic power injection, and/ or necessary pre and post-injection care specifically related to the injection procedure. This option includes all the components required for a vascular injection procedure, such as preparing the injection site, administering local anesthesia, inserting needles or catheters, injecting contrast media, and providing any necessary pre- and post-injection care.

48) Answer D - The answer is d) 33533, 33517, 35600. This operative report describes a coronary artery bypass grafting (CABG) procedure, which involves grafting conduits to bypass obstructed coronary arteries. In this case, the surgeon used conduits taken from the patient's left arm and right thigh to bypass the chronically occluded right coronary artery and the moderately diseased left anterior descending artery. The procedure code for CABG with two arterial grafts is 33533. The surgeon also cannulated the patient's aorta and atrium, which is coded as 33517. Finally, the surgeon used a radial artery conduit, which is coded as 35600.

49) Answer A - The correct answer is a) 92928-RC, 92978-RC. The clinical summary describes a coronary intervention procedure that involved the placement of a drug-eluting stent in the ostial/proximal segment of the right coronary artery. The codes that represent this procedure are: 92928-RC: Percutaneous transcatheter placement of intracoronary drug-eluting stent(s), right coronary artery or branch, including radiological supervision and interpretation; with intraprocedural pharmacological adjunctive therapy (List separately in addition to code for primary procedure). 92978-RC: Transcatheter therapy, coronary, by intravascular stent(s), with coronary angioplasty when performed; single major coronary artery or branch. The use of IVUS (intravascular ultrasound) and heparin

during the procedure is not separately billable and therefore not included in the codes reported.

Therefore, the correct answer is a) 92928-RC, 92978-RC.

50) Answer D - The correct answer is d) 43246.

The percutaneous endoscopic direct placement of a tube gastrostomy is a procedure in which a feeding tube is inserted through the abdominal wall into the stomach under endoscopic guidance. In this case, the patient had a previous partial esophagectomy, which likely made it difficult for them to take in food orally, necessitating the placement of a feeding tube.

CPT® code 43246 describes the percutaneous endoscopic gastrostomy (PEG) tube placement procedure, which involves the placement of a feeding tube through the abdominal wall and into the stomach under endoscopic guidance. This code includes the dilation of the gastrostomy tract and placement of a gastrostomy tube. It is important to note that this code is specific to the placement of a percutaneous endoscopic gastrostomy tube and not a percutaneous endoscopic jejunostomy (PEJ) tube. Therefore, the correct CPT® code for the percutaneous endoscopic direct placement of a tube gastrostomy in this patient who previously underwent a partial esophagectomy is 43246. The additional code 43116, which is used for partial esophagectomy, is not reported in this case because it is not relevant to the gastrostomy tube placement procedure. Answer choice c) 49440 is also incorrect as it describes a different procedure, namely the placement of a non-tube gastrostomy. Answer choices a) and b) include code 43116 which is not relevant to this procedure.

51) Answer B - The correct answer is b) 43244, K74.60, I85.10.

CPT® code 43244 describes the ligation of esophageal varices by endoscopy. This code includes the use of a flexible endoscope to visualize the varices, as well as the placement of one or more rubber bands around the varices to prevent bleeding. The procedure is performed through the mouth and esophagus, and does not require any incisions.

ICD-10-CM code K74.60 is used to report cirrhosis of the liver without mention of esophageal varices. This code is appropriate because the patient has a history of cirrhosis, which is a common cause of esophageal varices.

ICD-10-CM code I85.10 is used to report esophageal varices without bleeding. This code is appropriate because the patient presented with coffee ground emesis, which is a sign of bleeding from the esophageal varices. However, since the bleeding was not ongoing at the time of the procedure, the code for varices without bleeding is the most appropriate.

52) Answer A - he correct answer is a) 47140, 47146, 47147, 47135.

CPT® code 47140 describes the procurement of a liver from a donor. This code includes the removal of the liver from the donor, as well as any associated procedures, such as vascular dissection or reconstruction.

CPT® codes 47146 and 47147 describe the reconstruction of the graft, including both venous and arterial anastomoses. These codes are used to report the backbench reconstruction of the graft, which involves connecting the donor liver to the recipient's blood vessels.

CPT® code 47135 describes the orthotopic allotransplantation of the liver. This code is used to report the actual transplantation of the liver into the recipient. This procedure involves making an incision in the recipient's abdomen, removing the recipient's diseased liver, and replacing it with the donor liver.

53) Answer D - The correct answer is d) 54161, 14040.

CPT® code 54161 describes circumcision with adjacent tissue transfer. This code includes the circumcision procedure, as well as the transfer of adjacent tissue to cover the surgical site.

CPT® code 14040 describes the adjacent tissue transfer. This code is used to report the transfer of tissue from a nearby area to cover a surgical site. In this case, the adjacent tissue transfer is an integral part of the circumcision procedure and should be reported together with the circumcision code.

54) Answer C - The correct answer is (c) 51728, 51797, 51741. Explanation: The provided scenario involves multiple procedures, including complex CMG cystometrogram with voiding pressure studies, intrabdominal voiding pressure studies, and complex uroflow. These procedures are reported with CPT codes 51728, 51797, and 51741, respectively. Code 51726 only describes a simple uroflow study and is not appropriate for this scenario. Code 51728 includes the voiding pressure studies, so it is not necessary to report code 51726 along with it.

55) Answer D - The correct answer is (d) 52648, 52224-59. Explanation: The provided scenario involves cystoscopy, bladder biopsies, and GreenLight laser ablation of the prostate. Cystoscopy with bladder biopsy is reported with CPT code 52224. The modifier -59 is added to indicate that this code is being used for a separate and distinct procedure from the GreenLight laser ablation. GreenLight laser ablation of the prostate is reported with CPT code 52648. Code 52647 is used for laser vaporization of the prostate tissue, but in this scenario, GreenLight laser ablation was performed. Code 52649 is used for laser enucleation of the prostate, which is a different procedure from GreenLight laser ablation.

56) Answer B - The correct answer is (b) Colp/o. Explanation: Colp/o is the root word for vagina. Uter/o is the root word for uterus. Hyster/o is the root word for uterus as well, but it

is more commonly used as a combining form. Metri/o is the root word for uterus in some contexts, such as in the term "endometrium," which refers to the lining of the uterus.

57) Answer C - The correct answer is (c) 56440. Explanation: The provided scenario involves incision and drainage (I&D) of a recurrent Bartholin's gland cyst, with tacking of the edges to prevent recurrence. This procedure is reported with CPT code 56440. Code 56405 is used for incision and drainage of a vulvar abscess, but in this scenario, a cyst is being treated. Code 56420 is used for marsupialization of a Bartholin's gland cyst, which involves creating a permanent opening in the cyst to allow drainage, but in this scenario, the edges are being tacked together to create an open pouch instead. Code 56740 is used for excision of a Bartholin's gland cyst, which involves removing the cyst entirely, but in this scenario, only an I&D procedure is performed.

58) Answer A - The CPT® code used to report a complete unilateral removal of the vulva and deep subcutaneous tissues is 56630. This code is used for vulvectomy, complete, unilateral, radical, with or without inguinal lymphadenectomy. This procedure involves the complete removal of the vulva, including the clitoris, labia majora, labia minora, and perineal body, as well as deep subcutaneous tissues. This procedure is typically performed in cases of vulvar cancer or other malignancies of the vulva.

59) Answer D - Vulvar intraepithelial neoplasia (VIN) is a precancerous condition of the vulva that can progress to vulvar cancer. VIN is classified into three grades based on the degree of dysplasia and abnormal cell growth. VIN I is the least severe form of VIN, while VIN III is the most severe. Therefore, the correct answer is D, VIN III. VIN III is also referred to as high-grade squamous intraepithelial lesion (HSIL) and is characterized by severe dysplasia and

abnormal cell growth throughout the full thickness of the epithelium.

60) Answer A - The CPT® code reported for laparoscopic tubal ligation with falope ring is 58671. This code is used to report laparoscopy, surgical; with application of Falope ring or band to tubes for sterilization. This procedure involves the placement of a small clip or ring on the fallopian tubes to prevent the eggs from traveling down the fallopian tubes and being fertilized by sperm. This is a permanent form of contraception and is commonly referred to as "getting your tubes tied."

61) Answer D - In this scenario, the correct answer is D, 58240. This code is used to report a total abdominal hysterectomy with bilateral salpingo-oophorectomy. In addition, this procedure involves the removal of the bladder (cystectomy), creation of an ileal conduit (urinary diversion), and partial colectomy (removal of a portion of the large intestine). This procedure is typically performed in cases of advanced cervical cancer where the cancer has spread beyond the cervix.

62) Answer C - The correct answer is C, yes, since the doctor did the work, even though the outcome was unsuccessful. The code to report this procedure is 59412, which is used to report an attempt at external cephalic version after 37 weeks gestation. This procedure involves the external manipulation of the fetus to attempt to turn it from a breech position to a head-down position for a vaginal delivery. Even if the procedure is unsuccessful, it is still billable.

63) Answer A - The four lobes of the brain are the frontal lobe, parietal lobe, temporal lobe, and occipital lobe. The frontal lobe is responsible for movement, planning, and judgment. The parietal lobe is responsible for sensory information, such as touch and pressure. The temporal lobe

is responsible for hearing and memory, while the occipital lobe is responsible for vision.

64) Answer C - The correct answer is C, 61584, 61600-51. Code 61584 is used to report the excision of an extracranial non-dural arteriovenous malformation (AVM) or arteriovenous fistula (AVF), which is located outside the dura mater. Code 61600 is used to report the transcranial approach for the excision of an AVM or AVF located within the cranial cavity. Modifier 51 is appended to indicate that multiple procedures were performed during the same session.

65) Answer A - The correct answer is a) 60520.
CPT® code 60520 describes the surgical removal of the thymus gland through a transcervical approach, which involves dividing the blood supply to the thymus and dissecting it free from the pericardium. This is the most accurate code to report for the given procedure.
CPT® code 60521 is used for a similar procedure, but with a sternotomy (opening of the sternum) approach. CPT® code 60522 is used for a thymectomy performed during an extended transsternal or transthoracic approach, which involves additional chest wall resection. CPT® code 60540 is used for a thymectomy performed for myasthenia gravis in a patient under age 18.

66) Answer B - The correct answer is b) 63056, 63057.
CPT® code 63056 describes a decompression of the nerve root(s) in the lumbar spine through a transpedicular approach involving one or two segments. Since the given scenario involves two segments, this code can be used. Additionally, CPT® code 63057 can be reported as an add-on code for each additional segment decompressed through the same approach. Therefore, both codes are reported.
CPT® codes 63030 and 63035 are not applicable to this scenario as they describe spinal cord decompression procedures through a laminotomy/laminectomy approach.

67) Answer B - The correct answer is b) 63020, M50.20.

CPT® code 63020 describes a cervical laminotomy (partial removal of the vertebral lamina) for the purpose of decompressing the spinal cord or nerve root(s) at a single interspace. This code is appropriate for the given scenario.

ICD-10-CM code M50.20 is used to report a cervical disc disorder with radiculopathy. This code accurately describes the patient's condition and the reason for the surgery.

CPT® code 63035 is not applicable to this scenario as it describes a more extensive procedure involving a laminectomy (complete removal of the vertebral lamina) and/or facetectomy (removal of the facet joint) for spinal cord decompression.

68) Answer D - The correct answer is d) 64483.

CPT® code 64483 is used to report an injection of an anesthetic agent and/or steroid into the epidural or subarachnoid space, cervical or thoracic; single injection site.

In this case, the injection was performed at the L5-S1 level, which is in the lumbar region, not the cervical or thoracic region. Therefore, codes 64493 and 64494 (which are used for injections in the cervical or thoracic region) are not appropriate.

Code 64484 is used for injection(s) at each additional level of the lumbar spine after the first level, and it is not appropriate because only one level was injected in this case. Therefore, the correct code to report for this procedure is 64483.

69) Answer B - The correct answer is b) 64493-50, 64494-50, 64495-50, M54.5.

CPT® code 64493 is used to report an injection of an anesthetic agent and/or steroid into the facet joint(s), cervical or thoracic; single level. CPT® code 64494 is used for each additional level injected at the same level and side as the first level, and CPT® code 64495 is used for each additional level injected at a different level and/or side.

In this scenario, the injection was performed at three levels on both sides of the lumbar spine, so the appropriate codes to report are 64493-50 for the first level on one side, 64494-50 for the second and third levels on the same side, 64495-50 for the first level on the other side, and 64494-50 and 64495-50 for the second and third levels on the other side.

The ICD-10-CM code to report for lumbar pain is M54.5.

Therefore, the correct codes to report for this procedure are 64493-50, 64494-50, 64495-50, and M54.5. The -50 modifier is used to indicate that the procedure was performed bilaterally.

70) Answer B - The correct answer is (b) 63085-62, 63086-62 x 2. This scenario involves two surgeons performing different portions of the same surgery, which is commonly known as a co-surgery or team surgery. In this case, one surgeon is performing the transthoracic approach, and the other is performing the vertebral nerve root decompressions. To report this correctly, you need to use the co-surgery modifier 62, which indicates that two surgeons worked together as primary surgeons.

The codes that should be used in this case are:

63085-62 - Corpectomy, anterior with decompression of spinal cord, pectoral girdle approach, thoracic; one vertebral segment

63086-62 - Corpectomy, anterior with decompression of spinal cord, pectoral girdle approach, thoracic; each additional vertebral segment (List separately in addition to code for primary procedure)

Both codes should be appended with modifier 62 to indicate that two surgeons worked together as primary surgeons. The second code, 63086, should be reported twice because the second surgeon performed three vertebral nerve root decompressions.

71) Answer D - The correct answer is (d) 62269, G95.0. In this scenario, the patient has muscle atrophy and was diagnosed with syringomyelia after a biopsy of the spinal cord was performed under fluoroscopic guidance. The correct CPT® code to report for a biopsy of the spinal cord is 62269 - Biopsy, spinal cord, percutaneous, by trocar or needle, single or multiple. There is no need for a modifier in this scenario.
The correct ICD-10-CM diagnosis code for syringomyelia is G95.0 - Syringomyelia and syringobulbia. The code R20.9 - Unspecified disturbance of skin sensation may be reported for the lack of pain sensation due to muscle atrophy, but it is not necessary to report in this case.

72) Answer A - The correct answer is (a) 62270. In this scenario, the patient presents with symptoms of meningitis, and a lumbar puncture is performed to obtain cerebral spinal fluid (CSF) for analysis. The code that should be reported for a lumbar puncture is 62270 - Spinal puncture, lumbar, diagnostic.
There is no need for a modifier in this scenario since only one physician performed the service. The fact that the patient was in the sitting position and received medication prior to the procedure does not affect the code selection. However, it is important to note that if a therapeutic injection was administered during the same session as the diagnostic lumbar puncture, a modifier may be necessary to indicate that the two services were distinct and separate.

73) Answer B - The correct CPT® code to report for the drainage of an abscess in the external auditory canal is 69105. This code describes an "incision and drainage of external auditory canal abscess; simple" which is appropriate for this procedure.
When a patient has an abscess in the external auditory

canal, it may require drainage in order to alleviate pain and prevent the spread of infection. The appropriate CPT® code to report for this procedure is 69105. This code specifically describes an "incision and drainage of external auditory canal abscess; simple." This code is appropriate for the procedure because it involves making an incision in the abscess to allow the pus to drain, which is a relatively straightforward and uncomplicated procedure.

74) Answer C - The correct CPT® code to report for the removal of a foreign body from the external auditory canal without general anesthesia is 69200. This code describes an "removal foreign body, external auditory canal; without general anesthesia" which is appropriate for this procedure. When a foreign body, such as an insect or debris, becomes lodged in the external auditory canal, it may need to be removed to prevent further complications. The appropriate CPT® code to report for the removal of a foreign body from the external auditory canal without general anesthesia is 69200. This code specifically describes the "removal foreign body, external auditory canal; without general anesthesia." This code is appropriate for the procedure because it involves the removal of the foreign object from the external auditory canal without the use of general anesthesia, which is a less complex procedure than using general anesthesia.

75) Answer B - The correct CPT® code to report for the biopsy of a cyst-like mass on the left external auditory canal using a microcup forceps is 69105-LT. This code describes an "biopsy, external ear, ear canal, or both; simple" which is appropriate for this procedure performed on the left side. The LT modifier is used to indicate that the procedure was performed on the left side. When a patient has a cyst-like mass in the external auditory canal, it may require a biopsy in order to determine whether the mass is cancerous or benign. The appropriate CPT® code to report for this procedure is 69105-LT. This code specifically describes a

"biopsy, external ear, ear canal, or both; simple" which is appropriate for a biopsy of tissue along the posterior superior canal wall in the left ear using a microcup forceps. The LT modifier is used to indicate that the procedure was performed on the left side.

76) Answer C - The correct ICD-10-CM code to report for acute kidney failure following labor and delivery is O90.4. This code describes "acute renal failure following delivery" which is the appropriate diagnosis for this scenario. Acute kidney failure following labor and delivery can be a serious condition that requires medical attention. The appropriate ICD-10-CM code to report for this diagnosis is O90.4. This code specifically describes "acute renal failure following delivery" which is the appropriate diagnosis for this scenario.

77) Answer C - The correct modifier to report for the extenuating circumstances of a surgery being discontinued due to complications prior to anesthesia administration is modifier 73. This modifier is used to indicate that the procedure was discontinued due to extenuating circumstances before the anesthesia was administered. It allows the provider to bill for the preoperative services they performed. When a planned surgery is discontinued due to complications before anesthesia administration, the provider may still bill for the preoperative services they performed. The appropriate modifier to report in this scenario is modifier 73, which is used to indicate that the procedure was discontinued due to extenuating circumstances before anesthesia was administered. This modifier allows the provider to bill for the preoperative services they performed and provides additional information to the insurance company about why the surgery was not performed as planned.

78) Answer D - To calculate the correct anesthesia charge for

this procedure, we need to follow a few steps:

Step 1: Calculate the base units.

The base value for code 00350 is 10 units. Since the patient is a P3 status, we can add one extra base unit, bringing the total to 11 units.

Step 2: Calculate the time units.

To calculate the time units, we need to determine the anesthesia start time and the ending anesthesia time in fifteen-minute increments. The anesthesia start time is reported as 11:02, which rounds to 11:00, and the ending anesthesia time is reported as 12:47, which rounds to 12:45. The difference between these two times is 1 hour and 45 minutes, or 7 fifteen-minute increments. Therefore, we can add 7 time units to the 11 base units, giving us a total of 18 units.

Step 3: Calculate the anesthesia charge.

To calculate the anesthesia charge, we multiply the total number of units (18) by the conversion factor ($100). Therefore, the correct anesthesia charge is:

18 units x $100/unit = $1,800.00

Therefore, the correct answer is (d) $1,800.00.

79) Answer A - The appropriate modifier to report for the CRNA services when personally performing a case with medical direction from an anesthesiologist is QY.

Modifier QY is used to identify anesthesia services that are personally performed by a CRNA with medical direction by an anesthesiologist. This indicates that both providers were involved in the anesthesia care of the patient during the procedure. It is important to note that the medical direction must be provided by an anesthesiologist, not another CRNA or physician.

Other anesthesia modifiers include:

QZ: This modifier is used to indicate that the anesthesiologist is providing medical direction to more than four concurrent anesthesia procedures. This is only applicable when the anesthesiologist is medically directing other anesthesia providers, such as CRNAs or anesthesiology residents.

QK: This modifier is used to indicate that the anesthesiologist is personally performing the anesthesia service. It is not used in conjunction with modifier QY.

QS: This modifier is used to indicate that a CRNA was involved in the anesthesia care of the patient, but the medical direction was not provided by an anesthesiologist. This may be used, for example, when a CRNA is working with a surgeon or another physician who is providing medical direction.

80) Answer B - To determine the total anesthesia time and anesthesia code for this case, we need to calculate the duration of the anesthesia and identify the appropriate anesthesia code based on the type of procedure.

Step 1: Calculate the duration of the anesthesia.

The anesthesia start time is reported as 0830, and the patient is released to the recovery nurse at 1015. The difference between these two times is 1 hour and 45 minutes, so the total anesthesia time is 1 hour and 45 minutes.

Step 2: Identify the appropriate anesthesia code.

Since the procedure described in the scenario is a laparoscopic tubal ligation, the appropriate anesthesia code is 00851. This code represents anesthesia for procedures on the female reproductive system, including tubal ligation.

Therefore, the correct answer is (b) 1 hour 45 minutes, 00851.

81) Answer A - The correct answer is A) 78815.

The given procedure description states that the patient underwent a PET-CT scan of the body from skull base to mid-thigh for restaging examination of rectal carcinoma. The procedure involved the intravenous administration of F-18 deoxyglucose and multiplanar image acquisitions of the neck, chest, abdomen, and pelvis.

CPT code 78815 (Positron emission tomography (PET) imaging; with concurrently acquired computed tomography (CT) for attenuation correction and anatomical localization imaging, skull base to mid-thigh) accurately describes the above-described procedure.

CPT code 96365 (Intravenous infusion, for therapy, prophylaxis, or diagnosis (specify substance or drug); initial, up to 1 hour) and CPT code 78816 (Positron emission tomography (PET) imaging; limited area, such as skull, chest, or pelvis) are not appropriate codes for the procedure described in the question.

Therefore, the correct answer is A) 78815.

82) Answer A - The correct answer is A) 76818.

The given scenario describes a 25-year-old pregnant woman who is in her last trimester and visits her obstetrician's office for a fetal biophysical profile (BPP). The BPP is performed using an ultrasound, which monitors the fetus's movements, breathing, non-stress test (NST), and amniotic fluid volume.

CPT code 76818 (Ultrasound, pregnant uterus, real-time with image documentation, fetal and maternal evaluation, after the first trimester (> or = 14 weeks 0 days), transabdominal approach; single or first gestation) is used to report the obstetric ultrasound examination performed to assess the fetal biophysical profile in this scenario.

CPT code 76819 (Ultrasound, pregnant uterus, real-time with image documentation, fetal and maternal evaluation plus detailed fetal anatomic examination, transabdominal or transvaginal approach; second and third trimester) is not applicable as the scenario does not describe a detailed fetal anatomical examination.

CPT code 76815 (Ultrasound, pregnant uterus, real-time with image documentation, transvaginal) is not appropriate as the scenario states that the transabdominal approach was used.

CPT code 59025 (Fetal non-stress test; with reactive non-stress test) is not applicable as it is reported separately for the non-stress test (NST) that is included as part of the BPP in this scenario.

Therefore, the correct answer is A) 76818, which is used to report the obstetric ultrasound examination performed to assess the fetal biophysical profile.

83) Answer C - The correct answer is c) 77373-26, Z51.0, C34.11.

The given scenario describes a 65-year-old female with a non-small cell lung cancer in her right upper lobe that is inoperable due to severe respiratory conditions. She will be receiving stereotactic body radiation therapy (SBRT) under image guidance, which will involve the delivery of 25 Gy per fraction for 4 fractions using beams arranged in 8 fields. CPT code 77373-26 (Radiation treatment delivery, stereotactic body radiation therapy, per fraction to one or more lesions, including image guidance, entire course not to exceed 5 fractions) accurately describes the SBRT treatment delivered in this scenario.

ICD-10-CM code C34.11 (Malignant neoplasm of upper lobe, right bronchus or lung) is appropriate to report the non-small cell lung cancer in the right upper lobe of the lung.

ICD-10-CM code Z51.0 (Encounter for antineoplastic radiation therapy) is also appropriate to report the encounter for radiation therapy.

CPT code 77435-26 (Stereotactic radiation treatment delivery, including image guidance, entire course of treatment) is not appropriate as this code is used to report stereotactic radiation therapy for lesions that cannot be treated with conventional radiation therapy.

CPT code 77371-26 (Radiation treatment delivery, stereotactic radiosurgery (SRS), complete course of treatment of cranial lesion[s], single session[s]) is not applicable as it is used to report stereotactic radiosurgery (SRS) for cranial lesions only.

CPT code 77431-26 (Radiation treatment management, 3-5 fractions) is not appropriate as it does not describe the stereotactic body radiation therapy treatment delivered in this scenario.

Therefore, the correct answer is c) 77373-26, Z51.0, C34.11.

84) Answer D - The correct answer is d) 79440-26, 77002-26, 20610.

The given scenario describes a patient with thickening of the synovial membrane who undergoes a fluoroscopic guided radiopharmaceutical therapy joint injection on their right knee. The procedure is performed in an ambulatory surgical center (ASC).

CPT code 79440-26 (Computed tomography guidance for placement of radiation therapy fields) accurately describes the fluoroscopic guidance used for the injection.

CPT code 77002-26 (Fluoroscopic guidance and localization of needle or catheter tip for spine or paraspinous diagnostic or therapeutic injection procedures (epidural or subarachnoid)) is also reported for the use of fluoroscopy.

CPT code 20610 (Arthrocentesis, aspiration and/or injection; major joint or bursa (e.g., shoulder, hip, knee joint, subacromial bursa)) is reported for the injection of the radiopharmaceutical into the knee joint.

Modifier 26 is appended to codes 79440 and 77002 to indicate that the professional component of the service is being billed.

Therefore, the correct answer is d) 79440-26, 77002-26, 20610.

85) Answer A - The correct CPT® code for the procedure described is 75825.

75825 is the CPT® code for "Transcatheter placement of an intravascular filter, lower vena cava". In this procedure, an intravascular filter is placed in the lower vena cava to prevent blood clots from traveling to the lungs. The procedure described in the question is consistent with this code because it involves the placement of a filter in the inferior vena cava.

The other answer choices are not appropriate for the described procedure.

75827 is the CPT® code for "Transcatheter placement of an intravascular filter, including radiological supervision and interpretation, upper vena cava or adjacent structures". This code is not appropriate because the filter was placed in the lower vena cava, not the upper vena cava.

75820 is the CPT® code for "Venography, radiological supervision and interpretation, retrograde, or antegrade, complete bilateral study". This code is not appropriate because the procedure involved the placement of a filter, not venography.

75860 is the CPT® code for "Transluminal balloon angioplasty, percutaneous; renal or other visceral artery". This code is not appropriate because the procedure did not involve angioplasty of the renal arteries or any other visceral artery.

Therefore, the correct answer is A) 75825.

86) Answer A - The appropriate radiology code for this series of clinical management fractions is 77427.

77427 is the CPT® code for "Radiation treatment management, five treatments". This code is used to report the management of a patient undergoing a series of conventional fractionated radiation treatments, where five treatments are administered over a period of one or more weeks.

In this case, the patient is receiving a total of seven treatments, with five on one day and two on the next. However, the number of treatments does not affect the code selection, as the code 77427 includes the management of up to five treatments.

Therefore, the correct answer is A) 77427, which would be reported once for the series of seven treatments. The other answer choices are not appropriate as they do not accurately reflect the nature of the treatment or the number of fractions being administered.

87) Answer D - The appropriate CPT® code for the described obstetrical ultrasound is 76815.

76815 is the CPT® code for "Ultrasound, pregnant uterus, real time with image documentation, fetal and maternal evaluation, after first trimester (>14 weeks 0 days), multiple gestation (e.g., twins, triplets, etc.)". This code is used to report a comprehensive ultrasound examination of a pregnant uterus with multiple gestations after the first trimester, which includes fetal and maternal evaluation, fetal heartbeats, and fetal position.

In this case, the patient is in her second trimester and has a triplet pregnancy. Therefore, the appropriate code to report the ultrasound is 76815, which includes the necessary components of the examination.

The other answer choices are not appropriate as they do not accurately reflect the nature of the ultrasound or the number of fetuses being evaluated.

Answer choice A (76805, 76810, 76810) includes codes for limited and complete obstetrical ultrasounds, but it does not include the multiple gestation component required for this case.

Answer choice B (76811, 76812, 76812) includes codes for detailed and complete fetal anatomical surveys, but it does not include the multiple gestation component required for this case.

Answer choice C (76815 x 3) reports three units of 76815, which is not appropriate as it is only one ultrasound examination being performed, regardless of the number of fetuses.

Therefore, the correct answer is D) 76815, which would be

reported once for the ultrasound.

88) Answer A - The correct answer is a) Cytopathology.

The Fluorescence in situ hybridization (FISH) test is a type of cytopathology test that involves the use of fluorescent-labeled DNA probes to identify specific chromosomal abnormalities or gene mutations in cells.

Therefore, codes for FISH testing can be found in the Cytopathology section of the Pathology chapter of CPT® (Current Procedural Terminology). The Cytopathology section of the Pathology chapter includes codes for various types of tests and procedures that involve the examination of cells for the diagnosis of disease, including tests such as Pap smears, fine needle aspirations, and FISH testing.

It is important for coders to select the appropriate code from the correct section of the CPT® codebook to accurately reflect the services provided, ensure proper reimbursement, and maintain compliance with coding guidelines.

89) Answer C - The correct answer is (c) 88300.

The CPT code 88300 is used for the examination of surgical specimens that do not require microscopic examination. In this case, the pathologist received several small pieces of bone for examination, but no microscopic sections were required. Since the pathologist did not perform any further testing, the appropriate code to use for this service is 88300.

Option (a) is incorrect because the service can be billed, and it is important to properly code and bill for services rendered.

Option (b) is incorrect because 88304 is used for a comprehensive examination of a single surgical specimen, including microscopic examination.

Option (d) is incorrect because 88309 and 88311 are used for specialized testing or stains that may be required for the examination of the specimen. Since no further testing was required in this case, these codes would not be appropriate.

90) Answer B - The correct answer is (b) 80076, 82565.

The physician has ordered a comprehensive metabolic panel (CMP) and a complete blood count (CBC) with differential to evaluate the patient's liver function and kidney function. The CMP includes the following tests: albumin, total bilirubin, direct bilirubin, alkaline phosphatase, total protein, alanine aminotransferase (ALT), aspartate aminotransferase (AST), and creatinine. The CBC with differential includes a measurement of the number and types of blood cells present.

CPT code 80076 is used to report the CMP, which includes the tests ordered by the physician. CPT code 82565 is used to report the CBC with differential. Both of these codes are used to report laboratory services and are appropriate for this scenario.

Option (a) includes several incorrect codes that are not relevant to the tests ordered by the physician in this scenario.

Option (c) includes only code 80076 for the CMP, but does not include the CBC with differential.

Option (d) includes modifier -22, which is not appropriate in this scenario. Modifier -22 is used to indicate that a service was more difficult or time-consuming than usual, and therefore requires additional payment. There is no indication in the scenario that the services performed required additional work, so this modifier should not be used.

91) Answer C - The correct answer is (c) 81025.

CPT code 81025 is used to report a qualitative pregnancy test. This code is appropriate for the scenario described, where a urine pregnancy test was performed using the Hybritech ICON test. The Hybritech ICON test is a visual color comparison test that provides a qualitative result (either positive or negative) for the presence of human chorionic gonadotropin (hCG) in urine, which is a hormone produced during pregnancy.

Option (a) is incorrect because 84703 is used to report a quantitative pregnancy test, which measures the amount of hCG present in the blood or urine. This is not the test that was performed in the scenario.

Option (b) is also incorrect because 84702 is used to report a semiquantitative pregnancy test, which provides a rough estimate of the amount of hCG present in the blood or urine. This is not the test that was performed in the scenario.

Option (d) includes code 81025, which is appropriate, but also includes code 36415, which is used to report the collection of a venous blood sample by venipuncture. This code is not applicable in this scenario, as the test was performed on a urine sample.

92) Answer C - The correct answer is (c) 99360.

CPT code 99360 is used to report attendance at a high-risk delivery or cesarean section. This code is appropriate for the scenario described, where the pediatrician was present in the delivery room for a baby at risk for complications, but the baby was born completely healthy and did not require the services of the pediatrician.

Code 99219 is used for a hospital admission, and is not applicable in this scenario.

Code 99252 is used for a prolonged service in the office or other outpatient setting, and is not applicable in this scenario.

Option (d) includes two units of code 99360, which is not appropriate in this scenario. Only one unit of this code should be reported for the 45 minutes the pediatrician spent in the delivery room.

Therefore, the correct CPT code to report in this scenario is 99360, which describes the pediatrician's attendance at the high-risk delivery.

93) Answer C - The correct answer is (c) 99291, 31500, 36510, 94610.

In this scenario, the pediatrician provided critical care services to a critically ill premature infant while waiting for air transport to a higher level of care. The services provided included intubation, administration of surfactant, bagging on 100% oxygen, and continuous monitoring of vital signs, ECG, pulse oximetry, and temperature. The pediatrician also placed an umbilical vein line for fluid administration and emergency medication needs.

CPT code 99291 is used to report critical care services for the first 30-74 minutes of a critically ill patient's care. This code is appropriate for the 45 minutes of care provided by the pediatrician in this scenario.

Code 31500 is used to report intubation of a patient, which was performed in this scenario.

Code 36510 is used to report placement of a peripheral intravenous line or catheter for infusion therapy or phlebotomy. However, in this scenario, the pediatrician placed an umbilical vein line, which is not considered a peripheral IV line. Therefore, code 36510 is not appropriate, and a more specific code should be used instead.

Code 94610 is used to report the initial nebulization treatment for a patient, and is not applicable in this scenario.

Therefore, the correct codes to report in this scenario are 99291 for the critical care services provided, 31500 for the intubation, and a more specific code for the placement of the umbilical vein line (such as 36410 or 36425).

94) Answer B - The correct answer is b) 99391.

In this case, the patient is a four-month-old infant who is brought in for a well-child checkup. The physician conducts a comprehensive exam, including assessment of weight, height, head circumference, eyes, ears, nose, throat, lungs, heart, abdomen, and hip. The physician also addresses the mother's concerns about the infant's crying and breast milk supply, as well as diagnoses mild thrush and diaper rash. The plan includes treatment for the thrush and recommendations for advancing to baby foods and supplementing with Similac.

Based on the documentation, the appropriate E/M code to report is 99391, which is the code for a comprehensive preventive medicine evaluation and management service for a new patient under one year of age. The other options (a, c, and d) do not accurately reflect the level of service provided in this case.

95) Answer B – The 99204 is the correct code as moderate level of MDM.

96) Answer A - The correct answer is a) 92920, 92921 - LD.

PTCA stands for Percutaneous Transluminal Coronary Angioplasty, which is a minimally invasive procedure used to treat coronary artery disease (CAD) by widening narrowed or obstructed arteries. In this case, the PTCA was performed in the left anterior descending (LAD) and the first diagonal (D1) branches of the left anterior descending artery (LD).

CPT code 92920 is used to report PTCA of a single major coronary artery or branch, and code 92921 is used to report each additional branch treated in the same session. Therefore, in this case, we would report code 92920 for the PTCA of the LAD and code 92921 for the PTCA of the first diagonal (D1) branch of the LD.

Option b) 92920×2 is incorrect as it reports PTCA of the same artery or branch twice, which is not the case here.

Option c) 92924 is used to report atherectomy of the coronary arteries, which is a different procedure than PTCA.

Option d) 92925 is used to report atherectomy of a single major coronary artery or branch, and 92996 is used to report a thrombectomy procedure during a PTCA. Therefore, these codes are not appropriate for this scenario.

97) Answer A - The correct CPT code for Margaret's weekly allergen immunotherapy consisting of two injections prepared and provided by the physician is a) 95125.

CPT code 95125 is used to report the provision of two or more units of allergy immunotherapy on the same day. The code is appropriate for reporting both the preparation of the injection by the physician as well as the administration of the injections.

Option b) 95117 is used to report the administration of a single injection for allergen immunotherapy, which is not appropriate for this scenario where two injections were provided.

Option c) 95131 is used to report the professional services for the supervision of the patient's self-administered subcutaneous injection of allergen immunotherapy, which is not applicable in this scenario since the physician prepared and administered the injections.

Option d) 95146 is used to report the professional services for the supervision of a patient who is self-administering a sublingual allergen immunotherapy, which is not applicable in this scenario as the immunotherapy was administered through injections.

98) Answer B - The correct answer is b) 93581, Q21.0.

In this scenario, the physician performed a right heart catheterization and transcatheter closure of a ventricular septal defect (VSD) by percutaneous approach.

CPT code 93581 is used to report the transcatheter closure of a VSD, which involves the use of a catheter to deliver a device to close the hole in the heart.

ICD-10-CM code Q21.0 is used to report a VSD that is present at birth, which is the case for the baby in this scenario.

Option a) 93530, 93581-59, Q21.9 is incorrect because

code 93530 is used to report a diagnostic right heart catheterization, which was not the only procedure performed in this scenario. Additionally, the use of modifier 59 with code 93581 is not appropriate as it does not identify a distinct procedural service.

Option c) 93530, Q24.0 is incorrect because code 93530 is used to report a diagnostic right heart catheterization, but no information was provided to suggest the presence of a congenital heart defect associated with code Q24.0.

Option d) 93530, 93591-59, Q21.0 is incorrect because code 93591 is used to report a therapeutic injection procedure, which was not performed in this scenario. The use of modifier 59 with code 93591 is also not appropriate as it does not identify a distinct procedural service.

99) Answer C - The correct answer is c) 99203, 96372, J0558 x 12, L03.114.

CPT code 99203 (Office or other outpatient visit for the evaluation and management of a new patient) is appropriate for this encounter, as the patient is a new patient at the intermediate care center and a problem-focused history and examination were performed.

CPT code 96372 (Therapeutic, prophylactic, or diagnostic injection) is appropriate for the injection of Bicillin CR, which was administered to the patient.

CPT code J0558 (Injection, penicillin G benzathine and penicillin G procaine, 100,000 units) is appropriate for the injection of Bicillin CR. The dosage given was 1,200,000 units, so this code would be reported 12 times.

ICD-10-CM code L03.114 (Cellulitis of left hand) is appropriate for the diagnosis of cellulitis of the left hand, which was the reason for the patient's visit.

Therefore, the correct codes are: 99203, 96372, J0558 x 12, L03.114.

100) Answer B - The correct answer is b) 93458-26.

The patient was taken to the cardiac catheterization suite

for a left heart catheterization. This procedure involves the insertion of a catheter into the left side of the heart to assess the function of the heart and blood vessels. The procedure also involves the injection of contrast dye to obtain images of the heart and blood vessels.

CPT code 93458 (Catheterization and introduction of saline contrast followed by injection of contrast into at least one coronary artery or bypass graft, including imaging supervision and interpretation, when performed) is appropriate for the injection procedures for selective coronary angiography and left ventriculography, as well as the imaging supervision and interpretation for these procedures.

Modifier -26 (Professional component) is appended to indicate that only the professional component of the service was provided, as the cardiologist is in private practice.

Therefore, the correct code to report for these services is 93458-26. Code 93453-26 (Coronary angiography, including intraprocedural injection(s) for coronary angiography, imaging supervision and interpretation) and 93462 (Left heart ventricular angiography) are not appropriate for this scenario, as they do not accurately describe the services provided.

Thank You Readers!!!

Best of Luck for your CPC Exam!!!

Made in the USA
Coppell, TX
12 September 2023

21529579R00203